Injunctions Against Anti-social or Violent Individuals

The College of Law
of England and Wales

LIBRARY & INFORMATION SERVICES

Library Phone No.

The College of Law, Bishopthorpe Road, York YO23 2GA
Telephone: 01904 682052

01483 216169

Birmingham • Chester • Guildford • London • York

Injunctions Against Anti-social or Violent Individuals

Mathu Asokan
District Judge

Lorna Findlay
Barrister

Delia Truman
District Judge

JORDANS

Published by
Jordan Publishing Limited
21 St Thomas Street
Bristol BS1 6JS

British Library Cataloguing-in-Publication Data

A catalogue record for this book is available from the British Library.

ISBN 978 1 84661 079 0

Typeset by Letterpart Ltd, Reigate, Surrey

Printed in Great Britain by Antony Rowe Limited, Chippenham, Wiltshire

FOREWORD

Whether it be through Home Office statistics or the medium of the local newspaper, the unappealing message is clear: anti-social behaviour in its many aspects is rife. It will almost certainly take a wholesale change in contemporary attitudes for a more optimistic picture to emerge.

In the meantime, and perhaps in any event, the law has a significant part to play. The role of the civil injunction is central to the available processes.

For those called upon to handle the legal and practical issues arising, a readable and readily accessible source of guidance is essential. This book provides it. Every practitioner in the field should have a copy close at hand.

David Foskett
The Hon Mr Justice Foskett
Royal Courts of Justice
LONDON
5 February 2008

AUTHORS' NOTE

We would like to thank our colleagues at the Combined Civil Justice Centre Birmingham and St Philips Chambers Birmingham for sharing their views and experience in dealing with Injunctions.

We would like to extend a special thanks to His Honour Judge Platt and District Judge Tony Davies for kindly permitting the use of precedents/checklists which they had prepared.

Mathu would like to thank her husband and her daughters for their encouragement and patience. Lorna would like to thank her husband Jonathan Butler for taking the strain, her clerk Jenny Culligan for booking her some time out to write and her librarian Caroline Covington for listening to her.

We have endeavoured to state the law up to December 2007 but have included some later developments where possible. However, statutes are often amended and case-law is constantly evolving so practitioners are perhaps well advised to refer to the most recent versions of statutes and regulations.

Mathu Asokan
Lorna Findlay
Delia Truman

CONTENTS

TABLE OF CASES

References are to paragraph numbers.

TABLE OF STATUTES

References are to paragraph numbers.

TABLE OF STATUTORY INSTRUMENTS

References are to paragraph numbers.

Chapter 1

INTRODUCTION

1.1   An injunction, as defined by the Glossary in the Civil Procedure Rules, is 'a court order prohibiting a person from doing something or requiring a person to do something'. The former type of order would be a 'prohibitory' injunction and the latter a 'mandatory' one. Injunctions may be used in a wide variety of situations. This book endeavours to assist practitioners when dealing with orders which regulate violent or threatening behaviour, but other types of injunction may also be sought, such as to preserve the status quo pending a decision from a court. This could occur where monetary compensation after the event might not be proper recompense if the court should ultimately decide that the other party should not have done what they did . An injunction may be sought to prevent a person dissipating his assets pending a final court hearing (a 'freezing injunction') or from disclosing confidential information. Where an injunction is sought pending a final determination, it is known as an interim injunction. Once there has been such a final determination, any injunction granted, as part of that final decision, is a final injunction. It is far more common for an injunction to forbid someone from doing something than to require them to do something. Telling someone to do something requires a positive action on their part. Forbidding someone from doing something only requires them to refrain from what may be a wrongful act (for an interim injunction) or has been decided to be a wrongful act (for a final injunction). This book is generally concerned with prohibitory orders.

1.2   Injunctions are a discretionary remedy – the court does not have to grant them. The leading authority on the grant of interim injunctions is *American Cyanamid Co v Ethicon Ltd* [1975] AC 396. The general principle that applies when seeking an interim injunction is that the applicant does not have to satisfy the court that he would be successful at any final trial but he obviously has to provide sufficient evidence to show there is a serious question to be tried. The court will then consider where the balance of convenience lies, ie which party will be most inconvenienced/harmed by the grant or refusal of the interim injunction and, if it is granted, and the court then decides at trial that it should not have been, whether the affected party can be properly compensated in damages (this latter point will depend on the type of injunction granted – for example, it does not apply in some Family Law Act injunctions – see Chapter 6).

TYPES OF ORDERS AND WHO MIGHT APPLY

1.3   This book deals with a range of potential remedies under a variety of Acts, such as anti-social behaviour injunctions under the Housing Act 1996 (used by social landlords such as local authorities against unruly tenants or their visitors) and non-molestation injunctions under the Family Law Act 1996 (which may be used by a number of persons to prevent violence, threats of violence and harassment). Each type of injunction has its own procedure to be followed and its own requirements as to who may apply. Whilst the procedures may have a number of similarities, it is best to refer to the relevant chapter in order to avoid difficulties. Depending on the nature of the proceedings, the person seeking the remedy may be described as the 'complainant', the 'claimant' or the 'applicant' and the person against whom the remedy is sought may be referred to as the 'defendant' or the 'respondent'.

DURATION OF ANY ORDER GRANTED

1.4   This again will vary according to the type of injunction sought and reference should be made to the appropriate chapter. Some orders may have no time-limit on them and the person against whom they are made will remain bound without limit. Others may be made 'until further order' when the court will look at the matter again. Some may be granted for a specified period but may be extended on further occasions. Some may only be granted by law for a limited time in the first place (such as some occupation orders under the Family Law Act).

BREACH OF ORDER

1.5   The consequences of breaching an injunction depend on the nature of the breach and the Act under which the injunction was made. In the civil courts, breach of an injunction is generally punished as a contempt of court – the person who has breached the order (sometimes known as the 'contemnor') being punished for ignoring the order which was made, the ultimate penalty for which might be imprisonment. However, under the Family Law Act, breach of a non-molestation order is now a criminal offence and is thus more likely to be dealt with through the criminal system. As the system of enforcement varies according to the order breached, reference should be made to the chapter dealing with the type of order obtained.

AGE AND MENTAL CAPACITY

1.6   In the criminal courts, proceedings can be brought against persons under the age of 18 years where they are deemed to have the capacity to know the difference between right and wrong. Generally, children under the age of 10 years are not considered to properly appreciate the difference for the purpose of criminal acts. The Crime and Disorder Act 1998 makes it clear that proceedings for anti-social behaviour orders can be brought against children of 10 years and over. In civil cases, there can be problems in seeking injunctions against persons under 18 years of age. A 'litigation friend' (a properly responsible adult) will need to be appointed to assist them in the proceedings, and there are distinct difficulties with how any order might be enforced because of the restrictions on sentencing children to prison and the fact that they are unlikely to have assets which could be confiscated or from which fines could be paid. However, there may still be benefits in obtaining an injunction, for example, there might be a power of arrest attached to the order which means that the underage wrongdoer can at least be removed from the area, albeit temporarily, and thus perhaps a breathing space can be given to the victim of his behaviour.

1.7 Persons with limited capacity to understand either the order telling them not to do something or who have limited abilities to control their own behaviour are clearly likely to present procedural difficulties to the person seeking the remedy against them. The criminal system has the ability in certain cases to commit the defendant to a hospital when, for example, a serious offence has been committed but, because of the defendant's mental health problems, he cannot be dealt with through the usual enforcement routes. The civil system has greater restrictions on the steps it can take. The chapters dealing with the types of order which may be obtained also cover the question of underage respondents and those with mental health issues in relation to those types of orders.

STRUCTURE OF THIS BOOK

1.8 Although each potential remedy involves different statutes and different procedures, they all follow the same basic format, whereby the person seeking the remedy makes the appropriate application to the relevant court, there are one or more court hearings, and a decision is made as to whether the claim for the remedy has been made out. A final order is then made. This book endeavours to provide the practitioner with the statutory basis for the remedy sought, who may apply, against whom an order may be made and the procedure to be followed. In addition to quoting relevant legislation and rules, case-law has been cited to assist in showing how the law and procedure has developed, and precedents provided at the end of each chapter which may offer a framework which can be adapted to suit each individual matter.

Chapter 2

ANTI-SOCIAL BEHAVIOUR ORDERS

INTRODUCTION

2.1   In the 1990s anti-social behaviour was identified as a serious problem in urban housing estates and deprived inner city areas where young persons or groups of young persons caused fear, distress and misery to innocent people by their conduct. It was generally acknowledged that the criminal law offered insufficient protection to communities[1] and was not the most appropriate tool to deal with low level crime and nuisance behaviour. Dealing with anti-social behaviour became a government priority which resulted in the passing of the Crime and Disorder Act 1998 (CDA 1998) which gave legal force to the concept of the anti-social behaviour order (ASBO). This provided a legal mechanism for identifying instances where the public required protection from anti-social behaviour, and was supported by a special procedure that ensured matters could be dealt with speedily while minimising the risk to those who gave evidence to substantiate the allegations of nuisance and annoyance. ASBOs are not designed to replace existing legislation but complement existing measures to combat anti-social behaviour, and have become the main tool available to local authorities and the police in this area. They relate to issues that concern everyone in the community such as behaviour which cannot be discounted as generational issues and which impact upon the quality of life of the young and old alike. ASBOs are a statutory creation and have legal force.

2.2   The Police Reform Act 2002 introduced important changes, including the availability of ASBOs which extend across any defined area in England and Wales and the granting of power to a court to impose an order at the same time as passing sentence for a criminal conviction.

2.3   The Home Office has issued guides to ASBOs in 1999, 2002 and in August 2006

2.4   Defining anti-social behaviour is not easy. The only definition in *law* is contained in s 1(1) of the CDA 1998 which provides that 'anti-social behaviour' means acting in 'a manner that caused or was likely to cause harassment alarm or distress to one or more persons not of the same household as himself'. By contrast, anti-social behaviour is not 'run of the mill disputes between neighbours, petty intolerance or minor one-off acts'.[2]

---

[1]   *R (on the application of McCann) v Manchester Crown Court* [2003] 1 AC 787, per Lord Steyn.
[2]   Home Office Guidance 1999.

2.5   There has been criticism that the present wording is too wide. The House of Commons Select Committee considered this in its report on anti-social behaviour and reached the conclusion[3] that it would not be right to be more specific as:

- the definitions work well for enforcement purposes;

- exhaustive lists of behaviour which would be considered to be anti-social behaviour by central government would not be workable and anomalous; and

- inherently anti-social behaviour is a local problem and may take different forms in different localities.

The major strength of the current statutory description of anti-social behaviour is that the description is flexible.

2.6   ASBOs and anti-social behaviour injunctions are not wholly dissimilar to injunctions under the Family Law Act 1996,[4] in that they are intended to be preventative rather than punitive.

2.7   When s 1 of the CDA 1998 was enacted it was intended that the model of a civil remedy of an injunction should be adopted, with criminal sanctions for breach of the order. This aspect of ASBOs was, and still is, the most contentious aspect of the regime. CDA 1998 came into force on 1 April 1999. The initial use of ASBOs by relevant authorities was disappointing and the Government responded with a raft of legislative amendments[5] designed to improve the effectiveness and cost-efficiency of ASBOs. The result has been a dramatic take-up in the use of ASBOs since 2003.[6]

POTENTIAL COMPLAINANTS

2.8   Magistrates' courts are empowered by Pt 1 of the CDA 1998 to grant ASBOs and also three ancillary orders, namely intervention orders, individual support orders and parenting orders. Applications are made to magistrates' court sitting in its civil jurisdiction. The power to grant ASBOs has been extended to county courts since 1 April 2003.

2.9   Section 1(1) of the CDA 1998 provides:

---

[3]   House of Commons Select Committee, Anti-Social Behaviour, Fifth Report of Session Report 2004–05, recommendation 7.

[4]   For a full discussion of injunctions under the Family Law Act 1996, see Chapter 6.

[5]   Police Reform Act 2002, Anti-Social Behaviour Act 2003 and Serious Organised Crime and Police Act 2005.

[6]   For statistics see www.crimereduction.homeoffice.gov.uk/asbos/asbos2.htm.

'An application for an order under this section may be made by a relevant authority if it appears to the authority that the following conditions are fulfilled with respect to any person aged 10 or over, namely—

(a) that the person has acted, since the commencement date, in an anti-social manner, that is to say, in a manner that caused or was likely to cause harassment, alarm or distress to one or more persons not of the same household as himself; and

(b) that such an order is necessary to protect relevant persons from further anti-social acts by him.'

2.10 'Relevant authority', for the purpose of the Act (see ss 1A, 1B and 1E) means:

(1) council for a local government area;

(2) in relation to England, a county council;

(3) the chief officer of police of any police force maintained for a police area;

(4) the chief constable of the British Transport Police Force;

(5) any person registered under s 1 of the Housing Act 1996 as a social landlord who provides or manages any houses or hostel in a local government area;

(6) a housing action trust established by order in pursuance of s 62 of the Housing Act 1988;

(7) the Environment Agency;

(8) Transport for London; or

(9) any person or body of any other description specified in an order made by the Secretary of State.

2.11 The meaning of 'relevant persons' is dependent upon the applicant. In the event that the applicant is the local authority or local police, relevant persons would be those in the local authority area or local police area. If the applicant is the British Transport Police this would mean persons likely to be or persons in or on the vicinity of policed premises. Where the applicant is a social landlord this would mean persons residing in, or those who are on and likely to be on, premises, or persons in the vicinity of or likely to be in the vicinity of, premises managed by the social landlord.

2.12 Similar considerations would apply in the event that the applicant is the Environment Agency or Transport for London.

POTENTIAL DEFENDANTS

2.13   An order can be made against anyone who is aged 10 or over who has acted or is likely to act in an anti-social manner. ASBOs are issued against individuals and not against organisations.

2.14   The orders are tenure-neutral and therefore where the defendant lives is not of any consequence, ie orders are not made against only social housing tenants. As the order is specific to a person it remains in force even if the person moves home. This is because ASBOs are used against a variety of situations and settings. They are relevant to misconduct in public places such as parks, shopping centres and the like.

2.15   In the event that the allegations relate to groups of people the case needs to be made against each individual although such cases can and are normally heard together.

CONDITIONS TO BE SATISFIED BEFORE ORDER IS MADE

2.16   Applications are made to magistrates' court by the complaint. The complaint must be made to the magistrates' court whose commission area covers the police commission area or local government area.

Precondition

2.17   It is a precondition that consultation should take place between local agencies, ie the local government for the area must consult with the chief officer of police for the area. *Failure to consult* is unlikely to render the application void. It is also not necessary for agreement to be reached between the parties.

Notification to defendants

2.18   There is no precondition for potential defendants to be notified prior to commencing proceedings. Further, a failure to notify proposed defendants does not amount to a breach of or infringement of defendants' rights under Arts 6 and 8 of the ECHR,[7] especially where previous behaviour and history of the defendants is such that notification will not be productive.

---

[7]   *Wareham v Purbeck District Council* [2005] EWHC 358 (Admin).

TIME LIMITS FOR MAKING AN APPLICATION

2.19 A 6-month time limit applies to applications that are made by way of complaint to the magistrates' courts. Section 127(1) of the Magistrates' Courts Act 1980 states that:

> 'Except as otherwise expressly provided by any enactment and subject to subsection (2) below, a magistrates' court shall not try an information or hear a complaint unless the information was laid or the complaint made within six months from the time when the offence was committed, or the matter of complaint arose.'

Hence, it must be proven by the applicant that at least one act of anti-social behaviour has been committed within 6 months of the complaint. Incidents that pre-date the 6-month stipulation may be used to demonstrate a course of conduct. Such acts may also be relevant to the issue as to whether the defendant has behaved in an anti-social manner within s 1(1)(a) so that they amount to similar fact evidence and may be used as evidence to demonstrate the necessity for making an order under s 1(1)(b) of the CDA 1998.[8]

2.20 Section 1(5A) of the CDA 1998 provides that s 127 of the Magistrates' Courts Act 1980 shall not be affected, namely limitation of time in relation to information laid or complaints made in magistrates' courts. Section 127 is not about admissibility of evidence but is about jurisdiction. Upon jurisdiction being established the court can receive evidence about acts committed beyond the 6-month period as background information for the reasons set out in **2.19**.

INTERIM ORDERS

2.21 The court may, pending final determination of an application before it, make an interim order if it is *just* to do so.

2.22 An interim order must only be made for a specified period and will cease upon a final decision being made. It may be varied, renewed or discharged prior to the making of a final order. The order will prohibit the defendant from doing anything specified in the order.

2.23 The application must be made as set out in Sch 5 to the Magistrates' Courts (Anti-Social Behaviour Orders) Rules 2002.[9] However, it is not crucial to use the form.

2.24 The application is made on notice to the defendant or with the leave of the justices' clerk on a without notice basis. In the latter instance leave will only

---

[8] *Stevens v South East Surrey Magistrates' Court* [2004] EWHC 1456 (Admin).
[9] SI 2002/2784 (as amended by the Magistrates' Courts (Miscellaneous Amendments) Rules 2003, SI 2003/1236).

be granted if is *necessary* for such an application to be made. The court may direct the application be made on notice where it refuses to make an interim order.

2.25 Upon an interim order being made the following documents *must be personally served* upon the defendant:

(1)   the main application;

(2)   the interim order;

(3)   the summons, endorsed with the date for the defendant to attend court.

Service of the above documents must be effected as soon as possible after the interim order is made and, until such time as personal service is effected, the order will not take effect.

2.26 In the event that the interim order is not served within 7 days of the order being made it ceases to have effect.

2.27 If the defendant makes an application to vary or discharge the order he must be given an opportunity to make oral representations and, until this is done, his application cannot be dismissed.

FULL ORDERS

2.28 The consequences of an ASBO are serious and hence procedural fairness requires that the defendant should have notice of the allegations against him.[10]

2.29 Application is made by complaint against the defendant by the relevant authority to a magistrates' court whether the defendant is a young person or child.

2.30 The application may be made in the form prescribed in Sch 1 to the Magistrates' Courts (Anti-Social Behaviour Orders) Rules 2002. The use of the form is optional.

2.31 A summons is issued to the relevant authority whose responsibility it is to effect service of the summons on the defendant. Service of the summons may be effected by personal service or by mailing the summons to the defendant's last known address. The summons is deemed served if personal service is effected or if it is posted unless proved to the contrary by the defendant. The summons directed to the defendant requiring him to attend before a magistrates' court should be in the form set out in Sch 2 to the Magistrates' Courts (Anti-Social Behaviour Orders) Rules 2002.

---

[10]   *W v Acton Youth Court* (unreported) 26 April 2005, per Pitchers J.

2.32 It may be *prudent* to effect personal service and file an affidavit of service to avoid later doubts as to service.

2.33 Home Office Guidance (August 2006) recommends that the following documents be served upon the defendant with the summons:

(1) completed application form;

(2) evidence of statutory consultation;

(3) guidance as to how the defendant can obtain legal advice and representation;

(4) notice of hearsay evidence;

(5) details of evidence in support; and

(6) a warning to the defendant that it is an offence to pervert the course of justice and that witness intimidation is liable to lead to prosecution.

2.34 As far as possible service of the summons should be effected on the defendant in person. In the event that this is not possible, service should be effected at the last known address of the defendant.

2.35 Where proceedings relate to a child or young person a copy of the summons should be effected on the person with parental responsibility. 'Parent' has the same meaning as under s 1 of the Family Law Reform Act 1987.

2.36 Prior to evidence being disclosed the applicant should consult with the police and other authorities/agencies to ensure that reasonable steps have been taken to provide witness support and prevent witness intimidation. Evidence should not be disclosed without the witnesses express permission. Evidence that is not disclosed may not be relied upon.

2.37 In addition to the above it is good practice to add a copy of the proposed order, although the precise terms and duration are entirely a matter for the court.

DIRECTIONS

2.38 It is advisable and good practice to request an early hearing date of the first hearing of an application so that it can be ascertained whether the application is contested. In the event that the application is to be contested the issues can be identified at this early stage.

2.39 It is also advisable to request the court to grant directions at a hearing, or, if appropriate, at the hearing for an interim order (although this will be rare given that the defendant may not be present or represented and the issues may not be known at this stage especially if it is an application made without notice). Directions as to the further conduct of the matter would assist, although the Civil Procedure Rules 1998 do not apply to magistrates' courts and the Criminal Procedure Rules 2005 do not apply as the proceedings are civil.

2.40 Directions will assist in securing an early date for the final hearing – be fair and effective and hopefully avoid unnecessary delays in the final determination of the matter.

2.41 Home Office Guidance (August 2006) recommends that a minimum of eight identical court bundles should be prepared as follows:

- three for the magistrates;

- one for the legal adviser;

- one for the applicant's solicitor;

- one for the defendants solicitor;

- one for the witness;

- one for the defendant.

The bundles should be indexed and paginated, and contain:

- the summons for the order and proof of service;

- the application for the order;

- the defendant's details;

- the defendant's previous convictions;

- the defendant's acceptable behaviour contract agreements;

- a map and description of the exclusion zone;

- an association chart (if the action relates to anti-social behaviour by a group of persons);

- documentation of statutory consultations;

- supporting statements from multi-agency consultation;

- statement of the officer in the case;

- any other witness statements;

- hearsay notices;

- a draft order for approval by court; and

- a home circumstances report where the defendant is a child or young person.

2.42 The contents of the bundle should be agreed with the defendant's solicitor if possible prior to the pre-trial review and served upon the defendant as soon as possible after the summons is served.

2.43 Disclosure should be transparent and complete.

2.44 Suggested directions include:

(1) filing and service of defence;

(2) disclosure of documents (there is no formal requirement for disclosure. However, it is advisable that the applicant should provide disclosure voluntarily whether or not such disclosure supports the application, as failure to do so may result in a finding that the defendant's rights under Art 6 of the ECHR have been breached);

(3) filing of evidence by both parties and the time scales thereof;

(4) the issue as to whether witness statements will stand as witnesses' evidence in chief;

(5) the determination of applications for special measures directions;

(6) reporting restrictions for children and young persons;

(7) filing of agreed and paginated bundle of documents by the applicant, such bundle to include case summary, schedule of issues and the order sought by each party and the timescale for filing the bundle;

(8) in appropriate instances filing of skeleton arguments.

THE FINAL HEARING

2.45 Any magistrate or judge may hear the case. Evidence will be given on oath (s 98 of the Magistrates' Courts Act 1980). At the final hearing the issues before the court will be:

(1)   whether the defendant has acted in such a manner as to cause harassment, alarm or distress;

(2)   whether an order is necessary to protect relevant persons;

(3)   details of the prohibitions that must be specified in the order;

(4)   duration of the order.

Evidence

2.46   Home Office Guidance (August 2006) suggests that evidence on behalf of the applicant may include the following:

(1)   evidence of breach of an acceptable behaviour contract;

(2)   witness statements from persons affected by the behaviour;

(3)   police, landlord or similar agencies' record of incidents and attendance at the property;

(4)   police officers statements;

(5)   statement from professional witnesses such as the truancy officer, health visitor or council official;

(6)   video or CCTV footage;

(7)   reports from other agencies such as the probation service;

(8)   copies of custody records of previous arrests relevant to the application;

(9)   previous convictions;

(10) evidence of complaints recorded by the police, housing providers or other agencies;

(11) relevant civil proceedings such as eviction for similar behaviour;

(12) information from witness diaries.

Hearsay evidence

2.47   The House of Lords' judgment in *R v Crown Court at Manchester ex parte McCann*[11] provides confirmation that hearsay evidence is admissible. Lord Steyn stated as follows:

---

[11]   [2002] UKHL 39.

'Having concluded that proceedings in question are civil under domestic law and article 6, it follows that the machinery of the Civil Evidence Act 1995 and the Magistrates' Courts (Hearsay Evidence in Civil Proceedings) Rules 1999 allow the introduction of such evidence under the first part of section 1.

... use of the Civil Evidence Act 1995 and the Rules in cases under the first part of section 1 are not in anyway incompatible with the Human Rights Act 1998.

... pragmatism dictates that the task of the magistrates should be made more straight forward ... by ruling that they must in all cases under section 1 apply the criminal standard ... hearsay evidence will often be of crucial importance. For my part, hearsay evidence depending on its logical probativeness is quite capable of satisfying the requirements of section1 (1).'

2.48 Hearsay evidence is generally admissible. The admissibility of hearsay evidence is governed by the Civil Evidence Act 1995. The court will have to assess the reliability of hearsay evidence and the factors set out in s 4(2) of the 1995 Act are important. They are:

'(a) whether it would have been reasonable and practicable for the party by whom the evidence was adduced to have produced the maker of the original statement as a witness;

(b) whether the original statement was made contemporaneously with the occurrence or existence of the matter stated;

(c) whether the evidence involves multiple hearsay;

(d) whether any person involved had any motive to conceal or misrepresent matters;

(e) whether the original statement was an edited account, or was made in collaboration with another or for a particular purpose;

(f) whether the circumstances in which the evidence is adduced as hearsay are such as to suggest an attempt to prevent proper evaluation of its weight.'

The Magistrates' Courts (Hearsay Evidence in Civil Proceedings) Rules 1999[12] deal with the procedure for admitting hearsay evidence. Essentially a party who desires to give hearsay evidence at the hearing must, at least 21 days before the hearing, serve a copy upon all parties and file a copy of the notice at court by serving it on the justices' clerk. The notice must:

(a) state it is a hearsay notice;

(b) identify the proceedings in which the hearsay evidence is to be tendered;

(c) state that the party proposes to adduce hearsay evidence;

(d) identify the hearsay evidence;

(e) identify the person who made the statement which is to be given in evidence; and

---

[12] SI 1999/681.

(f)   state why the person will not be called to give oral evidence.

The court can make a direction of its own motion. The court may, on an application being made, allow another party to call and cross-examine the person who made the statement on its contents.

2.49   It is a matter for the judge or magistrate to decide what weight he or she attaches to hearsay evidence. Section 1(1) of the 1995 Act provides that in civil proceedings evidence shall not be excluded on the ground that it is hearsay.

2.50   Hearsay is defined as a statement made otherwise than by a person while giving oral evidence in the proceedings which is tendered as evidence of matters stated (s 1(2)(a)). Multiple hearsay is also admissible although the weight attached is likely to be less.

2.51   Notice of intention to rely upon hearsay evidence must be given by the party who intends to rely on such evidence to the other parties (s 2(1)). Failure to comply will not render such evidence inadmissible but may affect the weight given to it. In estimating the weight to be given to hearsay evidence in civil proceedings the court shall have regard to any circumstances from which any inference can reasonably be drawn as to the reliability or otherwise of the evidence.

2.52   Hearsay evidence shall not be admitted if or to the extent that it is shown to consist of, or to be proved by means of, a statement made by a person who at the time he made the statement was not competent as a witness (s 5). A person will not be a competent witness if he suffers from such mental or physical infirmity, or lack of understanding, as would render him incompetent as a witness in civil proceedings. A child will be treated as competent as a witness if he satisfies the requirements of s 96(2)(a) and (b) of the Children Act 1989.

2.53   In any application for an ASBO the use of hearsay evidence will be unavoidable and will be essential to enable magistrates to make an informed decision about the scale and nature of the alleged behaviour and the prohibitions that must be imposed.

2.54   Hearsay allows a police officer to give evidence on behalf of a witness who wants to remain anonymous. It could include details such as dates, times, places, description of actions, who was present and what was said.

2.55   Hearsay can also include evidence from the person taking the statement and evidence of the witness' demeanor. Such evidence could also be based upon the person's own judgment of the situation.

2.56   Professional witnesses such as council officials, railway staff, health visitors, doctors and police officers can give evidence about their assessment of the defendant and his behaviour.

Previous convictions

2.57 The defendant's previous convictions can be used to prove that he has acted in an anti-social manner and as evidence that an order is necessary. Section 11(1) of the Civil Evidence Act 1968 provides that reliance may be placed upon previous convictions which are relevant to the issues in the proceedings.

Special measures directions

2.58 Witnesses have a right to give their best evidence and it is the best protection they have. Section 29 of the Youth Justice and Criminal Evidence Act 1999 permits witnesses to give their evidence with the help of an intermediary. In appropriate cases the court will make a special measures order.

2.59 Special measures directions may be sought on an application for an ASBO to include interim orders.

2.60 A witness will be eligible for special measures directions if:

(a) he is under the age of 17 at the time of the hearing;

(b) he suffers from any disability (mental or physical) which may render the quality of the evidence to be diminished;

(c) the quality of the evidence may be affected due to fear or distress in having to give evidence.

2.61 Pursuant to s 16 of the Youth Justice and Criminal Evidence Act 1999 vulnerable witnesses are either:

(a) a child under the age of 17; or

(b) a person who is suffering from a mental or physical disability, or disorder or significant impairment of intelligence and social functioning by reason of which the court considers that the quality of evidence given by him is likely to be diminished.

2.62 The witness' needs should be picked up at an early stage. Intermediaries are speech and language professionals such as social and medical professionals, therapists and teachers. Their expertise is in assessing the needs of children and vulnerable adults and establishing a rapport with them.

2.63 In cases involving such witnesses it is best for trial counsel and the judge to hold a hearing with the intermediary to establish the grounds rules, such as the manner in which the witness is to be questioned, need for a TV link, need for transcripts for the jury, etc.

Reporting restrictions

2.64   As these are proceedings for a civil order in the magistrates' court there are no reporting restrictions. Applicants may wish to publicise both interim and final orders as such publicity may be a further deterrent and enhance the prospect of enforcement. There is however no 'naming and shaming' since ASBOs are not intended to punish individuals but to protect communities. The public do have an interest in knowing who is committing anti-social acts. Note, however, that the court has a discretion under s 39 of the Children and Young Persons Act 1933 to impose restrictions. The principles have been set out in *R v Winchester Crown Court ex parte B*.[13] These were referred to by Elias J in *R (T) v St Albans Crown Court and others*[14] and he expressed his approval of them in the context of ASBOs. The court should consider:

(1)   whether there are good reasons for disclosing the name of the defendant;

(2)   the age of the defendant and whether public identification as a criminal is likely to cause damage;

(3)   the welfare of the child or young person (s 44 of the Children and Young Persons Act 1933);

(4)   the interests of the public to know the identity of convicted criminals;

(5)   whether naming individuals who have been convicted may be a deterrent to others;

(6)   whether the order made is interim or final (it is more likely that the court will make a restriction order in respect of an interim order, ie until the allegations against the defendant are proven);

(7)   whether there is an appeal pending.

2.65   The principles that emerge in the judgment of Kennedy LJ in *R (Stanley, Marshall and Kelly) v Commissioner of Police for the Metropolis and Chief Executive of London Borough of Brent*[15] (*Stanley v Brent*) are as follows:

(1)   ASBOs are not intended as a punishment or embarrassment to individuals (no naming and shaming) but are intended to protect communities.

(2)   There is an implied power in the CDA 1998 and Local Government Act 2000 to publicise an order for effective enforcement.

(3)   Publicity helps in tackling anti-social behaviour.

---

[13]   [2000] 1 Cr App R 11.
[14]   [2002] EWHC 1129 (Admin).
[15]   [2004] EWHC 2229 (Admin).

(4)　Orders protect local communities.

(5)　The effectiveness of the order will depend on people's knowledge of it.

(6)　Information about orders keeps the community informed that action is being taken to tackle problems in the area.

(7)　A case-by-case approach should be adopted and each case must be decided on its merits. Publicity should be expected in most cases.

(8)　It is necessary to balance the human rights of the individuals against whom the order is obtained against those of the community as a whole.

(9)　Publicity should be the norm and not the exception. The individual against whom the order is made should understand that the community is likely to learn about it.

(10)　Publicity should be reasonable and proportionate to the nature and extent of the anti-social behaviour and take account of the vulnerability of the individual involved.

2.66　Section 1C(9C) of the CDA 1998 provides that s 49 of the 1933 Act does not apply in respect of a child or young person who is convicted and a resultant order is made if the proceedings relate to the making of the order. This means that details of the child or young person may be published but the criminal offence in respect of which the order was made still remains subject to automatic reporting restrictions.

2.67　Pursuant to s 141 of the Serious Organised Crime and Police Act 2005 the automatic reporting restrictions for breaches committed by children and young persons are disapplied for proceedings in court in respect of breaches of anti-social behaviour orders by children and young persons. The court, however, retains a discretion to apply reporting restrictions.

2.68　Pursuant to s 144 of the Serious Organised Crime and Disorder Act 2005 a magistrates' court is empowered to make a parental compensation order where a child under the age of 10 has taken or caused loss or damage to property in the course of behaving anti-socially.

2.69　Procedure relating to the final hearing is governed by s 55 of the Magistrates' Courts Act 1980 (conducting the hearing in the absence of the defendant) and r 14 of the Magistrates' Courts Rules 1981 (procedure at the hearing).

Conducting the final hearing without the defendant

2.70　Pursuant to s 55 of the Magistrates' Courts Act 1980 the court may proceed with the hearing in the absence of the defendant if it is satisfied as to proper service of the proceedings and notification of the hearing upon the defendant. Proceedings should also have been served within a reasonable time before the hearing or the defendant may have attended court previously to answer the complaint and is clearly aware of the proceedings. The court may choose to adjourn the hearing and issue a warrant for the defendant's arrest. The same precautions as to service apply if a warrant is issued.

THE HEARING

2.71 The hearing will usually begin with the applicant opening the case followed by evidence being adduced by the applicant. The defendant then has the right to address the court whether he intends to rely upon any evidence. The defendant will not usually address the court at this stage unless the applicant's case is so weak or the case is flawed to such an extent as to cause the defendant to make an application for the case to be dismissed. It is then open to the defendant to call his evidence. Following this the defendant may address the court.

2.72 Both parties may, with the leave of court, address the court for a second time. If such an opportunity is offered to one party the court must offer a similar opportunity to the other party. Note, however, that if the defendant obtains the leave of court to address it for the second time this must be done before the applicant's second address, if any.

2.73 *It would be helpful if the court outlines the procedure that will be adopted, especially if the defendant attends court unrepresented.* This may be done by the judge or alternatively the legal representatives.

Conditions

2.74 Section 1(4) of the CDA 1998 provides that:

> '(4) If, on such an application it is proved that the conditions mentioned in subsection (1) above are fulfilled, the magistrates' court may make an order under this section (an "anti-social behaviour order") which prohibits the defendant from doing anything described in the order.'

2.75 When considering the acts said to have been committed by the defendant the court:

(1) will not try an information or hear a complaint if 6 months have elapsed since the offence was committed or the matter of complaint arose;

(2) will disregard any act of the defendant which he shows was reasonable in the circumstances (s 5 of the CDA 1998);

(3) will disregard the defendant's intention;

(4)   will not make an order merely on the basis that the defendant consents;

(5)   will make an order, if appropriate, on the basis of just one act of anti-social behaviour;

(6)   will make an order even where the conduct complained of has ceased by the time the application is made.[16]

Burden of proof

2.76 These are civil proceedings. They are matters heard by magistrates' courts sitting in their civil jurisdiction. Nevertheless, the applicant must prove *beyond reasonable doubt* that the defendant has acted in an anti-social manner within s 1(1)(a) of the CDA 1998.

2.77 In *R (McCann) v Manchester Crown Court*[17] the House of Lords, while confirming that ASBOs are civil orders, stated that the standard of proof is as follows:[18]

> 'they [magistrates] must in all cases under section 1 apply the criminal standard ... it will be sufficient for the magistrates, when applying section 1(1)(a) to be *sure* that the defendant has acted in an anti-social manner, that is to say in a manner which caused or was likely to cause harassment, alarm, or distress to one or more persons not of the same household as himself.'

2.78 The issue as to whether an order is *necessary* within s 1(1)(b) does not need to be proven beyond reasonable doubt as it is *a question of judgment*. In *R (McCann) v Manchester Crown Court* (above) Lord Steyn said:

> 'The inquiry under section 1(1) (b), namely that such an order is necessary to protect persons from further anti-social acts does not involve a standard of proof: it is an exercise of judgment or evaluation ...'

Decision as to defendant's behaviour

2.79 It is a *question of fact* whether the defendant's conduct has caused or is likely to cause harassment, alarm or distress. These words are given their ordinary and natural meaning.

•   The words 'likely to cause' in s 1(1)(a) of the Act enable the applicant to prove the defendant's anti-social behaviour in appropriate cases without calling witnesses who have been subjected to such behaviour.[19]

---

[16]   *S v Poole Borough Council* [2002] EWHC 244 (Admin).
[17]   [2002] UKHL 39.
[18]   Per Lord Steyn, at [37].
[19]   *R (Gosport Borough Council) v Farenham Magistrates' Court* [2006] ECWA 3047 (Admin).

- The expression 'likely to cause' allows someone other than the victim to give evidence of the likelihood of it occurring. Thus professionals can be used to give evidence where victims who have been targeted are unwilling to give evidence for fear of reprisal.

2.80 Whilst the applicant does not have to prove intention he must show that harassment, alarm or distress *was caused to one or more persons not of the same household as the defendant*. 'Household' is given its ordinary meaning.

Examples of behaviour

2.81 Anti-social behaviour is not defined by the Act. Anti-social behaviour covers a wide range of behaviour and the lack of definition grants flexibility to courts in deciding what acts constitute anti-social behaviour. The term can include criminal behaviour. Much depends upon the alleged conduct and more particularly the consequences and effect of such conduct upon any member or members of the community within which it is taking place.

2.82 The Home Office has provided guidance (August 2006) as to the types of conduct that could justify granting an ASBO, and listed below are some examples. It should be noted that the list is not exhaustive:

- harassment of residents or passers-by;

- criminal damage;

- verbal abuse;

- noise nuisance;

- vandalism;

- engaging in threatening behaviour;

- writing graffiti;

- assault;

- prostitution;

- racial abuse;

- vehicle vandalism;

- substance misuse;

- begging;

- kerb-crawling;

- joyriding.

Necessity for order

2.83 ASBOs are intended to be preventative and not punitive. This is emphasised by the test of necessity. In every case of proposed prohibition the court *must be satisfied that an order is necessary to protect relevant persons* from being subjected to further acts of anti-social behaviour.

2.84 In *S v Poole Borough Council*[20] Simon Brown LJ said that 'once an ASBO has been made, its effect will be likely to deter future misconduct'.

2.85 An ASBO may be granted if no further conduct has ensued since the making of the interim order and if the conduct complained of ceased since the application was made.

2.86 Matters that should be considered when making an order include:

(1) the conduct;

(2) frequency and duration of such conduct;

(3) the impact of such conduct;

(4) the steps taken by applicant before making the application to prevent repetition;

(5) the possibility of repetition if an order is not made;

(6) whether any interim order made has been breached;

(7) the age, personal characteristics and relevant previous convictions of the defendant.

Interim order made on a without notice basis

2.87 An application for an interim order under s 1D of the CDA 1998 may, with the leave of the justices' clerk, be made without notice being given to the defendant. It is for the justices' clerk to decide whether it is necessary for an interim order to be made without notice to the defendant.

---

[20]   [2002] EWHC 244 (Admin).

2.88   The Divisional Court held in *R (Manchester City Council) v Manchester City Magistrates' Court*[21] that regard should be had to the following matters (note however that the list is non-exhaustive):

(1)   the likely response of the defendant upon receiving notice of the application;

(2)   whether such response was likely to prejudice the complainant, having regard to the complainants' vulnerability;

(3)   the gravity of the conduct complained of;

(4)   the urgency for the order;

(5)   the prohibitions sought;

(6)   the rights of the defendant to be notified of the application;

(7)   the ineffectiveness of the order until it is served and the time scale for the order;

(8)   the defendant's right to have the order varied or discharged.

Obtaining/granting interim order

2.89   Interim orders may be made pursuant to s 1D of the CDA 1998.[22] This is a temporary order obtained at an initial court hearing held in advance of the full hearing. It may contain the same prohibitions as a full order and carries the same penalties for breach as a full order.

2.90   The court has to consider whether it is *just* to make an interim order. Whether the application is made on notice or on a without notice basis, this decision is made by the magistrates alone. An interim order with leave of the justices' clerk can be made without notice of the proceedings to the defendant.

2.91   The benefit of the interim order is that it provides immediate protection against anti-social behaviour and will also reduce possibility of witness intimidation. The interim order:

•   will not have effect until it is served upon the defendant;

•   will cease if it is not served within 7 days of it being granted and have no effect;

•   can be varied or discharged on application by the defendant;

---

[21]   [2002] UKHL 39.
[22]   As amended by the Police Reform Act 2002, s 65 and the Serious Organised Crime and Police Act 2005.

- will cease to have effect if the application for an ASBO or county court order is withdrawn or refused;

- has the same penalties for breach as a full order;

- can extend over any defined area of England and Wales.

2.92 The issue as to whether it is just to make the order involves a consideration of all relevant circumstances, and when considering making an order on an interim basis whether there is a strong prima facie case against the defendant.

2.93 Seeking and making an interim order involves a balancing exercise of the following factors:

(1) the need to protect the public against anti-social behaviour;

(2) the seriousness of the behaviour complained of, the urgency to take steps to prevent further acts and the necessity for an interim order;

(3) the extent to which the defendant's rights as a free citizen are affected.

Similar provisions apply when the application is considered an on notice basis.

The order – terms of the order and duration

2.94 The order will impose prohibitions on the defendant and be effective for the period specified in the order.

2.95 The powers to deal with anti-social behaviour have been extended and strengthened by the Police Reform Act 2002. Orders can now also extend across any defined part of England and Wales.

2.96 The orders are not criminal sanctions and are not intended to punish the offender. They are community-based orders that involve local people in the collection of evidence and in enforcement.

2.97 Magistrates' courts, Crown Courts and youth courts can make orders against an individual who has been convicted of a criminal offence. These are known as orders on conviction (CRASBOs). Such orders will be considered at a civil hearing after the verdict. They will not be part of the sentence the offender receives for the criminal offence. A CRASBO can be made by the court of its own initiative or upon an application being made by the prosecutor (s 1C(3) of the CDA 1998). An order can be sought by the police or local authority who may make a request to the court. CRASBOs cannot be made where there is a deferred sentence for the relevant offence. They can only be made if the court sentences or conditionally discharges the offender for a relevant offence. Proceedings may be adjourned for the application to be made.

An interim order may be made pursuant to s 1D(1)(b) of the CDA 1998. A CRASBO is a civil order and has the same effect as obtaining the order following an application. In the event the offender is detained in custody the court can make provisions for the order to be effective upon the defendant's release. In such instances the order takes effect immediately but its terms will be suspended until his release.

2.98 Previously, orders extended only to the defendant's area and adjoining areas. Due to the changes introduced by the Police Reform Act 2002 an order can extend to any defined areas in England and Wales. The more serious the behaviour the greater the likelihood of the court granting a geographically wide order. Such orders will not be granted unless there is evidence that there is an actual or potential danger about the geographical extent of the problem.

Prohibitions

2.99 Once the court has decided that the order is necessary to protect persons from further anti-social acts by the defendant it should then consider what prohibitions are appropriate. Each order and in particular each prohibition should be targeted to the individual and the type of anti-social behaviour it is to prevent. Prohibitions imposed must be specified in the order. Only those prohibitions that are *necessary* to protect relevant person(s) must be imposed. ASBOs cannot be used as a form of punishment and cannot impose positive obligations. In particular:

(1)   Prohibitions cannot be mandatory. They must be prohibitory.

(2)   Each prohibition must be stated clearly and in language that can be readily understood by the defendant.

(3)   A map should be appended to the order showing clearly any exclusion zone.

(4)   Persons with whom the defendant must not associate or contact should be named.

(5)   Each prohibition must be in respect of specific anti-social behaviour which it seeks to prevent.

(6)   The prohibitions imposed must be proportionate and not a means of increasing the sentence the defendant may receive.

(7)   Prohibitions must not be in breach of Arts 8, 10 and 11 of the Human Rights Act 1998.

(8)   Prohibitions can include a stipulation that will prevent a criminal offence being committed, eg prohibit entry into a block of flats rather than preventing criminal damage in the building.

(9) Orders should be realistic and practical.

(10) Orders should be specific when referring to matters of time, for example requiring the defendant to be outside or in particular areas at certain times

(11) Orders must be in terms that make it easy to determine and prosecute a breach.

(12) Orders must contain a prohibition against inciting/encouraging others from indulging in anti-social acts.

(13) Orders must protect all persons in the area covered by the order from the behaviour.

(14) Orders may cover acts that are anti-social and those that are precursors to a criminal act, for example preventing the entry into a shopping centre, rather than on shoplifting.

(15) Orders may include a general condition prohibiting acts that are likely to cause harassment, alarm and distress. This may however be clarified further if appropriate.

(17) Orders may include a prohibition from approaching or harassing a witness named in the court proceedings.

Duration

2.100 The same considerations as to whether an order is necessary could equally apply to the duration of the order. The length of the order will depend upon the facts of each case.

2.101 A full order will remain in effect for a period (not less than 2 years) specified in the order unless it varied, discharged or a further order is made (s 1(7),(9) of the CDA 1998). There is no maximum period. Orders are issued for a minimum of 2 years and can be issued for an indefinite period pending a further order. Either party can apply to vary or discharge the order. Note, however, that the order cannot be discharged in the first 2 years unless all parties consent.

2.102 *An interim order* may be renewed, varied or discharged. It will remain in force until the making of a final order, whereupon it will cease to have effect.

Intervention orders

2.103 Magistrates' courts and county courts are empowered (by virtue of CDA 1998, ss 1G and 1H, as inserted by the Drugs Act 2005, s 20) to grant an intervention order against a defendant whose anti-social behaviour is connected with drug abuse. Such an order can be obtained against a defendant who is aged 18 years or above. Where such an order is sought the relevant authority should:

(1)   make an application for an ASBO;

(2)   obtain a report from a suitably qualified person as to the effect of drug misuse by the defendant; and

(3)   consult with such persons as the Secretary of State may prescribe in order that appropriate activities may be made available.

2.104 The relevant conditions that must be met for the court to grant an intervention order when making an ASBO are:

(1)   that such an order is desirable to prevent a recurrence of behaviour that led to an ASBO;

(2)   appropriate activities pertaining to the cause or trigger behaviour are available;

(3)   the defendant is not (at the time the intervention order is made) subject to another intervention order or to any other treatment relating to the trigger behaviour or its cause; and

(4)   the Secretary of State has notified the court that appropriate activities are available in the area where the defendant lives (this has been done by virtue of Home Office Circular 29/2006 and will remain effective until withdrawn).

2.105 The *maximum* duration of an intervention order is *6 months*. The order will require the defendant to comply with the requirements specified in the order and with the directions issued by an authorised person in order to implement the requirements.

Individual support orders

2.106 Individual support orders are similar to intervention orders in that they are intended to prevent a recurrence of the behaviour that led to an ASBO being made against the defendant. However, individual support orders can be obtained against children and young persons as well as persons aged 18 and above. The ethos of ASBOs is that they combine the twin-track approach of enforcement and support. Since May 2004 courts have been able to issue individual support orders to juveniles issued with ASBOs on application.

2.107 By virtue of s 1AA of the CDA 1998 (as inserted by the Criminal Justice Act 2003), a court must consider whether the following individual support conditions are fulfilled:

(1) an order is desirable to prevent repetition of anti-social behaviour;

(2) the defendant is not already subject to a similar order;

(3) the Secretary of State has notified the court that arrangements are available for implementing such orders in the area where the defendant lives (this has been done by virtue of Home Office Circular 25/2-004 and will remain effective until withdrawn).
If the above conditions are met, the court *must* make an individual support order.

2.108 The court must obtain a report from a social worker or a member of the youth offending team confirming that the above conditions are satisfied and the appropriate prohibitions against the defendant and the details of the defendant's obligations that must be included in the order.

2.109 In the event that the court is not satisfied that such an order should be made this must be stated in court.

2.110 The *maximum duration* of such an order is *6 months*. The order will require the defendant to comply with the requirements specified in the order and with any directions given by the responsible officer in order to implement the requirements.

2.111 Section 322(1AB) requires the court to explain clearly to the defendant the terms of the order in 'ordinary language'. When the ASBO ceases to have effect, so will the individual support order.

2.112 Breach of an individual support order is an offence and criminal penalties apply.

Parenting orders

2.113 Sections 8, 9 and 10 of the CDA 1998 deal with parenting orders. The nature of such orders is preventative rather than punitive, and is aimed at preventing a recurrence of the behaviour that led to an ASBO. A 'relevant authority' for these purposes was, until October 2007, a local education authority. However, the Police and Justice Act 2006 inserted a new s 26C into the CDA 1998 which widens the scope of 'relevant authority' to include local authorities and registered social landlords. The procedure is now contained in amended CPR Part 65.

2.114 The court *must* make a parenting order when it deals with a defendant under the age of 16 and *may* make such an order if the defendant is aged 16 or 17.

2.115 It is essential that parents and guardians take responsibility for the behaviour of their children. The court can decide to make a parenting order.

The consent of the parent or guardian is not needed. Parenting orders are civil orders and help to engage parents to address their child's offending behaviour, to establish discipline and to build a relationship with their child.

2.116 The court must, before it makes such an order, obtain and consider information relating to the family circumstances and also consider what, if any, effect such an order will have on the family.

2.117 The *maximum* duration of the order is *12 months*. The parents will be required by such an order to comply with the requirements specified in the order and to attend, for a concurrent period of 3 months, a counselling or guidance programme specified by the responsible officer.

2.118 There is a requirement pursuant to s 9 that the order and its effect should be explained to the parent in 'ordinary language', as is also the case with variation, discharge and breach of the order.

One year review of juveniles' ASBOs

2.119 Since young persons' circumstances change constantly, orders should be reviewed every year in order to provide support and prevent breach. This is an administrative exercise rather than judicial intervention. The review should be undertaken by the team that initiated the proceedings. Where practicable the youth offending team should provide an assessment of the young person. Depending upon the progress made an application to vary or discharge the order or to strengthen the prohibitions may be made. Applications to vary or discharge the order must be made to the court. The overriding considerations will be the needs and safety of the community. The community's view on the effectiveness of the order will have to be included in the review.

REMINDER/CHECKLIST FOR CONTENT OF ORDER

2.120 Where the court makes an order the order should:

(1)   record the facts;

(2)   state the reasons for making the order;

(3)   state the prohibitions (which must be valid) clearly and in precise terms so that any breach can be easily identified and proved;

(4)   use language that can be readily understood by the defendant;

(5)   have appended to it a copy of the map which must clearly delineate any exclusion zone;

(6)   be pronounced in open court;

(7)   state the consequences of the breach to the defendant;

(8)   state the duration of the order.

Where the defendant is a foreign national some courts consider it to be good practice to arrange for a translation of the order in the defendant's native tongue. ASBOs on juveniles should be reviewed every year

2.121 A copy of the order should be served upon the defendant before he leaves court. In appropriate instances consideration should be given to a translation of the order in the defendant's native language.

2.122 Any draft proposed order filed with the papers should include all the above.

Breach

2.123 A person will be guilty of an offence if he, without reasonable excuse, does anything which he is prohibited from doing by the court order.

2.124 Breach of an order is a criminal offence which is arrestable and recordable. Proceedings for breach may be heard in the magistrates' court or be committed to the Crown Court. The proceedings are the same whether they relate to interim or full orders obtained by making an application to the magistrates' court or county court or orders obtained on conviction in criminal proceedings.

2.125 A copy of the order form used by magistrates' court may be found at Appendix C of the Magistrates' Courts (Anti-Social Behaviour Orders) Rules 2002.

2.126 Upon the defendant being arrested the matter will be dealt with by the Crown Prosecution Service as the prosecuting authority (Prosecution of Offences Act 1985, s 3). Proceedings may also be brought by a relevant authority in which the defendant resides or is believed to be residing.

Court

2.127 Defendants aged under 18 will be brought before a youth court although the original order may have been made by a different court. These proceedings are not subject to automatic restrictions. The court may impose reporting restrictions if appropriate. Under s 98 of the Magistrates' Courts Act 1980 evidence will be given on oath. Evidence of a child under 14 will be unsworn. The attendance of a parent or legal guardian at court is required in respect of a child aged under 16 by s 34 of the Children and Young Persons Act 1933.

2.128 The court will require information about the young person's background, home surroundings and family circumstances prior to sentence. This information should be given by social services or the youth offending team.

2.129 Community penalties are available and the youth court should also consider whether to make a parenting order or amend the individual support order. Conditional discharge is not an available option.

2.130 Defendants aged 18 and over will be brought before the magistrates' court. The defendant may be committed to the Crown Court if the magistrates take the view that the offence is such that greater punishment should be granted than they have power to order.

The original order

2.131 A copy of the original order certified by a proper officer of court will be sufficient proof that the order was made. *Service* of the original order, whether it is a full order or an interim order, that is alleged to have been breached must be proven.

Standard of proof

2.132 The criminal standard of proof applies. Guilt must be established beyond reasonable doubt. Section 1(10) of the CDA 1998 permits the defendant to raise the defence of reasonable excuse; the onus is on the prosecution to prove lack of excuse.

Sentencing powers

2.133

(1)   On summary conviction the sentence imposed on an adult defendant is a maximum of 6 months' imprisonment and/or a fine up to the statutory maximum, which is presently £5,000.

(2)   An adult may be sentenced on conviction on indictment to a maximum of 5 years' imprisonment and/or a fine.

(3)   The maximum sentence that may be imposed on conviction in the youth court on a youth aged between 12 and 17 is a detention and training order for 2 years, 12 months of which will be served in custody and the balance in the community.

(4)   On conviction in the youth court of a person aged between 12 and 14 the same sentence as in para (3) applies save that the court must also be of the opinion that the defendant is a persistent offender.

(5) On conviction in the youth court, a defendant who is aged between 10 and 11 years may be made the subject of a community order.

Whilst the full range of disposals of the youth court is available custody is normally considered as a last resort for serious and persistent breach.

2.134 There is no power to make a conditional discharge order against adults or youths.

2.135 The sentencing powers outlined above apply to breach both of interim and final orders.

2.136 The sentence imposed should be proportionate and reflect the impact of the anti-social behaviour. It must relate to all relevant circumstances, such as the number of breaches and how the breach relates to the finding of anti-social behaviour.

2.137 When sentencing for breach of an order the court is likely to consider:

(1) the serious nature of the breach;

(2) an early guilty plea;

(3) whether a custodial sentence is necessary particularly for a first-time offender;

(4) whether the sentence is proportionate to the offence and reflects the impact of the anti-social behaviour;

(5) what, if any, help can be rendered to the offender to comply with the order.

2.138 The leading authority for the approach on sentencing is *R v Lamb*.[23] The court in that case drew a distinction between breaches of the terms of the order and breaches that amount to further anti-social behaviour. Where a breach does not involve harassment, distress or alarm a community order may help the defendant to learn to live with the terms of the ASBO. This is consistent with the guideline on breach proceedings issued by the Sentencing Guidelines Council, where it was emphasised that custody should be used as a last resort and the primary purpose of breach proceedings is to ensure that the order is observed. Where, however, there is a persistent breach without alarm or distress it may be important to impose a custodial sentence to preserve the courts' authority. In such instances the sentence should be as short as possible. In *Lamb* the individual sentences were reduced to 2 months in custody. Where the new breach amounts to further harassment, alarm or distress the court considered that orders of 8 months on a guilty plea were appropriate.

---

[23]   [2005] EWCA Crim 2487.

2.139 When the defendant has been found guilty of breaching the order, and prior to sentencing, the court may take reports from the local authority or police and any particular agency. The court should also consider the original reason for making the order.

Variation and discharge of order

2.140 Pursuant to s 1(8) of the CDA 1998 the applicant or the defendant can apply *by complaint* for the order to be varied or discharged. The application must be made to the original court that made the order. An application to vary or discharge an order made on conviction in criminal proceedings may be made to any magistrates' court within the same petty sessions area as the original court that made the order.

2.141 An anti-social behaviour order cannot be discharged before the *end of the period of 2 years beginning with the date of service of the order except with the consent of the parties* (s 1(9) of the CDA 1998). An order made on conviction cannot be discharged before the end of two years. Prohibitions can be varied, removed or added within the initial 2 years.

2.142 The application, which must include the reasons why the applicant wishes the order to be varied or discharged, must be made to the court that made the order.

2.143 The court may determine the application if there are no grounds upon which the order should be varied or discharged without a hearing.

2.144 If the application relates to an interim order made without notice such an application must not be dealt with on paper as the defendant must be afforded an opportunity to make oral representations in court.

2.145 Where it appears to the court that there are grounds for varying or discharging the order the court must issue a summons requiring the parties to attend the hearing and give at least 14 days notice in writing of the hearing.

2.146 With regard to interim orders the test will be whether it was *just* to make the order pending resolution of the matter and thus the burden of proof is not shifted to the defendant.

APPEALS

2.147 Section 4(1) and (2) of the CDA 1998 deal with appeals. Section 4 grants the defendant a right of appeal against an order made in respect of a stand alone ASBO. Section 108 of the Magistrates' Courts Act 1980 grants the defendant a right of appeal against a CRASBO. In both instances the appeal is to the Crown Court.

2.148 Rules 74 and 75 of the Magistrates' Courts Rules 1981 and rr 6–11 of the Crown Court Rules 1982 relate to appeals against orders.

2.149 The court has power pursuant to s 142 of the Magistrates' Courts Act 1980 to rectify mistakes made in orders when dealing with an offender in criminal proceedings. This power applies only to orders made on conviction rather than on a stand alone application.

Applicant

2.150 An applicant (ie the relevant authority) may only ask the magistrates' court to state a case for the opinion of the High Court under s 111 of the Courts Act 1980 where it fails to get an order.

Defendant

2.151 The defendant can appeal against the *making* of the order and against the *terms* of the order. The appeal is made to the Crown Court.

Appeal hearing

2.152 The appeal hearing is a full hearing before a circuit judge. By virtue of s 79(3) of the Supreme Court Act 1981 an appeal is by way of a rehearing of the case. Both parties may rely upon additional evidence.

2.153 Crown Court Rules 1982, r 7 provides that notice of appeal must be given in writing to the designated officer of the court and the applicant body within 21 days of the order. The Crown Court has a discretion to grant permission to appeal out of time (r 7(5)). The Crown Court should have before it a copy of the original application, the order and the notice of appeal.

2.154 The Crown Court may vary the order or make a new order. Any order that is made by the Crown Court shall for the purpose of any later application for variation or discharge be treated as the original order by the magistrates' court unless it is an order which directs the application to be re-heard by the magistrates' court.

2.155 The Crown Court may suspend a prohibition pending the outcome of the appeal. There is, however, no provision for an automatic stay pending the appeal and therefore the order will remain in force, and a breach of the order if proven will be a criminal offence even if the appeal succeeds.

2.156 An appeal against the order by the Crown Court will be to the High Court by way of case stated (s 28 of the Supreme Court Act 1981) or by application for judicial review (s 29(3)).

2.157 The defendant could ask the magistrates' court to state a case for the opinion of the High Court under s 111 of the Magistrates' Courts Act 1980. In this instance the defendant will lose his right of appeal to the Crown Court.

2.158 In limited instances an application for judicial review of the magistrates' decision may be made. Judicial review considers the lawfulness of actions and decisions. An application is made to the High Court for consideration as to whether there was an improper exercise of jurisdiction by the magistrates' court or whether it erred in law.

2.159 The application must be made promptly and in any event within 3 months from the date when the grounds for the application arose.

2.160 If the defendant consented to the making of the order it will not be a bar to the appeal but will count against him on the merits.

Appeals to the High Court

2.161 Any party to the proceedings, or any party who is aggrieved by the order, conviction, determination or other proceedings of the court, may question the proceedings on the basis that it is wrong in law or in excess of jurisdiction. The court can be asked to state a case for the opinion of the High Court. In such an instance the case stated is heard by at least two High Court judges and, often, three judges sit to include the Lord Chief Justice. No evidence is adduced and the matter proceeds purely on submissions on legal arguments by counsel. The High Court can make such order as it deems fit and may reverse, affirm or amend the original determination. The matter can also be remitted to the justices with the opinion of the court.

COSTS

2.162 Magistrates may make a costs order under s 64 of the Magistrates' Courts Act 1980. Costs are at the courts' *discretion*. It should be just and reasonable to make a costs order. Costs orders are enforceable like any civil debt.

Representation

2.163 Defendants have a right to be represented as Art 6 of the ECHR is clearly engaged. Criminal public funding is available for any proceedings under ss 1 and 4 of the CDA1998 for applications relating to ASBOs to include interim orders whether they are magistrates' courts proceedings or appeals to the Crown Court.

2.164 The Legal Services Commission (LSC) will treat any application under ss 1 and 1D of the CDA 1998 as criminal proceedings and hence the right to representation may be granted. Advocacy assistance is available for ASBOs, interim orders and variation and discharge of orders. The general criminal contract under which solicitors provide legal services to the LSC will provide the grant. There are no financial criteria that need to be satisfied for the grant of advocacy assistance. Solicitors can self-grant advocacy assistance. Advocacy assistance may not be granted if it appears unreasonable that approval should be granted or if the interests of justice test, set out in Sch 3 to the Access to Justice Act 1999, is not met. The further factor to be considered when applying this test is whether there is a real risk of imprisonment if an ASBO is made and subsequently breached.

2.165 An application can be made to the LSC for a representation order. Provision for representation is made under regs 3(2) and 6(3) of the Criminal Defence Service (General) (No 2) Regulations 2001.[24]

2.166 Application on Form CDS3 must be made to the Commission. When considering the grant of representation the Commission will take into account the availability of advocacy assistance. Written reasons must be given by the Commission when refusing a representation order, together with the procedure for the appeal process. The applicant can renew the application in writing to the Funding Review Committee, which may or may not grant the application.

2.167 Where an appeal is made under s 4 of the CDA 1998, advocacy assistance is available for proceedings in the Crown Court. The merits test in such an instance and is based on the general reasonableness test. Advocacy assistance may not be granted if in the particular circumstances it appears unreasonable to grant approval. The prospects and merits of an appeal should be considered, as well as whether the individual has reasonable grounds for taking the proceedings.

2.168 Representation is available for an appeal against an order under s 4 of the CDA 1998. An application should be made to the LSC, which will consider the grant against the availability of advocacy assistance.

2.169 Any challenge of the ruling of the Crown Court to the High Court by way of case stated or by application for judicial review falls outside the scope of criminal funding. An application for legal representation should be made to the LSC in accordance with the Funding Code procedures. Although it is within the General Criminal Contract this work will be funded through the Community Legal Service.

2.170 Advocacy assistance is available for breach of interim and full orders. Representation is also available on application to the Commission as set out above.

---

[24]   SI 2001/1437.

Orders in the county court

2.171 Applications for ASBOs can be made in the county court. The statutory authority is contained in ss 1–1D of the CDA 1998 as amended by ss 61–66 of the Police Reform Act 2002 and the Anti-Social Behaviour Act 2003.

2.172 There are very many similarities in the law governing the grant of ASBOs in the county court and the grant of civil orders in the magistrates' court. The basis upon which an order is made and the definition of 'relevant persons' are the same.

2.173 The provisions relating to proceedings in the county court are set out in s 1B(1), (2) and (4) of the CDA 1998, which provides:

'(1) This section applies to any proceedings in the county court ("the principle proceedings").

(2) If a relevant authority—

(a) is a party to the principle proceedings, and

(b) considers that the party to those proceedings is a person in relation to whom it would be reasonable for it to make an application under section 1,

it may make an application in those proceedings for an order under subsection (4).

…

(4) If, on an application for an order under this subsection, it is proved that the conditions mentioned in section 1(1) are fulfilled as respects that other party, the court may make an order which prohibits him from doing anything described in the order.'

Further:

(1) A relevant authority may be joined in the principle proceedings so that an order can be obtained against a party in the proceedings (s 1B(3) of the CDA 1998).

(2) A relevant authority may make an application to join a person who is not a party to the principle proceedings for the purpose of obtaining an order against him. Note however that this can only be done if his anti-social acts are material to the principle proceedings (s 1B(3A) and (3B) of the CDA 1998).

2.174 There can be no free-standing applications in the county court for ASBOs. Where proceedings are brought in the county court they are parasitic to existing proceedings. The applicant and the person against whom the order is sought must be parties to the 'principal proceedings'.

2.175 Where the applicant is the claimant in the principal proceedings the application for the order must be made in the claim form. Where the applicant is the defendant in the principal proceedings the application should be made by an application notice, which should accompany the defence.

2.176 Where the relevant authority is not a party to the proceedings an application to be made to a party and an application for an order must be made as soon as possible after the authority becomes aware of the principal proceedings.

2.177 Where the alleged perpetrator is not a party and the relevant authority believes that his anti-social acts are relevant to the principal proceedings, an application may be made to join that person and apply for an order.

2.178 As county courts are empowered to make orders, the need to make a separate application to the magistrates' court is removed and protection against anti-social behaviour is afforded quickly and efficiently.

2.179 An example of the usefulness of a county court order is that it will prevent a person who has been evicted from his accommodation for harassing his neighbours and/or others from continuing this behaviour by returning to the same area.

2.180 The application can be dealt with by a district judge or deputy district judge by virtue of CPR, r 8.1A PD 2B.

INTERIM ORDER

2.181 The procedure relating to interim orders is set out in CPR Part 25. The application is made under s 1D of the CDA 1998. The application can be made:

(1)   in the claim form;

(2)   by an application notice seeking an order;

(3)   on notice to the defendant;

(4)   without notice to the defendant if there are good reasons.
      Written evidence in support must be filed and state reasons for seeking an order.

2.182 The considerations for granting an interim order, whether it is on notice or without notice, are the same as in the magistrates' court.

2.183 The order can be varied, discharged or renewed. Such an application must be made under CPR Part 23.

Full order

2.184 An application for an order may be made pursuant to s 1B(2) of the CDA 1998.The procedure is governed by CPR Part 65 and CPR PD65. The application is made in the claim form.

2.185 If the relevant authority is a defendant in proceedings the application should be made by application notice in Form N244 and this must be filed with the defence. If a defence has been filed the application must be made as soon as possible thereafter. At least 3 days' notice of the application must be given.

2.186 Where a person is not a party to the principle proceedings the relevant authority must make an application under CPR Part 19 to join that party to the principle proceedings. Such an application must be *on notice* and Form N244 must contain reasons as to why the conduct of the party to be joined is material and give details of alleged behaviour.

Duration

2.187 The order will be effective for 2 years or until further order. There is no maximum period. The order must be served personally upon the defendant. It is good practice to file a certificate of service.

Interim order

2.188 An application for an interim order may be made pursuant to s 1D of the CDA 1998. An application for an interim order may be made on notice or, if there are good reasons justifying it, on a without notice basis, an application should be made in accordance with CPR Part 25. Written evidence filed with the application *must* provide reasons as to why the application is made on a without notice basis.

2.189 The order must be for a fixed period. An application under CPR Part 23 should be made to vary, renew or discharge the order.

2.190 Conditions for making the order, the decision to make the order, the prohibitions imposed and the duration of order are similar to the matters outlined earlier in the section relating to magistrates' courts.

Evidence in support

2.191 The relevant sections are ss 1B(4) and 1E of the CDA 1998. They relate to written evidence and consultation requirements respectively. The court must consider whether the relevant authority has complied with the requirements.

2.192 The application must be accompanied by written evidence which can be set out in Part C of the application. The normal practice, however, is to file separate witness statements with the application.

2.193 The provisions of the Civil Evidence Act 1995 apply. Hearsay evidence is admissible. It is advisable to:

(1) State by oral evidence (such as from the housing officer) the reasons why the makers of the original statements are unable to give direct evidence (eg tenants/neighbours unwilling to give evidence).

(2) If reliance is placed upon multiple hearsay, it should be traced to the source of the information.

Breach

2.194 Breach of an ASBO made in the county court will be a *criminal offence* and will be dealt with as such. It may be for this reason that ASBOs are now rarely dealt with in the county court.

Variation/discharge of order

2.195 Unless the parties consent the order cannot be discharged for 2 years from the date of service of the order. An application under CPR Part 23 must be made to vary or discharge the order.

Appeals

2.196 The relevant procedure is contained in CPR Part 52. An appeal from a district judge is to a circuit judge. An appeal from a circuit judge is to the High Court.

2.197 In the event that the matter has been allocated to the multi-track and the decision is final an appeal from the circuit judge will be to the Court of Appeal.

Permission to appeal

2.198 Permission to appeal is required from the first instance judge or appeal judge. The time limit for lodging the appeal if permission is granted from the first instance judge is 21 days. Permission to appeal must be sought within 21 days from the appeal judge.

Costs

2.199 The costs rules contained in CPR Parts 43–48 apply. The court will in appropriate cases make a summary assessment of costs. Enforcement of unpaid costs will be in accordance with CPR.

CHECKLISTS, FORMS AND PRECEDENTS

2.200 Checklists, forms and precedents relating to anti-social behaviour orders are reproduced below.

1. APPLICATION FOR ANTI-SOCIAL BEHAVIOUR ORDER UNDER THE CRIME AND DISORDER ACT 1998

☐   There are principal proceedings. *[CDA s1B(1)]*

☐   Applicant is a relevant authority. *[CDA s1B(2), s1B(3), s1(1A)]*

☐   Applicant is a party to principal proceedings or applies to be joined. *[CDA s1B(2), s1B(3); CPR 65.24]*

☐   The respondent/defendant is a party *[CDA s1B(2), s1B(3) ; CPR 65.22]*
    ☐   **OR** there is an application to join him or her *[CDA s1B(3B); CPR 65.23]*
    ☐   **AND** the prospective new party's anti-social acts are material to the principal proceedings *[CDA s1B(3A)(b)), s1B(3C)]*

☐   The respondent /defendant is 18 or over – except in a pilot scheme court when
    ☐   if under 18 has litigation friend **OR**
        ☐   Order made under CPR 21.2(3) permitting the child to conduct proceedings without a litigation friend

☐   The application is made
    ☐   in claim form [CPR 65.22(1)(a)]
    ☐   or by application notice by defendant filed with the defence [CPR 65.22(1)(b)]
    ☐   or by application notice by existing party as soon as possible after it becomes aware of the circumstances that lead it to apply for an order after its claim is issued or its defence filed [CPR 65.22(2)]
    ☐   or in the same application notice as application to have relevant authority or new respondent/defendant joined as party [CPR 65. 23(1)(b), 65.24(1)(b)]

☐   [If application by relevant authority to join a person to the principal proceedings] application notice must contain the relevant authority's reasons for claiming that the person's anti-social acts are material in relation to the principal proceedings AND details of the anti-social acts alleged. *[CPR 65.23(2)]*

☐   Application for ASBO accompanied by written evidence *[CPR 65.25]*

☐ **INCLUDING** evidence of consultation (e.g. that applicant local authority has consulted with chief officer of police; that applicant registered social landlord consult with council and with police) *[CDA s1E; CPR 65.25]*

☐ Satisfied as to service. [Normal CPR service rules apply and CPR Part 65 requires that applications "should normally be made on notice to the person against whom the order is sought". If application made in Claim Form only and fixed hearing date given on issue, 21 days notice – *CPR 55.5(3)(c)*. If application by way of application notice, 3 days notice – *CPR 23.7(1)(b)*.]

☐ The respondent/defendant has acted in a manner that caused or was likely to cause harassment, alarm or distress to one or more persons not of the same household as himself. *[CDA s1(1)(a)]*
　　☐ **AND** the such an order is necessary to protect *relevant persons* from further anti-social acts by him. *[CDA s1(1)(b)]*

☐ *Relevant persons* as defined (e.g. within the local government area of the applicant council; persons who are residing in or who are otherwise on or likely to be on premises provided or managed by the applicant registered social landlord or persons who are in the vicinity of or likely to be in the vicinity of such premises). *[CDA s1(1B)]*

2. APPLICATION FOR INTERIM ANTI-SOCIAL BEHAVIOUR ORDER

☐ Main application for an ASBO *[CDA s 1D(1)]*

☐ Application support by evidence including evidence of consultation in connection with the main application *[CPR 65.25, 25.3(2)]*

☐ Application in [CPR 65.26(2)(a)]
    ☐ Claim form **OR**
    ☐ Application notice

☐ Satisfied as to service. [Normal CPR service rules apply. *CPR 65.26(2)(b)* provides that application "should normally be made on notice to the person against whom the order is sought". If application made in Claim Form only and fixed hearing date given on issue, 21 days notice – *CPR 55.5(3)(c)*. If application by way of application notice, 3 days notice – *CPR 23.7(1)(b)*. If made without notice, court may grant an interim remedy if it appears to the court that there are good reasons for not giving notice – *CPR 25.3(1)*; but evidence in support must state the reasons why notice has not been given – *CPR 25.3(3)*]

☐ Is it just to make an order pending determination of the main application? *[CDA s1D(3)]*

3. ASBO AND ASBI CASE MANAGEMENT DIRECTIONS

(1) Pursuant to CPR 65.3(1) and CPR 8.9 (c) the claim is treated as allocated to the Multi-track. It may be tried by a District Judge. Allocation questionnaires and pre- trial checklists are dispensed with.

(2) List for trial on the first open date after t/e . . . . The trial shall take place in open court.

(3) Each party shall give to every other party standard disclosure of documents by serving a list with a disclosure statement by . . . . Any request to inspect or for a copy of a document must be made by . . . .

(4) No party may call a witness at trial without the permission of the trial judge unless a witness statement, verified by statement of truth, setting out his evidence, has been served by . . . .This includes the evidence of the parties themselves.

(5) No expert evidence being necessary, no party has permission to call or rely on expert evidence.
OR:- (and only exceptionally)
The parties have permission to rely on the written evidence of a single joint expert in . . . .[field]. The expert's report must be limited to matters relating to . . . . [issue] and delivered to both parties by . . . . Pending any order as to costs, each party shall pay half of the expert's charges. If the parties are unable to agree any matter in relation to the choice of expert, or the joint instructions to be given, an application must be made urgently. Both parties must provide any facilities required by the expert for access or inspection promptly on request.

(6) The claimant must lodge at court at least 7 days before the trial,
 – an indexed bundle of documents (contained in a suitable binder), with each page clearly numbered,
 - a case summary (which should not exceed 500 words) and schedule of outstanding issues, referring where appropriate to the relevant documents,
 [- a trial template (subject to the approval of the trial Judge) which must include time for the Judge to consider, give judgment, and to deal with costs]
 The claimant must seek to agree the above with the other party(ies)

• The bundle must include a Scott Schedule itemising each material allegation upon which a finding of fact is sought by the parties in support of their position. The schedule must in respect of each allegation:-
 (a) set out the contentions of each party;
 (b) include a cross reference to the relevant paragraph[s] in the Particulars of Claim and/or Defence;

    (c)   identify any relevant witnesses, specifying the page numbers in the trial bundle containing the relevant parts of their statements;

    (d)   provide a column for use by the Judge.

The Scott Schedule is required whether or not the Defendant has expressly put forward a defence or points of contention. The format and content of the Scott Schedule should be agreed between the parties and/or their legal representatives if possible.

(1)   The bundle must include drafts of the orders which the Claimant will seek on disposal of the claim. The Claimant must have at the hearing a Word copy of the draft order on disk or must have emailed such a copy to the court in advance of the hearing.

(2)   The parties shall file and exchange skeleton arguments no later than 3 days before the trial.

(3)   The claimant's solicitor must forthwith liaise with all other parties to determine details of the joint availability of all trial personnel for all parties within the trial window. If there are no, or only limited, dates of joint availability the reason for the non-availability of each party's trial personnel must be obtained. That solicitor must notify such availability to the court's Diary Manager (or case worker) by telephone number 0121 681 3120, by no later than . The hearing date will then be fixed.

4. DIRECTIONS ORDER IN ASBO CLAIM

In the Anytown County Court   Case Number [ ]

BETWEEN

[ ]

Claimant

-and-

[ ]

Defendant

Before District Judge . . . . . . on 200

Upon hearing [Counsel][the Solicitor] for the Claimant and
    [Counsel][the Solicitor] for the Defendant
    the Defendant in person
    the Defendant not attending
    without notice to the Defendant
    [others]

IT IS ORDERED that:

- In this order, the claim by the Claimant . . . . . . against the Defendant . . . . . . for possession of . . . . . . , and for associated remedies is referred to as 'the principal proceedings' and the application by the Claimantfor an Anti Social Behaviour Order (an 'ASBO') against the . . . . . . Defendant is referred to as 'the ASBO application'.

- is joined as . . . . . . Second Defendant so that the Claimant can make the ASBO application against him

- is joined as . . . . . . Second Claimant so that it can make the ASBO application against the . . . . . . Defendant

- The application to join as a party is adjourned to . . . . . . t/e . . . . The . . . . . . Claimant must serve that application and the ASBO application on the Defendant together with copies of all the statements of case and evidence filed to date and notice of the next hearing, not later than . . . . . . days before the hearing

- [The application to join . . . . . . as a party is dismissed][. . . . . . be removed as a party] on the ground that he is under 18 and the court has no jurisdiction to join him as a party to make an ASBO against him

- The principal proceedings will be heard together with the ASBO application and the following directions apply (unless expressly stated otherwise) to both of them

- Allocation Questionnaires are not required. The case is allocated to the [fast][multi-] track.

- *(if allocated to MT)* The final hearing may be listed before a District Judge, [because the principal proceedings are for recovery of land][because a District Judge has jurisdiction to hear the principal proceedings and the matter is suitable for trial before a District Judge][if the Designated Civil Judge consents, but otherwise must be listed before a Circuit Judge]

- [see separate form for interim ASBO]

5. ASBO UNDER SECTION 1B CDA 1998

ANTI-SOCIAL BEHAVIOUR ORDER Under section 1B Crime and Disorder Act 1998	IN THE ANYTOWN COUNTY COURT	
	Claim no:	
	Claimant	
	Defendant	

To:
of:

Seal

IF, WITHOUT REASONABLE EXCUSE, YOU THE DEFENDANT DO ANYTHING WHICH YOU ARE PROHIBITED FROM DOING BY THIS ORDER, YOU WILL BE GUILTY OF AN OFFENCE AND YOU WILL BE LIABLE ON CONVICTION TO A TERM OF IMPRISONMENT OR TO A FINE OR BOTH.

If you do not understand anything in this order, you should go to a Solicitor, Legal Advice Centre or a Citizens Advice Bureau.

Either party can apply to the court for this order to be varied or discharged. But you must obey the order unless it is varied or discharged by the court. Except with the consent of both parties, no such order can be discharged before the end of a period of two years beginning with the date of service of this order.

On Wednesday, 13 February 2008 the court considered an application for an order under section 1B Crime and Disorder Act 1998.

(Where marked* delete or complete as appropriate. If for a fixed term, this must be a minimum of 2 years.)

The court found that the Defendant had acted in the following anti-social manner which caused or was likely to cause harassment, alarm or distress to one or more persons not of the same household as the Defendant:-

And the court found that an order was necessary to protect persons in England and Wales from further anti-social acts by the Defendant.

The court ordered that the Defendant   is prohibited from:

The court further ordered that:

the order shall continue [until   *at 4pm] *or* [until further order]*.

Ordered by

On   Wednesday, 13 February 2008

6. ASBO UNDER SECTION 1D CDA 1998

INTERIM ANTI-SOCIAL BEHAVIOUR ORDER Under section 1D Crime and Disorder Act 1998	IN THE ANYTOWN COUNTY COURT

Claim no:	
Claimant	
Defendant	

To:
of:

Seal

IF, WITHOUT REASONABLE EXCUSE, YOU THE DEFENDANT DO ANYTHING WHICH YOU ARE PROHIBITED FROM DOING BY THIS ORDER, YOU WILL BE GUILTY OF AN OFFENCE AND YOU WILL BE LIABLE ON CONVICTION TO A TERM OF IMPRISONMENT OR TO A FINE OR BOTH.

If you do not understand anything in this order, you should go to a Solicitor, Legal Advice Centre or a Citizens Advice Bureau.

Either party can apply to the court for this order to be varied or discharged. But you must obey the order unless it is varied or discharged by the court.

On Wednesday, 13 February 2008 the court considered an application for an interim order under section 1D Crime and Disorder Act 1998.
The court considered it just to make an order under that section pending determination of the claimant's application for an order under section 1B Crime and Disorder Act 1998 ("the main application")

The court ordered that the defendant   is prohibited from:

The court further ordered that:
The order shall continue until   at 4pm or until determination of the
main application if sooner.

Ordered by

On   Wednesday, 13 February 2008

7. COMMITTAL OR OTHER ORDER UPON PROOF OF DISOBEDIENCE OF A COURT ORDER OR BREACH OF AN UNDERTAKING

Committal or Other Order upon Proof of Disobedience of a Court Order or Breach of an Undertaking

In the	**County Court**

Between _____ Applicant / Claimant / Petitioner

Claim No.	Always quote this

and _____ Respondent / Defendant

Before His (Her) Honour Judge
Sitting at   on *(date)*

(seal)

1   An application having been made by[1]   for committal of[2]   to prison
for disobeying the order [breach of the undertaking] dated   The relevant terms of the order
(undertaking) and the allegations made by the applicant are recited on the attached notice to show good reason

or

2   Whereas[21]   has been suspected of a breach of the attached order
dated   and has been arrested by a constable and brought before the Judge
under section 47(6) of the Family Law Act 1996.

or

3.   Whereas[22]   has been suspected of a breach of the attached
[undertaking] dated   and has been arrested under a warrant of arrest and brought before the Judge under
[section 47(8) of the Family Law Act 1996] [section 3(3) of the Protection from Harassment Act 1997].

---------------------------------- IMMEDIATE CUSTODIAL ORDER ----------------------------------

It is ordered that[20]   be committed for contempt to Her Majesty's Prison
(be detained under section 9(1) of the Criminal Justice Act 1982) at[3]   for a
(total) period of[6]   or until lawfully discharged if sooner, and that a warrant
of arrest and committal be issued forthwith.

And the contemnor can apply to the (court) (judge) to purge his contempt and ask for release.

[And, as the court by order dated   dispensed with service of the notice of application for a committal
order,
It is ordered that the contemnor be brought before a judge of this court as soon as practicable.]

---------------------------------- ALTERNATIVE DISPOSAL ----------------------------------

It is ordered that[2]   be committed for contempt to prison for a (total) period
of[6]

The order is suspended until   [19   ][20   ] and will not be put in force if during that time the
contemnor   complies with the following terms:

And it is further ordered that in the event of non compliance any application for issue of the warrant shall be made to a
judge (on notice to the contemnor)
It is ordered that[2]   be fined the sum of £
Such sum to be paid into the office of the court within 14 days of the date of this order.

It is ordered that consideration of the penalty for the contempts found proved be adjourned until   [19   ]
[20   ] and may be restored for decision if during that time[22]   does not comply with the
following terms

---------------------------------- PROVISION FOR COSTS ----------------------------------

And it is ordered that

Date
For record of service, hearing and contempts found proved, see overleaf

N79 Committal or other order upon proof and disobedience of a court order or breach of an undertaking (Family Law Act 1996) (Protection from Harassment Act 1997)

RECORD OF SERVICE, HEARING AND CONTEMPTS FOUND PROVED

At the hearing

(1)   [appeared personally] [was represented by solicitor / counsel] [did not attend]

(2)   [appeared personally] [was represented by solicitor / counsel] [did not attend]

The court read the affidavits of (Names)   Date affidavit(s) sworn

And the court heard oral evidence given by
Name(s)

And the court is satisfied having considered the facts disclosed by the evidence and/or admitted in court by him/her
that⁽ᵃ⁾   has been guilty of contempt of this court by disobeying the
order (breaking the undertaking) dated   by (and as set out in the attached schedule)

                                          And for the particular contempt the court
                                        imposed the penalty of:

1.   1.

2.   2.

————————————————RECORD OF SERVICE————————————————

Service of Injunction Order with Penal Notice incorporated or indorsed	**Service of Notice to show good reason in form N78**	**Arrest under warrant of arrest**
(Order dated [19][20]	(Order dated [19][20]	respondent arrested on
(for substituted) (dispensing with) service)	(for substituted) (dispensing with) service)	
Service proved by	Service proved by	by
☐ certificate of service	☐ certificate of service	
dated [19][20]	dated [19][20]	in accordance with a warrant
☐ certificate of bailiff	☐ certificate of bailiff	of arrest issued
☐ oral evidence of	☐ oral evidence of	

Service of Immediate Custodial Order

I *(name of Officer)*   certify that I served the contemnor with a copy of this order by:

☐ delivery by hand to the contemnor before he was taken from the court building or other place of arrest to the place of detention

☐ delivery by hand to the contemnor at *(time)*   on *(date)*   [19][20] at *(place)*

Where a suspended committal order is made, the applicant is responsible for service. (Rules of the Supreme Court Order 52 rule 7(2).)
Where there is suspended committal order or penalty is adjourned on terms, personal service is advisable.

The court office is open from 10 am to 4 pm Monday to Friday.

When corresponding with the court, please address forms and letters to the Court Manager and quote the case number.

Notes for completion of page 1

Terms or names that may be used more than once in the order are numbered in brackets as follows:

(1) Person making application for committal
(2) Person against whom the committal order is made (contemnor)
(3) Name of prison or young offender institution
(4) Period of detention

If the respondent has been brought before the court under a power of arrest (Family Law Act 1996) delete 1 and 3.

If the respondent has been brought before the court under a warrant of arrest (Family Law Act 1996 or Protection from Harassment Act 1997) delete 1 and 2.

In all other cases delete 2 and 3.

Enter the date of order (with penal notice incorporated or indorsed) or undertaking.

Date of form N78 Notice to show good reason (applies to 1 only).

Date of the warrant of arrest (applies to 3 only).

Note: A warrant of arrest cannot be issued on an undertaking under the Protection from Harassment Act 1997.

IMMEDIATE CUSTODIAL ORDER

Complete this section if an immediate custodial order is made otherwise delete and complete section below

Section 9(1) of CJA is for persons aged less than 21 and at least 18.

The total period of detention must be specified by the Judge. The maximum period for contempt of court (including a county court) is 2 years.

If the offence is failure to do a specific act and the judge decides that the application may be made to a district judge upon proof that the act has been done delete (judge) otherwise delete (court).

Complete only if order dispensing with service of notice of application was granted otherwise delete.

ALTERNATIVE DISPOSAL

Delete this section if an immediate custodial order is made otherwise delete alternatives not selected by judge.

Enter the exact terms of any suspended committal order or adjournment of penalty.

There are further possible alternative disposals, eg under sections 35, 37 and 38 of the Mental Health Act and sequestration.

COSTS

Enter any order for costs here or show that no order for costs has been made if applicable

Date the order here

Notes on completion of page 2 🖘
(Record of service, hearing and contempts found proved)

——————REPRESENTATION——————

The parties and their legal representative (advocate only)

——————AFFIDAVIT EVIDENCE——————

Only those affidavits which the judge has considered at the hearing. There is unlikely to be any affidavit evidence offered where the respondent has been brought to court under a power of arrest.

——————ORAL EVIDENCE——————

Only those witnesses sworn and examined

——————CONTEMPTS FOUND PROVED——————

List and give exact details of only those allegations of contempt which the judge has found proved.

If separate penalties are imposed for each contempt found proved these are to be recorded in the right-hand column showing whether or not periods of detention are to run consecutively or concurrently.

If necessary annex additional page and continue list on it. If an additional page is not used delete the words (and as set out in the attached schedule).

——————JUDGE'S APPROVAL——————

The Judge must be asked to initial the order here

——————RECORD OF SERVICE——————

Enter details of certificates of service.

Record of delivery of an undertaking need not be made on this document as it can be found on the form of undertaking.

A sealed copy of the approved order must be served on the contemnor, see Order 29 rule 1(5) recited opposite.

Where the respondent is brought before the court under a power of arrest delete record of service of form N78.
Where the respondent is brought before the court under a warrant of arrest delete record of service of form N78 and complete record of service of warrant of arrest.

Disobedience of a Court Order or Breach of an
Undertaking   **(Form N79)**

Notes for Guidance
on Completion

The Court Officer responsible for the forms completion should note the following:

- **Where the respondent is brought before the court after being arrested under a power of arrest (Section 47(6) of the Family Law Act 1996)** a sealed copy of the injunction order giving the power of arrest (not Power of Arrest form FL406) with penal notice indorsed becomes part of form N79 and must be attached to the approved order.

- **Where the respondent is brought before the court after being arrested under a warrant of arrest (section 47(8) of the Family Law Act 1996) (section 3(3) of the Protection from Harassment Act 1997)** a sealed copy of the injunction order becomes part of form N79 and must be attached to the approved order.

- **In all other cases** Form N78 (notice to show good reason why an order for committal should not be made) becomes part of form N79 and a sealed copy of N78 must be attached to the approved order.

- **In all cases the warrant is in form N80.**

- **When the form has been fully completed it must be passed to the judge for approval. If the judge** is available he/she should be asked to approve and initial or sign the final (typed) version. If this is not possible the judge must be asked to initial or sign the final hand-written draft. In either case the document endorsed by the judge **must be retained on the court file.**

- Before the order is served it must also be checked by an officer of no less than HEO grade.

- Before the order is served these notes should be detached, they are for the guidance of Court Staff only.

When an immediate custodial order is made:

- A copy of N79 (with attached N78 or injunction) must be sent to the Office of the Official Solicitor.

- A sealed copy of the approved order must be served on the contemnor. Order 29 rule 1(5) CCR states:

    If a committal order is made, the order shall be for the issue of a warrant of committal and unless the judge otherwise orders:-

    (a)   a copy of the order shall be served on the person to be committed either before or at the time of the execution of the warrant; or

    (b)   where the warrant has been signed by the Judge, the order for issue of the warrant may be served on the person to be committed at any time within 36 hours after execution of the warrant.

Chapter 3

ANTI-SOCIAL BEHAVIOUR INJUNCTIONS

INTRODUCTION

3.1   This chapter deals with housing injunctions for anti-social behaviour under the Housing Act 1996 ('the 1996 Act'). Anti-social behaviour injunctions (ASBIs) confer a power on social landlords which was previously only available to local authorities. As a result, social landlords can now deal with anti-social behaviour in a much more proactive manner.

3.2   An ASBI is a civil order obtained from the county court which can control and remedy anti-social behaviour. The injunction can require an adult over the age of 18 not to do something and/or prevent a particular action or behaviour. An injunction can be applied against tenants and non-tenants, and where there have been threats of violence, actual violence or significant risk of harm the defendant can be excluded from a specified area. If an injunction is breached it will be dealt with by way of civil proceedings and, if proven, the court can impose an unlimited fine and/or commit the defendant to prison for a period up to 2 years.

3.3   An injunction is a discretionary remedy and it is for the court to decide whether an injunction should be issued. Injunctions are being used increasingly to control anti-social behaviour *in situ* rather than displacing the problem, for example, by evicting the nuisance tenant who could then continue the offending behaviour unchecked in another property.

3.4   The relevant statutory provisions are contained in the 1996 Act, Part V, Ch III, as amended by the Anti-Social Behaviour Act 2003. Sections 152,153, 154, 155(1) and (2)(a), 157 and 158 of the 1996 Act deal with applications for injunctions to restrain anti-social behaviour and came into force on 1 September 1997. Section 152 provides:

> '(1)   The High Court or county court, may on an application by a **local authority**, grant an injunction prohibiting a person from —
>
> (a)   engaging in or threatening to engage in conduct causing or likely to cause a nuisance or annoyance to a person residing in, visiting or otherwise engaging in a lawful activity in residential premises to which this section applies or in the locality of such premises;
>
> (b)   using or threatening to use residential premises to which this section applies for immoral or illegal purposes; or
>
> (c)   entering the residential premises to which this section applies or being found in the locality of any such premises.

(2)   This section applies to residential premises of the following descriptions —
   (a)   dwelling-houses held under secure or introductory tenancies from the local authority;
   (b)   accommodation provided by that authority under Part VII of this Act or Part III of the Housing Act 1985(homelessness).
(3)   The court **shall not** grant an injunction under this section **unless** it is of the opinion that —
   (a)   the respondent has used or threatened to use violence against any person of a description mentioned in subsection 1(a); **and**
   (b)   there is a significant risk of harm of that person or of a person of similar description if the injunction is not granted.
(4)   An injunction under this section may —
   (a)   in the case of an injunction under subsection (1)(a) or (b), relate to particular acts or to conduct, or types of conduct, in general or to both, and
   (b)   in the case of an injunction under subsection (1(c), relate to particular premises or to a particular locality;
   and may be made for a specified period or until varied or discharged.
(5)   An injunction under this section can be varied or discharged by the court.
(6)   The court may attach a power of arrest to one or more of the provisions of an injunction which it intends to grant under this section.'

3.5   Sections 152 and 155 in Part V of the 1996 Act entitled 'Conduct of Tenants' confers powers on local authorities in a housing context. The regime for introductory tenancies is contained in Chapter 1 of Part V. Chapter 2 increases the powers of local authorities to obtain possession of their properties. Chapter 3, which includes ss 152 and 155, deals with anti-social behaviour injunctions.

3.6   In June 2004 Part II s 13 of the Anti-Social Behaviour Act 2003 introduced new provisions which enable housing action trusts and registered social landlords to apply for ASBIs. Sections 152 and 153 of the 1996 Act were repealed and introduced new provisions to enable social landlords to apply for ASBIs. These provisions are covered in ss 153A, 153B, 153C, 153D and 153E of the 1996 Act, which came into force on 30 June 2004.

Injunctions under the Housing Act 1996

3.7   The amended 1996 Act provides for three types of injunctions, each requiring the landlord to meet specified conditions before the court will grant the injunction.

(1) Anti-social behaviour (s 153A)

3.8   This is for conduct which:

(a)   is capable of causing nuisance or annoyance to any person; and

(b)   directly or indirectly relates to or affects the housing management functions of the landlord.

(2) Unlawful use of premises (s 153B)

3.9   This is for conduct which relates to the use or threatened use of housing accommodation owned or managed by a relevant landlord for unlawful purpose. Examples of such conduct include drug dealing, running a brothel and harbouring stolen goods.

(3) Breach of tenancy agreement (s 153D)

3.10   This relates to conduct which amounts to a breach or anticipated breach of the tenancy agreement and where the tenant is:

(a)   engaging or threatening to engage in conduct that is capable of causing nuisance or annoyance to another person; or

(b)   allowing, inciting or encouraging any other person to engage or threaten to engage in such conduct.

3.11   Applications for ASBIs are usually combined with proceedings for an order for possession by the relevant landlord. This is because landlords may seek to apply for other measures alongside an application for a housing injunction. Social landlords also have the right to apply for a demotion order to end a secure or an assured tenancy and replace it with a demoted form of tenancy. The demotion order is intended to issue a serious warning to the tenant that continued misbehaviour will lead to swift action being taken to end the tenancy. It removes a number of tenancy rights. In the event that the tenant stops causing problems he will be able to regain a higher level of security and rights.

3.12   The Anti-Social Behaviour Act 2003 places a requirement in Part 2 upon all social landlords to prepare and publish statements and summaries of their policies and procedures in relation to anti-social behaviour.

Possession claims against secure and assured tenants

Housing Act 1985 (s 82)

3.13   Section 82 of the Housing Act 1985 provides that:

'(1)   A secure tenancy which is either
 (a)   a weekly or other periodic tenancy, or
 (b)   a tenancy for a term certain but subject to termination by the landlord, cannot be brought to an end by the landlord except by obtaining an order mentioned in **subsection (1A)** for the possession of a dwelling-house or an order under **subsection (3).**

(1A)   The orders are –
 (a)   an order of the court for the possession of the dwelling-house;
 (b)   an order under subsection (3);
 (c)   a demotion order under section 82A.

(2)   Where the landlord obtains an order for possession of the dwelling-house the tenancy ends on the date on which the tenant is to give up possession in pursuance of the order.

(3)   Where a secure tenancy is a tenancy for a term certain but with a provision for re-entry or forfeiture, the court shall not order possession in pursuance of that provision, but in a case where the court would have made such an order it shall instead make an order terminating the tenancy on a date specified in the order and section 86 (periodic tenancy arising on termination of a fixed term) shall apply.

(4)   Section 146 of the Law of Property Act 1925 (restriction on and relief against forfeiture), except subsection (4) (vesting in under-lessee), and any other enactment or rule of law relating to forfeiture, shall apply in relation to proceedings for an order under subsection (3) of this section as if they were proceedings to enforce a right of re-entry or forfeiture.'

Housing Act 1988 (s 1)

3.14   Section 1 of the Housing Act 1988 provides that:

'(1)   A tenancy under which a dwelling-house is let as a separate dwelling is for the purpose of this Act an assured tenancy if and so long as
  (a)   the tenant or, as the case may be, each of the joint tenants is an individual: and
  (b)   the tenant, or as the case may be, at least one of the joint tenants occupies the dwelling-house as his only or principle home: and
  (c)   the tenancy is not one which, by virtue of subsection (2) or (6) below, cannot be an assured tenancy.

(2)   Subject to subsection 3 below, if and so long as a tenancy falls within any paragraph in Part I of Schedule 1 to this Act, it cannot be an assured tenancy; and in that Schedule –
  (a)   "tenancy" means a tenancy under which a dwelling-house is let as a separate dwelling;
  (b)   Part II has effect for determining the rateable value of a dwelling-house for the purposes of Part I; and
  (c)   Part III has effect for supplementing paragraph 10 in Part I.

(2A)   The Secretary of State may by order replace any amount referred to in paragraphs 2 and 3A of Schedule 1 of this Act by such amount as is specified in the order ; and such an order shall be made by statutory instrument which shall be subject to annulment in pursuance of a resolution of either House of Parliament.

(3)   Except as provided in Chapter V below, at the commencement of this Act, a tenancy—
  (a)   under which a dwelling-house was then let as a separate dwelling; and
  (b)   which immediately before that commencement was an assured tenancy for the purposes of sections 56 to 58 of the Housing Act 1980 (tenancies granted by approved bodies),
shall become an assured tenancy for the purposes of this Act.

(4)   In relation to an assured tenancy falling within subsection (3) above—
  (a)   Part I of Schedule 1 to this Act shall have effect , subject to subsection (5) below, as if it consisted only of paragraphs 11 and 12; and
  (b)   sections 56 to 58 of the Housing Act 1980 (and Schedule 5 of that Act) shall not apply after the commencement of this Act.

(5)   In any case where—
   (a)   immediately before the commencement of this Act the landlord under a tenancy is a fully mutual housing association, and
   (b)   at the commencement of this Act the tenancy becomes an assured tenancy by virtue of subsection (3) above,
Then, so long as that association remains the landlord under that tenancy (and under any statutory periodic tenancy which arises on the coming to an end of that tenancy), paragraph 12 of Schedule 1 to this Act shall have effect in relation to that tenancy with the omission of sub-paragraph (1)(h).
(6)   (....)
(7)   (....) '

Demoted tenancies

3.15   The Anti-Social Behaviour Act 2003 confers power on the county courts to change secure and assured tenancies into demoted tenancies. Such tenancies will lack the rights that are associated with secure and assured tenancies.

POTENTIAL CLAIMANTS

3.16   Applications for ASBIs (1996 Act, ss 153A–153D) and possession claim applications can only be made by a 'relevant landlord'.

Section 153E defines 'a relevant landlord' as:

(a)   a housing action trust;

(b)   a local authority (within the meaning of the Housing Act 1985);

(c)   a registered social landlord.

Section 152 injunctions cannot be sought if the victim, ie the claimant, is an owner occupier.

POTENTIAL DEFENDANTS

3.17   ASBIs can be obtained whether or not there is any statutory or common law cause of action.

3.18   Applications for injunctions can be sought against any person whether or not he is a tenant.

3.19   Injunctions can only be obtained against those who have mental capacity to understand what they are doing and how to modify their behaviour.

3.20	Obtaining an injunction order against a minor is rare. Landlords will encounter difficulties in obtaining injunctions against children because these are generally unenforceable. Injunctions are usually enforced by imprisonment, fine or sequestration. In the case of a child only a fine or sequestration is lawful. It is unlawful to imprison a person under the age of 18 (Powers of Criminal Courts (Sentencing) Act 2000, s 89).

3.21	In *Wookey v Wookey*[1] the court distinguished between the 'recalcitrant teenager in good employment who may be appropriately injuncted' and the vast majority of children for whom the civil courts are not appropriate.

3.22	In *Harrow London Borough Council v G*[2] complaints were made against a 14-year-old and this culminated in obtaining an injunction against him under s 152 of the 1996 Act, together with a power of arrest. On appeal Roderick Evans J granted the appeal as G was too young to be sentenced to imprisonment for contempt. There was no evidence that G had income or goods that could be sequestrated. The court held that where an application for an injunction against a minor is made under the 1996 Act the applicant must provide the court with evidence of the minor's personal circumstances to demonstrate that the injunction is enforceable by fine or sequestration of assets.

3.23	The landlord must show that the injunction may be enforced against a minor and may therefore consider other routes by which the minor's anti-social behaviour may be curtailed, for example by entering into an acceptable behaviour contract or by obtaining an ASBO.

CONDITIONS

Free-standing applications

The 'conduct test' (s 153A)

3.24	The court must be satisfied that the alleged anti-social behaviour meets the following 'conduct test' when considering whether to grant an injunction under s 153A of the 1996 Act. The conduct :

(1)	must be capable of causing nuisance or annoyance to any person; and

(2)	must directly or indirectly affects the housing management function of the landlord.

The housing management functions of the landlord include:

(1)	functions conferred by or under any enactment;

---

[1]	[1991] Fam 121.
[2]	[2004] EWHC 17 (QB).

(2)   the powers and duty of the landlord as holder of an estate or interest in housing accommodation (s 153E(11)).

3.25   This is intended to be broad ranging and cover any activity which the landlord undertakes in the day-to-day and strategic management of the housing accommodation. Thus, the conduct complained of must be capable of causing nuisance or annoyance to one of the following:

(1)   a person with a right to reside in or occupy the housing accommodation owned or managed by the relevant landlord, eg tenant or licencees and their lodgers and families living with them (the tenant category);

(2)   a person with the right to reside in or occupy other accommodation in the neighbourhood owned or managed by the relevant landlord, eg owner occupiers or private sector tenants living in the neighbourhood (the neighbour category);

(3)   a person engaged in lawful activity in or in the neighbourhood of the housing accommodation owned or managed by the relevant landlord, eg postman, refuse collector, meter man category;

(4)   a person employed (whether or not by the relevant landlord) in connection with the relevant landlord's management functions, eg housing officer, persons responsible for maintenance and repair, collection of rent arrears.

The 'conditions' (s 153A)

3.26   In addition to the need for the court to be satisfied that the alleged anti-social behaviour meets the 'conduct test' the court may grant an injunction only if each of the following *two* conditions (which are set out s 153A(3) and (4)) are satisfied:

(a)   a person against whom an injunction is sought is engaging, has engaged or threatens to engage in conduct which is capable of causing nuisance or annoyance to any person or which directly or indirectly affects the housing management functions of a relevant landlord; and

(b)   the conduct is capable of causing nuisance or annoyance to:
  (i)   a person with a right to reside in or occupy other housing accommodation owned or managed by a relevant landlord; or
  (ii)   a person with a right to reside in or occupy other housing accommodation in the neighbourhood of such housing accommodation; or
  (iii) a person engaged in lawful activity in or in the neighbourhood of such housing accommodation; or

(iv) a person employed in connection with the exercise of the relevant landlord's housing management functions. Such a person does not have to be employed by the relevant landlord.

3.27 There *must* be:

(a) a *nexus* between the residential premises and the person who is to be protected.[3] Living in privately owned accommodation near such premises will *not* provide such nexus;[4]

(b) a connection or link between the activity in which the person or persons protected by the injunction are engaging and some identifiable local authority tenanted residential premises. There *need not be any nexus* between the respondent and the residential premises.[5]

3.28 Examples of anti-social behaviour include:

• noise nuisance;

• verbal abuse of staff, agents and/or tenants and neighbours;

• visitors causing nuisance to neighbours;

• untidy gardens;

• threats of violence or actual violence;

• vandalism.

3.29 The claimant *need not*:

(a) *prove* that nuisance or annoyance has *actually* been caused. That the conduct complained of is *capable* of causing nuisance or annoyance is sufficient;

(b) obtain witness statements from neighbours or other tenants in support of the application if they have witnessed the conduct complained of, as proof of actual nuisance or annoyance is not needed.

3.30 Neighbourhood is *not* defined. 'Neighbours' means those living and working in the neighbourhood and includes everyone who is close enough to be affected by the conduct.[6]

---

3   *Enfield London Borough Council v B* [2000] 1 WLR 2259; *Nottingham City County v Thames* [2002] EWCA Civ 1098.
4   *Manchester City Council v Lee* [2003] EWCA CIV 1256.
5   *Manchester City Council v Lee*; *Wigan Metropolitan Borough Council v G (A Child)* [2003] EWCA Civ 1256; *Nottingham City County v Thames* [2003] HLR 145, CA.
6   *Northampton Borough Council v Lovatt* (1998) 30 HLR 875.

3.31 Pursuant to s 153E housing accommodation *includes* the whole of the housing accommodation owned or managed by a relevant landlord in the neighbourhood and any common areas used in connection with the accommodation. Housing accommodation may relate to flats, lodging-houses, hostels and any yard, garden, outhouses and appurtenances that either belong to the accommodation or are enjoyed with it.

3.32 Where the conduct complained of occurred is *not* material. Consequently it is immaterial if the conduct occurred outside the locality of the housing accommodation so long as the conduct complained of is capable of causing a nuisance to the category of persons mentioned in s 153A(4) of the 1996 Act. For example, a landlord may apply for an injunction in order to protect a tenant who has been regularly harassed by other residents of an estate even if the incident itself which gave rise to the application for an injunction happened elsewhere. This is because the anti-social behaviour is connected with the home owned or managed by the relevant landlord. Similarly, if an employee of the landlord is subjected to anti-social behaviour but the incident occurred elsewhere, for example in a shopping centre, an injunction may still be sought against the perpetrators where a link with the management functions of the landlord is established. Note also that the staff affected need not be directly employed by the landlord.

Injunctions against unlawful use of premises (s 153B)

3.33 A 'relevant landlord' may obtain an injunction prohibiting anyone from *using or threatening to use* housing accommodation owned or managed by the landlord for an unlawful purpose.

3.34 Section 153D deals with injunctions for breach of tenancy agreements. Hence, injunctions under s 153B may be restricted to criminal behaviour such as drug use, prostitution, running a brothel or handling stolen goods.

3.35 There is no definition of 'unlawful purpose'.

3.36 In considering whether to grant an injunction the court must be satisfied that the person against whom the injunctions is sought has used or threatened to use the housing accommodation owned or managed by the relevant landlord for an unlawful purpose. The landlord need not prove that anyone has suffered or is capable of suffering from the defendant's activities. The 'conduct test' and the two conditions which apply to ASBIs under s 153A of the 1996 Act do not apply to s 153B injunctions.

Exclusion orders and powers of arrest (s 153C)

3.37 The court granting an ASBI pursuant to s 153A or an injunction against unlawful use of premises pursuant to s 153B is of the view that *either*:

(a)   the conduct consists of or includes the use or threatened use of violence; *or*

(b)   there is a significant risk of harm to the various classes of potential victims listed in s 153A(4).

3.38   The court *may* add a stipulation in the injunction that the person should be prohibited from entering or being in any premises specified in the injunction. It may have the effect of excluding the defendant from his normal place of residence (s 153E). It is irrelevant whether the defendant has a tenancy or licence of his place of residence. 'Harm' includes serious ill-treatment or abuse whether or not physical (s 153E(12)).

3.39   The court may attach a power of arrest to any part/s of the order. Actual violence need not be proven for a power of arrest to be imposed. The court needs to be satisfied that there has been use or threatened use of violence or that there is significant risk of harm.

3.40   Any question of the appropriateness of an exclusion order should normally be reserved to an on notice hearing.[7]

Injunction against breach of tenancy agreement (s 153D)

3.41   Section 153D relates to any tenancy agreement for occupation of residential premises which are either owned or managed by a relevant landlord and is in addition to the common law power to restrain breach of a covenant in a tenancy agreement.

3.42   A relevant landlord can apply for an injunction against a tenant for breach of or anticipated breach of a tenancy agreement on the grounds that the tenant is:

(a)   engaging or threatening to engage in conduct that is capable of causing nuisance or annoyance to any person; or

(b)   allowing, inciting or encouraging any other person to engage or threaten to engage in such conduct; and

(c)   that conduct includes the use or threatened use of violence; or

(d)   there is a significant risk of harm to any person.

Section 153D(5) defines 'tenancy agreement' as including any agreement for the occupation of residential accommodation owned or managed by a relevant landlord.

---

[7]   *Moat Housing Group-South Ltd v Harris* [2005] ECWA Civ 287.

The court must carry out the 'conduct test' in respect of matters set out in paras (a) and (b) above.

3.43 The court may include in the injunction an exclusion order and may attach a power of arrest to any provision of the injunction if it is satisfied about matters mentioned in paras (c) and (d) above.

3.44 Breach of a tenancy agreement need not relate to the landlord's housing management function. For example, the landlord can apply for an injunction if the tenancy agreement contains a clause that prevents threatening a member of staff even if the staff member threatened has nothing to do with the landlord's housing management function.

Possession claims

3.45 The court must be satisfied when considering a claim for possession of premises against secure and assured tenants[8] that a tenant residing in or visiting a dwelling house:

(1)   has been guilty of conduct causing or likely to cause a nuisance or annoyance to a person residing, visiting or otherwise engaging in lawful activity in the locality; or

(2)   has been convicted of:
    (a)   using the dwelling house or allowing it to be used for immoral or illegal purposes; or
    (b)   an arrestable offence committed in, or in the locality of, the dwelling house.

The court must also consider reasonableness.

Examples of court decisions

Bristol City Council v Mousah[9]

3.46 In this case the council standard tenancy agreement specifically provided that there should be no supply from, or in, the neighbourhood of any controlled drugs. There was evidence of drug dealing. It was held that where there is a serious breach of the tenancy agreement, in the absence of exceptional circumstances, it would be reasonable to make a possession order.

---

8   Housing Act 1985, Sch 2, ground 2; Housing Act 1988, Sch 2, ground 14, as amended.
9   (1997) 30 HLR 32, CA.

Greenwich London Borough Council v Grogan[10]

3.47 In this case a 17-year-old tenant pleaded guilty to handling stolen goods from the property. He was sentenced to 6 months youth custody. At the time the possession claim was heard there were no further allegations. The Court of Appeal allowed an appeal against an order for possession and made a suspended order for possession for 12 months. When exercising its discretion the court could take into consideration the *wider public interest*. A balance had to be achieved in considering, first, whether, if the tenant lost the tenancy, he would revert to a life of crime and, secondly the competing interests of the local authority in safeguarding the interests of the other tenants and the people on its waiting list.

Bristol City Council v Grimmer[11]

3.48 In this case the defendant, her husband and elder sons had indulged in a large number of incidents of anti-social behaviour resulting in an outright possession order being made. Hale LJ said that the decision as to whether a possession order should be made 'is pre-eminently a difficult judgment that has to be made by the judge who is hearing the evidence and seeing the parties'. The Court of Appeal would not interfere with the judge's discretion.

Demoted tenancies – secure tenancies

3.49 Local housing authorities, housing action trusts and registered social landlords are entitled, pursuant to s 82A of the Housing Act 1985, in the case of secure tenancies to seek a demotion order from a county court. Such an order will be made *only if*:

(a) a notice seeking a demotion order has been served or it is just and equitable to dispense with that requirement (Housing Act 1985, s 83, as amended);

(b) the court is satisfied that the tenant or a person residing in or visiting the dwelling-house has engaged or has threatened to engage in conduct to which s 153A or 153B of the 1996 Act applies (anti-social behaviour or using premises for unlawful purpose); and

(c) it is reasonable to make an order.

Demoted tenancies – assured tenancies

3.50 Section 6A of the 1996 Act provides a similar procedure as with secure tenancies in the case of assured tenancies.

---

[10] (2001) 33 HLR 140, CA.
[11] [2003] EWCA Civ 1582.

PROCEDURE

Injunctions

3.51 The procedure to be followed in respect of applications for injunctions to restrain anti-social behaviour under ss 152 and 153 of the 1996 Act is contained in CPR Part 65 and Practice Direction 65. CPR Part 65 also contains provisions in respect of demoted tenancies, ASBOs and the Protection from Harassment Act 1997.

3.52 Injunctions can be either final or interim. Final injunctions are granted, if appropriate, at the end of proceedings when the evidence has been heard in full and the court has considered all the issues between the parties. Interim injunctions may be applied for and may be granted at any time from the commencement of proceedings. An interim injunction is a temporary order pending resolution of the matter and is made in advance of the final hearing so that immediate protection can be afforded to the community from anti-social behaviour.

Which court?

3.53 Applications *must be made* in the court for the district in which the defendant resides (CPR, r 65.3). Issuing proceedings in the wrong court is unlikely to render the application invalid. In most cases the judge will transfer the matter to the right court.

Essential pleadings/documents/service

3.54 The following requirements must be met:

(1) Applications for injunctions under s 153A, 153B or 153D of the 1996 Act must be made subject to CPR Part 8 procedure and the relevant practice direction.

(2) Applications must be supported by a witness statement which must be filed with the claim form.

(3) The claim form must state:
    (a) the matters required in CPR, r 8.2:
        (i) the question which the claimant wants the court to decide; or
        (ii) the remedy which the claimant is seeking and the legal basis for the claim to that remedy; and
    (b) the terms of the injunction applied for.

3.55 The claim should set out in summary form the facts and the question or issue which the court is to decide or the remedy sought. Wherever possible the claimant should file a draft of the order sought. Applications for injunctions under ss 153A, 154B and 153D *must be made on Form N16A*.

3.56   The claim form should state that Part 8 applies. The burden that Part 8 is suitable is upon the claimant.

3.57   A completed Form 16A – application for injunction (general form) – must be filed. This form will set out the basic details of the case, including details of the claimant and defendant and terms of the injunction sought, ie details of prohibitions. The claimant may apply for a power of arrest to an injunction under ss 153A, 153B and 153D where appropriate. The grounds of the application may be set out in the application notice itself or the witness statement.

3.58   Unless directed otherwise applications *made on notice should be heard in public* (CPR, r 39.2).

3.59   In every application made on notice the court will enter details of the time and place of hearing.

Service

On notice applications

3.60   Pursuant to CPR, r 65.3(5) and (6) the application notice and witness statement *must be served personally* on the defendant. Applications *must be made on 2 days' notice unless the court directs otherwise.*

3.61   The defendant can take part in the hearing whether or not he has filed an acknowledgment of service (CPR, r 65.3(6)(b)).

3.62   The claimant must deliver a copy of the injunction with power of arrest to any police station for the area where the conduct occurred.

Without notice applications

3.63   An application may be made on a without notice basis (CPR, r 65.3).

3.64   The witness statement in support must state the reasons why notice of the application has not been given within the written evidence accompanying Form N16A. Injunctions may be made without notice to the respondent if the court considers that it is just and convenient to do so.

3.65   Where an application is made, CPR, rr 8.3, 8.4 (acknowledgment of service and failure to file it), 8.5(2)–(6) and 8.6(1) (service of witness statements by claimant and defendant),[12] 8.7 (requirement to obtain permission of court to make a Part 20 claim) and 8.8 (defendant's objection to using the Part 8 procedure) do not apply.

---

[12]   Note, however, the requirement of CPR, r 65.3(2)(b).

3.66 A without notice court order and power of arrest deserves early consideration. It is advisable to ascertain the practice followed by the court where proceedings are issued in respect of early return dates for such cases. These applications would normally be listed within 14 days in order to grant the respondent an opportunity to make representations. It is usual for the injunction and the power of arrest to run only until the return date.

3.67 An order obtained on a without notice basis must be served upon the defendant before delivering a copy of the injunction to a police station in the area where the conduct occurred. The claimant must immediately inform the police station if the injunction order containing a power of arrest is either varied or discharged.

Jurisdiction

3.68 District judges, deputy district judges and circuit judges have jurisdiction to grant ASBIs and to commit for contempt.

Possession claims

Possession claims against secure and assured tenancies

3.69 Possession claims against secure and assured tenancies are founded on the following grounds:

- Housing Act 1985, Sch 2, ground 2;

- Housing Act 1988, Sch 2, ground 14.

Procedure for possession claims is as set out in CPR Part 55.

Court

3.70 The claim must be started in the county court for the district where the property is situated (CPR, r 55.3(1)).

Claim form

3.71 The claimant must use Form N5 which must be verified by a statement of truth (CPR, r 22.1).

The particulars of claim must:

(a) identify the land to which the claim relates;

(b) state that the claim relates to residential premises;

(c) state the ground on which possession is claimed;

(d) state full details of the tenancy agreement;

(e) state full details of the conduct alleged.

If a power of arrest is sought, each provision of the proposed order to which it is sought must be specified. This can be sought in the claim form, acknowledgement of service or by a Part 23 application.

Date of hearing

3.72 The court will fix a hearing date when the claim is issued (CPR, r 55.5(1)). This is not usually less than 28 days from the date of issue of the claim form. The hearing will be fixed before the end of 8 weeks.

3.73 The time between service of the claim form and the hearing should be at least 21 days (CPR, r 55.5(3)).

3.74 The above timings can be shortened if appropriate by court under CPR, r 3.1(2)(a) and (b). Further, the Practice Direction to CPR Part 55 (CPR PD55, para 6(3.2)) provides:

'Particular consideration should be given to the exercise of this power if:

(1) the defendant, or the person for whom the defendant is responsible, has assaulted or threatened to assault:
   (a) the claimant;
   (b) a member of the claimant's staff; and
   (c) another resident in the locality;
(2) there are reasonable grounds for fearing such assault; or
(3) the defendant, or a person for whom the defendant is responsible, has caused serious damage or threatened to cause serious damage to the property or the home or property of another resident in the locality.'

In such instances the court will have to consider what steps are needed to list the matter for final determination as soon as reasonably practicable.

Acknowledgment of service/defence

3.75 The defendant need not file an acknowledgment of service. If the defendant fails to file a defence within 14 days of service of the claim form as required by CPR, r 15.4 he will be able to take part in the proceedings, but such failure may be relevant when the court decides the issue of costs (CPR, r 55.7(3)).

Hearing/case management directions

3.76 At the hearing the court will either decide the matter or grant case management directions to include:

(1) the date by which the defendant must file a defence;

(2) allocate to track if appropriate. Note that the claims are deemed to be allocated to the multi track;

(3) the date for exchange of lay witness evidence.

(4) fixing the date of trial with an appropriate time estimate.

Note that it will generally be appropriate for any interim injunction that has been granted to continue until the final hearing unless the defendant gives an undertaking.

Demotion claims

3.77 In any claim for a demotion order or suspension order (or both) made in the alternative to a possession order, the provisions of CPR Part 55 must be followed. That is where a demotion claim is coupled with a claim for possession, and the normal procedure as set out in CPR Part 55 applies.

3.78 Where the landlord seeks only a demotion order or suspension order CPR, r 65.14–19 applies. The structure of such claims is similar to proceedings under CPR Part 55.

3.79 The court must not entertain proceedings for a demotion order unless a notice has been served upon the tenant or the court thinks that it is just and equitable to dispense with service of the notice under s 5 of the Housing Act 1988 as amended.

3.80 Section 6 of the Housing Act 1988 provides that the notice must:

(1) provide details of the alleged conduct;

(2) state that proceedings will not begin before a certain date (not before the end of the period of 2 weeks beginning with the date of service of the notice);

(3) state that proceedings will not begin after 12 months beginning with the date of service.

The particulars of claim must be filed and served with the claim form.

3.81 Note the provisions of CPR PD65, paras 5.1–7.1 which are as follows.

(1) Demotion claims made in the alternative to possession proceedings (CPR PD65, para 5.1)

3.82   The particulars of claim in respect of a demotion claim relating to residential premises let on a tenancy must:

(a)   specify whether the demotion claim is made under s 82A(2) of the Housing Act 1985 or under s 6A(2) of the Housing Act 1988;

(b)   state whether the claim is by a local housing authority, a registered social landlord or a housing action trust;

(c)   provide details of any express terms of the tenancy agreement served upon the tenant under either s 82A(7) of the Housing Act 1985 or s 6A(10) of the Housing Act 1988;

(d)   give details of alleged conduct.

(2) Suspension claims that are coupled with possession claims (CPR PD65, para 5A)

3.83   In the case of a suspension claim relating to residential property let on a tenancy, the particulars of claim must:

(a)   state that the claim is made under s 121A of the Housing Act 1985;

(b)   provide details of the conduct alleged;

(c)   state why it is reasonable to make the order having regard to the matters stated in s 121(4) of the Housing Act 1985.

(3) Demotion or suspension claims (CPR PD65, para 6)

3.84

•   The claim has to be made in the county court for the district where the property is situated.

•   The claim must be made in the appropriate claim Form N6. Form N122 is for the particulars of claim.

•   The defence must be made in Form N11D.

•   The claimant's statement should give details of alleged conduct and any other matters that are to be relied upon.
    In a demotion claim, in addition to the matters set out above the particulars of claim must include parties to the tenancy, period of tenancy and details of the rent (amount and when payable) (CPR PD65, para 7).

Fixing the date of the hearing

3.85 The provisions relating to fixing the hearing date are comparable to the provisions relating to possession claims under CPR Part 55. The issues as to whether time should be abridged are also similar and are set out in CPR PD65, para 8.2.

3.86 In the event that the matter cannot be determined on the date of the hearing the court will consider granting directions in order to list the matter for a final hearing as soon as practicably possible.

The final hearing

3.87 Unless otherwise directed all applications made on notice will be held in public (CPR, r 39.2). The format is usually the same as any civil proceedings. The claimant's representative will open the case and state what the issues are. The claimant/landlord will present its evidence. The defendant will present his evidence. Closing submissions will be made by the defendant's representative and finally by the claimant's representative

3.88 The evidence from the claimant should demonstrate to the court the context of the anti-social behaviour and/or illegal activity and its effect or potential effect on others. In doing so it must make clear the link between the behaviour and the landlord's housing management functions.

3.89 Hearsay evidence is admissible. In civil proceedings the admission of hearsay evidence is governed by ss 1–7 of the Civil Evidence Act 1995 and CPR, rr 33.1–33.5.

3.90 Section 4(1) of the 1996 Act provides:

'(1)   In estimating the weight (if any) to be given to hearsay evidence in civil proceedings the court shall have regard to any circumstances from which any inference can reasonably be drawn as to reliability or otherwise of the evidence.

(2)   Regard may be had, in particular, to the following –
(a)   whether it would have been reasonable and practicable for the party by whom the evidence was adduced to have produced the maker of the original statement as a witness;
(b)   whether the original statement was made contemporaneously with the occurrence or existence of the matters stated;
(c)   whether the evidence involves multiple hearsay;
(d)   whether any person involved had any motive to conceal or misrepresent matters;
(e)   whether the original statement was an edited account, or made in collaboration with another or for a particular purpose;
(f)   whether the circumstances in which the evidence is adduced as hearsay are such as to suggest an attempt to prevent the proper evaluation of its weight.'

3.91 Adequate notice of a party's intention to rely upon hearsay evidence will be given by including such evidence in a witness statement (CPR, r 33.2(1)).

3.92 Where hearsay evidence is contained in a witness statement of a person who is not being called to give oral evidence, the party intending to rely upon such evidence must inform the other parties when serving the evidence that the person is not being called to give oral evidence and give reasons as to why the witness is not being called (CPR, r 33.2).

3.93 The court will normally adjourn the hearing to enable oral evidence to be adduced if the maker of a witness statement does not attend court and his evidence is disputed.

3.94 Evidence could include direct witness statements, professional witness statements, CCTV footage, hearsay evidence, letters of complaints to the landlord and other agencies such as the police.

3.95 A single act of serious anti-social behaviour may suffice for an order to be made.

Burden of proof

3.96 The burden of proof is to the civil standard. The civil standard (on the balance of probabilities) and not the criminal standard (beyond a reasonable doubt) applies to injunctions. This means that injunctions require a lesser burden of proof than a criminal prosecution which may lead to a more certain outcome. The aim is to stop anti-social behaviour rather than punish the perpetrator.

THE ORDER

Injunctions

3.97 The order will prohibit the defendant from engaging in conduct and/or activities specified in the order.

3.98 The order must identify the particular person/persons where there is risk of significant harm to that/those person/persons.

3.99 Order relating to injunctions must be framed in terms that are reasonable and proportionate to the facts of the case.[13]

3.100 The injunction order will be made using Form N16 (interim order made without notice) or Form N16(1)(order on notice). Where an interim injunction order is made it will specify the date, time and place when the court will further

---

[13]   *Manchester City Council v Lee* [2000] HLR 177.

consider the application. The order will specify conduct that is forbidden and state in clear terms that if the order is disobeyed the defendant will be guilty of contempt and may be sent to prison.

3.101 There is no requirement of form. Mummery LJ in *Manchester City Council v Lee* said:

> 'Careful consideration needs to be given by the court in each case to the scope of the injunction which is justified by the evidence. In the exercise of its discretion the court must ensure that the injunction granted is framed in terms appropriate and proportionate to the facts of the case. Thus if the judge finds that there is a risk of significant harm to a person or persons it would usually be appropriate for the injunction to identify that person or those persons, so that the respondent knows the circumstances in which he might be in breach of the injunction, and liable for contempt of court if he caused a nuisance or annoyance to them in the future.
>
> In order to justify granting a wider injunction against a respondent restraining him from causing a nuisance or annoyance to "a person of a similar description", it would normally be necessary for the judge to make a finding that there had been use or threats of violence to persons of similar description, and that there was a risk of significant harm to persons of a similar description if an injunction was not granted in respect of them.'

3.102 The terms of the order must be clear and capable of being readily understood by the defendant:[14]

> 'It cannot be sensible or a proper exercise of the statutory power to grant an injunction in terms that are not readily understandable by those whose conduct they are intended to restrain. Further an injunction which leaves doubt as to what can and cannot be done is not a proper basis for committal proceedings.'

3.103 Note that guidance has been given by the Court of Appeal in *Moat Housing Group-South Ltd v Harris*[15] as follows:

(1)   The test for making an anti-social behaviour order was one of necessity to protect the public from further anti-social acts by the offender.

(2)   The terms of the order must be precise and be capable of being understood by the offender.

(3)   The findings of fact that have led to the order being made must be recorded.

(4)   The order must be explained to the offender.

(5)   The terms of the order must be pronounced in open court.

---

[14]   *Manchester City Council v Lee* [2000] HLR 177, per Chadwick LJ.
[15]   [2005] ECWA Civ 287.

(6)   The written order must reflect the order that was pronounced accurately.

(7)   Where it is reasonable to make a possession order, consideration should be given to suspend where appropriate.

3.104 With effect from April 2007, s 26 of the Police and Justice Act 2006 inserts a new s 153A into the Housing Act 1996. This has been introduced to avoid some courts interpreting the legislation narrowly so as to preclude the making of injunctions unless specified individuals (those the injunction is intended to protect) are named in its terms.

3.105 The intention is to remove all doubts as to Parliament's intention that injunctions should be available to protect the wider community, including those who do not wish to be identified.

Duration of order/variation/discharge

3.106 ASBI orders are normally for 6 or 12 months. They can be for a specified period as the court deems fit or until varied or discharged. They can remain in force for an indefinite period.

3.107 An injunction may be varied or discharged by the court on application made in Form N244 by the person against whom the order was made or by a relevant landlord.

Injunction without notice

3.108 In *Moat Housing Group-South Ltd v Harris*[16] Brooke LJ stated:

> 'A grant of an injunction without notice was to grant an exceptional remedy. It would be best if judges in the county court, in deciding whether to exercise their discretion to make an antisocial behaviour injunction without notice, followed the guidance given in section 45(2)(a) of the Family Law Act 1996.
>
> They should bear in mind that:
>
> (i)   to make an order without notice was to depart from the normal rules as to due process and warranted the existence of exceptional circumstances;
> (ii)   one such exceptional circumstance was that there was a risk of significant harm to some person or persons attributable to conduct of the defendant if the order was not made immediately;
> (iii) the order must not be wider than was necessary and proportionate as a means of avoiding the apprehended harm.'

3.109 It was held that a without notice injunction is an exceptional remedy and, as a matter of general principle, no order should be made in civil or family proceedings without notice to the other side, unless there is a good reason for

---

[16]   [2005] EWCA Civ 287.

departing from the general rule. The more intrusive the order, the stronger the reasons must be for departure from the general rule.

3.110 The guidance given in the case of *Moat House* (above) must be followed when without notice applications are considered. In essence an injunction granted on a without notice basis can be stipulated to run for 6 months if at the same time an early 'on notice' hearing is fixed.

Exclusion orders (s 153C)

3.111 The order must clearly state the areas of exclusion (which could be specified premises and/or a specified area), and a map clearly delineating the exclusion zone should be appended to the order.

3.112 A person may be excluded from his normal place of residence (s 153E(2)(b)) but such an order must be reasonable and proportionate for the protection of the rights and freedoms of others (s 8(2) of the Human Rights Act 1998).

3.113 Ouster and exclusion orders must be dealt with on notice if possible.

Powers of arrest (s 153C; Form N110A)

3.114 A power of arrest is available where:

- there has been a threat of violence;

- there is a significant risk of harm – this could include emotional or psychological harm.

Consequently, a power of arrest will be available in some cases where there has been no actual or threatened violence, for example in cases of violent hate behaviour including racial and sexual harassment.

3.115 The order will state clearly that the defendant will be arrested without warrant if a constable has reasonable cause to suspect that any of the terms of the order to which a power of arrest is attached has been breached.

3.116 The purpose of attaching a power of arrest to an order or specific parts of an order is protection. In *Moat Housing Group-South Ltd v Harris* (above) Brooke LJ said:

'A court should attach a power of arrest to one or more provisions contained in an order made without notice if it was satisfied that:

(a)   the defendant had used or threatened violence against some person or persons of a description mentioned in section 153 A(4), as inserted; and

(b)   there was a significant risk of harm to one or more of those persons attributable to the conduct of the defendant, if the power of arrest was not attached to those provisions immediately.'

3.117 Section 154 provides that in determining whether to attach a power of arrest in respect of without notice applications the court shall have regard to the following:

(a)   whether the applicant is likely to be prevented or deterred from seeking the exercise of the power if the power is not exercised immediately; and

(b)   whether there is reason to believe that the respondent is aware of the proceedings and is evading service and the applicant or the persons mentioned in s 154A(4) will be seriously prejudiced if a power of arrest is not attached until substituted service is effected.

3.118 Where the court attaches a power of arrest it must afford an opportunity at a hearing that must be fixed as soon as possible for the respondent to make representations in respect of the order. *A without notice court order with a power of arrest must be listed for hearing ideally within 14 days.* The time limit for the injunction and power of arrest is normally until the return hearing.

3.119 Power of arrest may be attached to *any* term/provision of the order *but the term/provision must not* contravene s 5 of the HRA 1998.

3.120 Summary arrest and detention is a serious interference with a person's private life and can be justified only by an order which is 'particularly precise'.[17]

3.121 Power of arrest is usually attached to paragraphs prohibiting violence or physical proximity.[18]

3.122 Each provision which is subject to a power of arrest must be set out in a separate clause. The power of arrest *must* be confined to specific paragraphs alone.

3.123 Powers of arrest may:

(a)   last for shorter periods (s 157(1));

(b)   be extended on application (s 157(2));

(c)   be discharged on application and have no effect on the injunction (s 157(4)).

---

[17]   *Kopp v Switzerland* (1998) 27 EHRR 91.
[18]   *Hale v Tanner* [2000] 3 FCR 62.

Undertakings

3.124 Undertakings may be given by the defendant in respect of the injunctions and exclusion orders sought by the landlord. Undertakings should be considered as a way of resolving the litigation. Breach of an undertaking will attract the same penalties as breach of an injunction.

Funding

3.125 Legal representation to defend an application for an anti-social behaviour injunction will generally only be granted where:

(a) there are serious allegations;

(b) the allegations are denied wholly or substantially;

(c) the matter cannot reasonably be dealt with by an undertaking.

Legal representation may be justified if there is some question of inability to defend, eg the mental capacity of the defendant is in question.

Possession orders

3.126 The court *must* consider (and the judgment must reflect this) in particular when deciding whether it is *reasonable to make a possession order*:

(1) the effect the nuisance or annoyance has had on persons other than the person against whom the order is sought;

(2) the continuing effect which such nuisance or annoyance will have on such persons;

(3) the effect such nuisance or annoyance will have/is likely to have on such persons if the conduct is repeated.

3.127 The court has very wide discretion and will make a possession order if it is reasonable to do so. In considering reasonableness the court will consider all the circumstances of the case. This broad discretion does not entitle the courts to consider the availability of other remedies such as injunctions. This was confirmed in *Newcastle City Council v Morrison*[19] where it was held that the recorder was wrong to see the question of reasonableness as turning on the notion that there was an alternative and, as he thought, more appropriate remedy available. May J stated that the views of Ralph Gibson J in *Sheffield City Council v Jepson*[20] applied to cases of anti-social behaviour:

---

[19] (2000) 32 HLR 891.
[20] (1993) 25 HLR 299.

'although the authority could have obtained an injunction rather than seeking possession (there is) no reason why a council should be required or expected to take that course. It is in the public interest that necessary and reasonable conditions in tenancy agreements of occupiers or public housing should be enforced fairly and effectively.'

3.128 However, it is right that injunctions should be considered when the court exercises its discretion to suspend a possession order. Kay LJ in *Cantebury City Council v Lowe*[21] said that:

'the issue of whether to suspend must be very much a question of the future. There is no point in suspending an order if the inevitable outcome is a breach. Any factor which is relevant as to whether there will be future breaches must, in my judgment, be relevant to the question of suspension. This would include the fact that following an injunction things had considerably improved or that the person is likely to observe an injunction if one was granted at the same time.'

Suspended order

3.129 Where the court is of the view that it is *reasonable* to make a possession order it should proceed to consider whether the order should be suspended on terms.

3.130 The provisions of the Disability Discrimination Act 1995 must be considered if relevant as follows:

(1) A determination must be made on whether the person who complains of disability discrimination is a 'disabled person'.

(2) Consideration must be given as to whether the person has been treated differently by reason of his disability.

(3) Consideration must be given as to whether the landlord's treatment of that person is justified. Such treatment will be justified only if it is in the interests of the health and safety of any persons living in neighbouring properties and it is reasonable in all the circumstances for the landlord to hold such an opinion.

In such proceedings the disabled person can counterclaim for a declaration that he has been unfairly discriminated against and/or counterclaim for injunctive relief. The Court of Appeal has stated that in instances involving secure tenants or if the tenancy relates to an assured tenancy the better course would be for the defendant to assert that it would be unreasonable for the court to make a possession order.

---

[21]   (2001) 33 HLR 583, at 590.

3.131 Landlords who hold a secure or assured tenancy should, in view of the difficulties, liaise closely with local social services prior to making a decision to serve a notice seeking possession.

3.132 Where a person is disabled by reason of mental health problems under the Mental Capacity Act 2005 such a person may be a 'protected person'.

Demotion order

Secure tenancies

3.133 Where the court makes a demotion order it has the following effects:

(1) The tenancy is terminated with effect from the date specified in the order.

(2) If the tenant remains in occupation and the landlord is a registered social landlord the tenancy becomes a demoted assured shorthold tenancy.

(3) Any arrears of rent that have accrued prior to the tenancy being demoted remain payable.

(4) There will no security of tenure. However, prior to starting a possession claim the landlord must serve a notice of proceedings which should state:
    (a) that the court will be asked to make a possession order;
    (b) the reasons for the landlord's decision to apply for an order; and
    (c) the date after which proceedings may be started.

Note the provisions as set out in s 143F for an internal review of the decision to seek possession.

3.134 Section 143D provides that if the procedure for internal review has been followed the court *must* make a possession order.

3.135 In most instances where the tenant has remained in occupation since the making of the demotion order for a period of one year the tenancy will revert to a secure tenancy (ie at the end of a period of one year starting from the date when the demotion order takes effect).

3.136 In the case of *assured tenancies* s 6A of the 1996 Act provides a similar procedure. In such instances the procedure for obtaining possession is as with assured shorthold tenancies (2 months' notice must be given pursuant to s 21 of the Housing Act 1988) save that the possession order *can* take effect within 6 months of the start of the tenancy.

Drinking banning orders

3.137 Drinking banning orders are sought under the Violent Crime Reduction Act 2006 (CPR, r 65.30). The 1996 Act empowers those aged 16 and over who are responsible for alcohol-related disorder to be excluded from pubs and clubs in a defined geographic area under a drinking banning order for a specified time. The duration of the order may be reduced if the person successfully completes an approved course to address the alcohol misuse behaviour.

3.138 The conditions for making the order are (a) the person has indulged in criminal or disorderly conduct whilst under the influence of alcohol and (b) there is a need to protect others from further such conduct by him whilst he is under the influence of alcohol.

3.139 Application may be made by the local authority, the chief officer for a police area, and the chief constable of the British Transport Police Force.

3.140 An application may be made where the relevant authority is a party to the principal proceedings or alternatively as soon as the relevant authority that is not a party to the principal proceedings becomes aware of the proceedings. The application is normally made on notice. Further, an application can also be made by a relevant authority to join a person to the principal proceedings if the person's conduct is material to the principal proceedings and the details of the conduct are set out in the application.

Breach

3.141 A breach of an injunction will be dealt with by way of civil proceedings for contempt. The claimant can, upon becoming aware of a breach, make an application on Form N244.

3.142 If the court is satisfied that the defendant has breached the term/terms of the order it may impose a fine or a period of imprisonment on the defendant. The imprisonment is for contempt of court and not for the conduct that has led to the breach of the order.

3.143 The person who has been committed to prison can write to the court to purge his contempt. The prisoner must apologise to the court for the contempt, acknowledge that the contempt had to be punished, demonstrate remorse and contrition and undertake to comply with the terms of the order in future. In the event that the court is satisfied that the contempt has been purged the prisoner will be released before the end of the sentence.

3.144 Section 155(1) provides the procedure to be followed if a power of arrest is attached to certain provisions of the court order by virtue of s 153(c) or (d).

- A constable may arrest without warrant a person whom he has reasonable cause for suspecting has breached the order.

- A person who has been arrested must be brought before a judge within 24 hours.

- In reckoning any period of 24 hours no account shall be taken of Christmas day, Good Friday or any Sunday.

- The defendant shall not be released within the period of 24 hours unless the judge so directs.

- A constable must immediately inform the person who applied for the injunction.

3.145 At the initial hearing the judge may grant bail or remand the arrested person in custody. This is a matter for the court

3.146 Section 155(3) provides that if no power of arrest is attached or if a power of arrest is attached to only certain provisions of the order the applicant may, at any time he considers that the respondent has not complied with the order, apply to the relevant judge for the issue of a warrant for the respondent's arrest. The application for a warrant must be made in accordance with CPR Part 23 and may be made without notice. The applicant must:

(a) file an affidavit setting out the grounds for the application; or

(b) give oral evidence as to the grounds for the application.

In such an instance the judge will not issue a warrant unless (CPR PD65, para 2.1):

(a) the application is substantiated on oath; and

(b) there are reasonable grounds for believing that the respondent has failed to comply with the injunction.

If the matter is not disposed with forthwith, the judge may remand the person. The court will require the person to comply with such terms as may be necessary. It is usual for the terms to be the stipulations contained in the original order.

3.147 The county court has power to review a decision to grant bail or to remand in custody particularly where there has been a change in circumstances. Therefore, on appeal against a refusal to grant bail the Court of Appeal will review the decision rather than hold a rehearing.

3.148 The court has power to remand a person if it considers that a medical report may be required.

Time scales in the case of adjournment or remand

Adjournment (CPR, r 65.6(4))

3.149 Where proceedings are adjourned and the arrested person is released the matter must be dealt with within 28 days (whether by the same judge or another judge). A committal application for contempt of court of the arrested person can be issued if the defendant is not dealt with within this period (CPR, r 65.6(5)).

Remand on bail (Sch 15, para 4)

3.150 A defendant cannot be remanded on bail for longer than 8 clear days unless the parties consent. Bail, if granted, will usually be subject to conditions. These may include the arrested person:

(1) remaining away from specified persons until the next hearing;

(2) being ordered to pay his own recognisance (a sum of money that he must pay immediately into court, or if he fails to attend at a future hearing pay into court as a forfeit); or

(3) having a surety (a person who agrees to be responsible for the person on bail) who agrees to pay a specified sum of money on his behalf either immediately or if he fails to attend a hearing; or

(4) being remanded in custody until the recognisance is paid or proof that money is available is provided to court (known as postponing recognisance).

Remand in custody

3.151 Remand in custody cannot exceed 8 clear days. If the remand is for no more than 3 clear days the person can be remanded into police custody.

Remand for medical examination/report

3.152 Where the court is of the view that a medical report is required the court can exercise any power under s 155 of the 1996 Act to remand a person for the purpose of a medical examination and report to be obtained. In such a case the matter shall not be adjourned for more than 4 weeks and the period of remand in custody is for a maximum of 3 weeks. If there is reason to suspect that the person arrested is suffering from a mental illness or severe mental impairment the judge is empowered under s 35 of the Mental Health Act 1983 to remand the person for a report on the accused's mental condition. The person remanded may be detained in hospital or a place of safety pending admission to hospital. Section 35(8) of the Mental Health Act 1983 provides that a person so remanded to a hospital may obtain a medical report at his own expense from a registered medical practitioner chosen by him and apply to the court on the basis of it for his remand to be terminated under s 35(7) of that Act. The Official Solicitor must be notified if appropriate.

Applications for bail

3.153 A person arrested under a power of arrest attached to an injunction order or a warrant of arrest which has been issued pursuant to s 155(3) may make an application for bail either orally or in an application notice. Such an application must state:

(1) the applicant's full name;

(2) the address of the place where the person making the application has been detained;

(3) the address where the person would reside if the application were granted;

(4) the amount of any proposed recognisance;

(5) the grounds for making the application;

(6) full details of any change in circumstances if a previous application has been refused.

A copy of the application must be served upon the person who obtained the injunction (CPR PD 65, para 3).

3.154 Where the court fixes the recognisance and the person is bailed subject to it, the recognisance may be taken by a judge, Justice of the Peace, Justices' clerk, police officer or the governor of prison (CPR, r 65.7). The person who has custody of the applicant must release him if satisfied that the recognisances have been taken.

Committals and contempt

3.155 A defendant who is found to have breached an ASBI order will be liable for civil contempt.

3.156 Where a person disobeys a judgment or order requiring him to abstain from doing an act, the order may be enforced by a committal order (CCR Ord 29, r 1(1)).

3.157 Where an alleged contempt of court is based upon disobedience of an order made in the county court the court has power to punish the breach (SCPD52, para 1.2).[22]

---

[22] Practice Direction to CCR Ord 29 and RSC Ord 52.

3.158 The rights of the individual under the European Convention of Human Rights should be borne in mind (SCPD52, para 1.4).

3.159 The standard of proof in committal proceedings is 'beyond reasonable doubt'.

3.160 The court may waive any procedural defect in the commencement or conduct of a committal application if satisfied that no injustice has been caused to the respondent by the defect (SCPD52, para 10).

3.161 The purpose of committal in the event of breach of an undertaking/ injunction is twofold:

(a)   to punish for disobedience of an undertaking/order of the court; and

(b)   to secure compliance with undertaking/orders in the future.[23]

3.162 A CPR Part 23 application must be made by a party to the litigation. The application must be made *to the court which made the order or took the undertaking* which is alleged to have been breached. The application must be accompanied by *an affidavit* which must state the grounds of the application.

3.163 It is essential that the application notice give details of the provisions which are said to have been breached. It is not enough that the affidavit contains the information, since the defendant *must know* the case he has to meet.

3.164 Upon breach of an anti-social behaviour order or terms of the tenancy pursuant to ss 152 and 153 of the 1996 Act the court may impose a sentence of up to 2 years and/or a level 4 fine.

PROCEDURAL REQUIREMENTS

3.165 The defendant should be personally served with the injunction unless he was present in court when the injunction was granted *and* was made aware of the penal consequences if the order is breached. The defendant can be notified by telephone or other means. The court may dispense with service; however, this is rare as it will have human rights implications.

3.166 The alleged contemnor arrested pursuant to a power of arrest must be given written notice of the alleged contempt.[24] Contempt applications are heard in public.

---

[23]   *Enfield London Borough Council v Mahoney* [1983] 2 All ER 901.
[24]   *Newman v Modern Bookbinders Ltd* [2000] 2 All ER 814,CA.

Legal representation

3.167 The defendant should be made aware of his right to legal representation. He should be warned of the possible penalty and invited to consider whether he wants legal representation. If the defendant wishes to obtain legal advice the judge can require his clerk to contact a solicitor who has a contract for providing help at court, or provide details as to how the defendant can contact a solicitor for advice. If the defendant already has a solicitor he should be afforded the opportunity to have the solicitor present. Often, for practical reasons, the court will adjourn the matter to enable the defendant to take advice.

3.168 In *King v Read and Slack*[25] the prison sentence imposed was set aside as there was a failure on the part of the judge to inform the respondent of his right to legal aid. This was considered to be a material irregularity.

Legal aid

3.169 Section 12 of the Access to Justice Act 1999 states:

'(1) The Commission shall establish, maintain and develop a service known as Criminal Defence Service for the purpose of securing that individuals involved in criminal investigations or criminal proceedings have access to such advice, assistance or representation as the interests of justice require.

(2) In this part "Criminal Proceedings" means –
    ...
    (f) proceedings for contempt or alleged to have been committed, by an individual in the face of the court; ... '

3.170 Schedule 3(which makes provision concerning the grant of a right to representation in criminal proceedings) has effect. The Commission shall fund representation to which an individual has been granted a right in accordance with Sch 3.

3.171 Section 15(1) provides that an individual who has been granted a right to representation in accordance with Sch 3 may select any representative or representatives willing to act for him. The Commission must comply with the duty imposed by s 14(1) by funding representation by the selected representative or representatives.

The Criminal Defence Service (Funding) Order 2001[26] provides that:

'(6) Where a court grants representation to a person for the purposes of proceedings for contempt, it may assign to him, for the purpose of those proceedings, any representative who is within the precincts of the court.'

---

[25] [1999] 1 FLR 425.
[26] SI 2001/855.

The Criminal Defence Service (General) (No 2) Regulations 2001[27] define the power of the court:

> '15. The Court may grant a representation order for representation by an advocate alone:
>
> (a)   in any proceedings referred to in section 12(2)(f) of the Act. ...'

Whilst the proceedings are civil the criminal standard of proof applies.

Conditions

3.172 The court will need to be satisfied that:

(1)   the respondent knew of the order;

(2)   the respondent's conduct amounts to a breach of the terms of the order as literally construed;

(3)   the conduct was deliberate and not just an intention to breach the terms of the order.

The court will dismiss the application if:

(1)   the arrest is unlawful. An arrest is lawful only if:
    (a)   the order is endorsed with a power of arrest;
    (b)   the alleged conduct if proven will amount to a breach of that part of the order to which a power of arrest is attached;
    (c)   the police officer had reasonable grounds to suspect that there has been a breach of the order.

(2)   more than 24 hours has elapsed since the arrest and the time the respondent was brought before a judge. In such a case the court has no jurisdiction;

(3)   there is no proof of service of the original order;

(4)   if the conduct alleged is so trivial that punishment is not warranted or if the period already spent in custody is sufficient;

(5)   the application amounts to an abuse of process.

The court may not impose a sentence if it forms the view that the injunction should not have been granted.

---

[27]   SI 2001/1437.

Absence of parties

Applicant

3.173 If the applicant fails to attend, the court may dismiss the application or adjourn. The matter may be dealt with if the respondent admits the breach.

Respondent

3.174 If the respondent fails to attend it is very likely that the hearing will be adjourned because although the hearing can proceed (subject to satisfying the court about service) and if the breach is found there will still have to be a rehearing when the respondent attends. Alternatively, where the contemnor has been served the court may deal with the matter and direct that the contemnor should be brought to court on his way to prison if committed.

3.175 There is no obligation on the contemnor to give evidence.

3.176 After giving evidence the contemnor should be asked if he wants to rely upon any further evidence.[28]

Absence of witnesses

3.177 The hearing can proceed if the allegations have been reduced to writing, and the parties have had reasonable time to consider the allegations and investigate, gather evidence and consider calling evidence. In most cases the matter will be adjourned to give an opportunity to the parties to call their witnesses.

The judgment/order

3.178 The judgment/order will:

(1) review the evidence;

(2) make findings in respect of each allegation;

(3) give reasons for the findings;

(4) identify the parts of the order that have been breached;

(5) identify the allegations that are not pursued, not proven or withdrawn.

3.179 The order *must* be approved and signed by the judge. This will enable the clerk to draw up the warrant of committal for the bailiffs.

---

[28] *Shoreditch County Court Bailiffs v de Madeiros* (1988) *The Times*, February 24, CA.

3.180 Where there is immediate committal the order must be handed to the contemnor before he is taken from the building. In any other case to include suspended committal the applicant will be responsible for service unless the court directs otherwise.

3.181 If it is necessary to adjourn it is imperative that at each stage after arrest the court considers why bail should not be given and give reasons for that decision. The factors which are relevant are the seriousness of the allegations and the risk of further breaches of the injunction.[29]

Punishment

3.182 The court's sentence is in respect of the contempt alone as the court is dealing with a civil contempt and not with what may amount to criminal behaviour. The maximum period a county court can imprison is 2 years. The maximum sentence includes suspended sentences that have been activated and consecutive sentences.

3.183 The decision as to the period of committal has no bearing on whether the sentence should be suspended. Every breach has to be identified, is punishable separately and can be dealt with by concurrent or consecutive sentence.

3.184 The sentence imposed will normally be 14 days or more, but never less than 8 days. The length of the sentence has no bearing on the history of the case but should reflect and be proportionate to the proven acts of breach.

3.185 Imprisonment is not an automatic consequence of breach. Further, it does not follow that on the first breach the court will be minded to suspend the sentence. The court may extend the injunction for a longer period or make an injunction order in stronger terms.

3.186 The rules of natural justice require that an opportunity must be given to all parties to address the court. The applicant's views should be heard since the evidence and submissions may assist in demonstrating to the court the seriousness of any breach. The defendant must be afforded an opportunity to mitigate and apologise for any breach before the court imposes the sentence.[30] The committal order can be made forthwith or suspended. Committal to prison should be considered as a last resort. In most instances sentence imposed is likely to be between 28 days and 6 months.

3.187 A judge giving a suspended sentence of imprisonment should explain the consequences of the breach to the defendant. The purpose of a suspended sentence is to ensure that the defendant has a constant reminder of the consequences of the breach of the order.

---

[29]   *Newham London Borough Council v Jones* [2002] EWCA Civ 1779.
[30]   *Manchester City Council V Worthington* [2000] 1 FLR 411.

3.188 Time spent in custody on remand is not deducted from time served but is taken into account when sentencing.

3.189 The court may either impose an unlimited fine or a term of imprisonment for up to 2 years. The case of *Leicester City Council v Alvin Spencer Lewis*[31] provides that once a breach is proved, sentencing is a matter wholly at the discretion of the court. Clarke LJ gave the following guidance regarding matters that must be taken into consideration when sentencing for breach:

(a) the behaviour the injunction was aimed at protecting people from;

(b) the strength of the case against the respondent in the original injunction application;

(c) the consideration the judge granting the injunction gave to the terms of the injunction;

(d) whether the breach was deliberate and the frequency;

(e) whether the respondent was arrested if there is an exclusion order;

(f) whether the respondent attempted to stop or leave the situation that caused the breach of the injunction;

(g) whether the respondent is of previous good character.

The above guidance needs to be modified to suit each case. Other factors may be relevant to the question of sentencing.

3.190 The court has the power to impose consecutive sentences in respect of separate incidents of contempt. A suspended sentence must be for a fixed term. The period for which the order is suspended must also be fixed.

Purging contempt

3.191 Under CPR 29 where a person is under custody for a warrant or order (other than a warrant for committal) and wishes to apply for his discharge he can make an application in writing attested by the governor of the prison (or any officer not below the rank of a principal officer) showing that he has purged or wishes to purge his contempt. He must not serve the notice upon the party who obtained the warrant or order less than one day before the hearing.

---

[31]   (2001) 33 HLR 37, CA.

3.192 If the committal order:

(1)   does not direct that any application for discharge shall be made to a judge; or

(2)   was made by the district judge under s 118 of the 1996 Act,

any application for discharge may be made to the district judge.

Hammerton v Hammerton

3.193 *Hammerton v Hammerton*[32] is an important recent decision. The appeal related to procedural errors which led to depriving the appellant of the protection he was entitled to before being sent to prison. These errors arose from a combination of the appellant being unrepresented and the decision of the judge to hear Mrs Hammerton's application for committal and Mr Hammerton's application for a contact order at the same time.

3.194 In his judgment Moses LJ stated:

'I should set out a number of principles in relation to committal hearings which are well settled ...

(i)   By virtue of s.6 of the Human Rights Act 1998, it is unlawful for the court, as a public authority for the purposes of s.6(3) of the 1998 Act, to act in a way incompatible with the defendant's rights enshrined in article 6 of the Convention for the Protection of Human Rights and Fundamental Freedoms ...

(ii)   Proceedings for committal are a criminal charge for the purpose of article 6 ...Thus the defendant to such proceedings has the right enshrined in article 6 (3)(c):
"to defend himself in person or through legal assistance of his own choosing or, if he has not sufficient means to pay for legal assistance to be given it free when the interests of justice so require"
... A defendant's intransigence in unreasonably failing to co-operate with whatever legal assistance is offered, or in refusing it, may make it impossible for legal assistance to be continued ... If he is unrepresented then an adjournment should, save in circumstances of extreme urgency, be granted so that representation may be obtained.

(iii)   Since committal proceedings involve a criminal charge against a defendant, the burden of proving guilt lies on the person seeking committal.

(iv)   A defendant in committal proceedings is not obliged to give evidence. His right against self-incrimination under article 6.1 applies ...

(v)   In the event the facts constituting contempt are proved, the seriousness has to be marked by reference not merely to the intrinsic gravity of the conduct, but also to secure compliance in the future ...

---

[32]   [2007] EWCA Civ 248.

13 ... there was no reason why the hearing of the committal should not be adjourned to enable him to afford such representation.

14 ... the second source of error. That was the decision of the judge to hear both the application for contact and the committal proceedings at the same time ...

15 ... The court was obliged to warn him that he did not need to give evidence. No such warning was given. But the evidence he gave about the alleged breaches of the undertakings and of the order was clearly relevant to the issue as to whether any form of contact was appropriate in the interests of the children. Accordingly, if Mr Hammerton exercised his right not to give evidence in the committal proceedings, he would inevitably fail in his claim for some form of contact.

16 ... there is no hint ... of the judge reminding himself of the different burden and standard of proof in the two applications. ...

18 ... the better course would have been for another judge to hear the committal proceedings.

19 ... the important rights enshrined in article 6 must not be sacrificed in the interests of time and costs ...

21 ... the judge did not have the benefit of mitigation or submissions ...

23 ... In *Re K*[33] Hale LJ concluded her judgment by observing that legal representation:

> "might have made a difference. I do not say that it would make a difference, but it might have done."

Wall LJ in the same case said:

> "here may well be cases in which the factual matrix for the committal proceedings is so inter-twined with that giving rise to the Part II proceedings, that there is no sensible alternative but to hear them together ...".'

3.195 A claim for possession for anti-social behaviour and the committal application for breach of an ASBI which was granted earlier are often listed at the same time. The facts are usually inextricably intertwined. However, in the event that the defendant/respondent is unrepresented utmost care must be exercised.

APPEALS

3.196 A uniform system of appeals was created by CPR Part 52, which came into force 2 May 2000. The appellant or respondent requires permission to appeal (CPR, r 52.3). Such permission may be sought from the lower court at

---

[33] *Re K (Contact: Committal Order)* [2003] 1 FLR 277.

the hearing at which the decision was made or to the appeal court in an appeal notice. The application may be made orally at the hearing. Where the lower court refuses permission a further application for permission to appeal may be made to the appeal court. Where the appeal court refuses permission on paper the person seeking permission may request a reconsideration of the decision at a hearing.

3.197 Permission to appeal is given only if (a) the appeal has a real prospect of success or (b) there is some other compelling reason why the appeal should be heard (CPR, r 52.3(7)).

3.198 The court has a discretion whether to grant permission. This must be exercised in accordance with the overriding objective.

Appeals against committals

3.199 Permission to appeal is not required in respect of an order by which a party is committed to prison. Any other order or decision made by a court in the exercise of jurisdiction to punish for contempt requires the grant of permission. Such orders are within the ambit of the Administration of Justice Act 1960, s 13, whether they relate to an adjournment of the whole or part of the application or of 'no order save as to costs'. An appeal in respect of a decision by a circuit judge in the county court with regard to a committal order or other order in contempt proceedings will lie with the Court of Appeal. If a district judge makes a committal order or other order in contempt proceedings, the appeal will ordinarily lie with the circuit judge. Exceptionally, an appeal may lie to the Court of Appeal either by the application of *King v Read and Slack*[34] or through the transfer operation contained in CPR, r 52.14. The criteria for leapfrogging an appeal direct to the Court of Appeal is where (a) there is an important point of principle or practice or (b) there is some other compelling reason.

COSTS

3.200 Costs orders may be made. Proceedings relating to possession claims and ASBIs are usually multi-track proceedings and therefore, unless costs are agreed, will be subject to detailed assessment. It is arguable that where any hearing lasts one day or less, costs should be summarily assessed. If invited the court may proceed to assess costs. In practice costs orders in these claims are rarely pursued.

---

[34]   [1999] 1 FLR 425.

CHECKLISTS, FORMS AND PRECEDENTS

3.201 Checklists, forms and precedents relating to anti-social behaviour injunctions are reproduced below.

1. APPLICATION FOR ANTI-SOCIAL BEHAVIOUR INJUNCTION UNDER SECTION 153A HOUSING ACT 1996

☐ Relevant landlord as Claimant. *[HA s153A(2), s153E(7)]*

☐ Application in Form N16A. *[PD1.1]*

☐ Commenced in court for district in which the defendant resides or the conduct complained of occurred. *[CPR 65.3(2)(b)]*

☐ Defendant is 18 or over

☐ **OR** if under 18 has litigation friend **OR**
    ☐ Order made under CPR 21.2(3) permitting the child to conduct proceedings without a litigation friend
    ☐ **AND** (if Defendant under 18) there is "evidence as to the personal circumstances of the minor which would make enforcement by way of fine or sequestration of assets an effective sanction for breach" *[London Borough of Harrow v G [2004] EWHC 17 Roderick Evans J.]*

☐ Supported by witness statement filed with the claim form. *[CPR 65. 3(2)(c)]*

☐ If on notice, served personally not less than 2 days before the hearing. *[CPR 65.3(5), (6)]*

☐ Person against whom injunction is sought is engaging, has engaged or threatens to engage in housing-related[35] conduct[36] capable of causing a nuisance or annoyance to *[HA s153A(3)]* :
    ☐ Person with a right to reside in or occupy housing accommodation owned or managed by a relevant landlord (paragraph (a) accommodation) or
    ☐ Person with a right to reside in or occupy other housing accommodation in the neighbourhood of paragraph (a) accommodation or

---

[35] Directly or indirectly relating to or affecting the housing management functions of a relevant landlord *[HA s153A(1)]*.
[36] Conduct anywhere *[HA s153A(1)]*.

☐ Person engaged in lawful activity in or in the neighbourhood of paragraph (a) accommodation or

☐ Person employed (whether or not by a relevant landlord) in connection with the exercise of a relevant landlord's housing management functions

2. SECTION 153C PRE-CONDITIONS FOR EXCLUSION ORDER AND/OR POWER OF ARREST IN RESPECT OF INJUNCTIONS UNDER SECTIONS 153A AND 153B

☐ The conduct consists of or includes the use or threatened use of violence. *[HA s153C (1)(a)]*

☐ **OR** there is a significant risk of harm to a person mentioned in "second condition" above. *[HA s153C(1)(b), s153A(4)]*

3. APPLICATION FOR INJUNCTION AGAINST UNLAWFUL USE OF PREMISES UNDER SECTION 153B HOUSING ACT 1996

☐ Relevant landlord as claimant. *[HA s153B(2), s153E(7)]*

☐ Application in Form N16A. *[PD1.1]*

☐ Commenced in court for district in which the defendant resides or the conduct complained of occurred. *[CPR 65.3(2)(b)]*

☐ Defendant is 18 or over

☐ **OR** if under 18 has litigation friend **OR**
　　☐ Order made under CPR 21.2(3) permitting the child to conduct proceedings without a litigation friend
　　☐ **AND** (if Defendant under 18) there is "evidence as to the personal circumstances of the minor which would make enforcement by way of fine or sequestration of assets an effective sanction for breach" *[London Borough of Harrow v G [2004] EWHC 17 Roderick Evans J.]*

☐ Supported by witness statement filed with the claim form. *[CPR 65. 3(2)(c)]*

☐ If on notice, served personally not less than 2 days before the hearing. *[CPR 65.3(5), (6)]*

☐ Conduct consists of or involves using or threatening to use housing accommodation owned or managed by a relevant landlord for an unlawful purpose. *[HA s153B(1)]*

4. SECTION 153C PRE-CONDITIONS FOR EXCLUSION ORDER AND/OR POWER OF ARREST IN RESPECT OF INJUNCTIONS UNDER SECTIONS 153A AND 153B

☐ The conduct consists of or includes the use or threatened use of violence. *[HA s153C (1)(a)]*

☐ **OR** there is a significant risk of harm to a person mentioned in "second condition" above. *[HA s153C(1)(b), s153A(4)]*

5. APPLICATION FOR INJUNCTION AGAINST BREACH OF TENANCY AGREEMENT UNDER SECTION 153D HOUSING ACT 1996

☐ Relevant landlord as Claimant. *[HA s153D(1), s153E(7)]*

☐ Application in Form N16A. *[PD1.1.]*

☐ Commenced in court for district in which the defendant resides or the conduct complained of occurred. *[CPR 65.3(2)(b)]*

☐ Supported by witness statement filed with the claim form. *[CPR 65. 3(2)(c)]*

☐ If on notice, served personally not less than 2 days before the hearing. *[CPR 65.3(5), (6)]*

☐ Defendant a tenant of the claimant. *[HA s153D(1)]*

☐ Breach or anticipated breach of tenancy agreement. *[HA s153D(1)]*

☐ **ON GROUNDS THAT** the tenant is engaging or threatening to engage in conduct that is capable of causing nuisance or annoyance to any person *[HA s153D(1)(a)]*
  ☐ **OR** is allowing, inciting or encouraging any other person to engage or threaten to engage in such conduct. *[HA s153D(1)(b)]*

☐ Pre-conditions for exclusion order and/or power of arrest under section 153D

☐   The conduct includes the use or threatened use of violence *[HA s153D(2)(a)]*

☐   **OR** there is a significant risk of harm to any person *[HA s153D(2)(b)]*

6. APPLICATIONS UNDER HOUSING ACT 1996 ON SHORT NOTICE OR EX PARTE

☐   Does witness statement in support state the reasons why no notice given? *[CPR 65.3(4)(a)]*

☐   Does court consider it just and convenient to grant the injunction? *[HA s153E(4)]*
> ☐   Do exceptional circumstance exist? *[Moat Housing]*
> ☐   For instance is there a risk of significant harm to some person or persons attributable to the conduct of the defendant if the order is not made immediately? *[Moat Housing]*
> ☐   Is the intended order no wider than is necessary and proportionate as a means of avoiding the apprehended harm? *[Moat Housing]*

☐   Has date been fixed for defendant to make representations? *[HA s153E(5)]*

Power of arrest ex parte

☐   Has the defendant used or threatened violence against some person or persons of a description mentioned in section 153A(4) *[Moat Housing]***AND**

☐   Is there a risk of significant harm to one or more of those persons, attributable to conduct of the defendant, if the power of arrest is not attached to those provisions immediately. *[Moat Housing]*
> ☐   Have regard to all circumstances including *[HA s154(1)]*
> > ☐   Whether the Applicant will be deterred or prevented from seeking the exercise of the power if the power is not exercised immediately
> > ☐   And whether there is reason to believe the Respondent is aware of the proceedings but is deliberately evading service and the Applicant and relevant person will be seriously prejudiced by delay until substituted service is effected.
> ☐   Has date been fixed for defendant to make representations? *[HA s154(2)]*

7. APPLICATION FOR ANTI-SOCIAL BEHAVIOUR ORDER UNDER THE CRIME AND DISORDER ACT 1998

☐ There are principal proceedings. *[CDA s1B(1)]*

☐ Applicant is a relevant authority. *[CDA s1B(2), s1B(3), s1(1A)]*

☐ Applicant is a party to principal proceedings or applies to be joined. *[CDA s1B(2), s1B(3); CPR 65.24]*

☐ The respondent/defendant is a party *[CDA s1B(2), s1B(3) ; CPR 65.22]*
    ☐ **OR** there is an application to join him or her *[CDA s1B(3B); CPR 65.23]*
    ☐ **AND** the prospective new party's anti-social acts are material to the principal proceedings *[CDA s1B(3A)(b)), s1B(3C)]*

☐ The respondent /defendant is 18 or over – except in a pilot scheme court when
    ☐ if under 18 has litigation friend **OR**
    ☐ Order made under CPR 21.2(3) permitting the child to conduct proceedings without a litigation friend

☐ The application is made
    ☐ in claim form [CPR 65.22(1)(a)]
    ☐ or by application notice by defendant filed with the defence [CPR 65.22(1)(b)]
    ☐ or by application notice by existing party as soon as possible after it becomes aware of the circumstances that lead it to apply for an order after its claim is issued or its defence filed [CPR 65.22(2)]
    ☐ or in the same application notice as application to have relevant authority or new respondent/defendant joined as party [CPR 65.23(1)(b), 65.24(1)(b)]

☐ [If application by relevant authority to join a person to the principal proceedings] application notice must contain the relevant authority's reasons for claiming that the person's anti-social acts are material in relation to the principal proceedings AND details of the anti-social acts alleged. *[CPR 65.23(2)]*

☐ Application for ASBO accompanied by written evidence *[CPR 65.25]*
    ☐ **INCLUDING** evidence of consultation (e.g. that applicant local authority has consulted with chief officer of police; that applicant registered social landlord consult with council and with police) *[CDA s1E; CPR 65.25]*

☐ Satisfied as to service. [Normal CPR service rules apply and CPR Part 65 requires that applications "should normally be made on notice to the person against whom the order is sought". If application made in Claim Form only and fixed hearing date given on issue, 21 days notice – *CPR 55.5(3)(c)*. If application by way of application notice, 3 days notice – *CPR 23.7(1)(b)*.]

☐   The respondent/defendant has acted in a manner that caused or was likely to cause harassment, alarm or distress to one or more persons not of the same household as himself. *[CDA s1(1)(a)]*

       ☐   **AND** the such an order is necessary to protect ***relevant persons*** from further anti-social acts by him. *[CDA s1(1)(b)]*

☐   ***Relevant persons*** as defined (e.g. within the local government area of the applicant council; persons who are residing in or who are otherwise on or likely to be on premises provided or managed by the applicant registered social landlord or persons who are in the vicinity of or likely to be in the vicinity of such premises). *[CDA s1(1B)]*

Application for Interim anti-social behaviour order

☐   Main application for an ASBO *[CDA s 1D(1)]*

☐   Application support by evidence including evidence of consultation in connection with the main application *[CPR 65.25, 25.3(2)]*

☐   Application in *[CPR 65.26(2)(a)]*
    ☐   Claim form **OR**
    ☐   Application notice

☐   Satisfied as to service. [Normal CPR service rules apply. CPR 65.26(2)(b) provides that application "should normally be made on notice to the person against whom the order is sought". If application made in Claim Form only and fixed hearing date given on issue, 21 days notice – CPR 55.5(3)(c). If application by way of application notice, 3 days notice – CPR 23.7(1)(b). If made without notice, court may grant an interim remedy if it appears to the court that there are good reasons for not giving notice – CPR 25.3(1); but evidence in support must state the reasons why notice has not been given – CPR 25.3(3)]

☐   Is it just to make an order pending determination of the main application? [CDA s1D(3)]

8. ARREST UNDER POWER OF ARREST FOR BREACH OF INJUNCTION UNDER CHAPTER III OF PART V HOUSING ACT 1996

☐   Has a copy of the injunction been personally served?

☐ Or is service admitted or dispensed with?

☐ Does it contain a power of arrest?

☐ Was the power of arrest within its period of validity?

☐ Is lawful arrest admitted?

☐ Is lawful arrest proved?

☐ Can further attendance of the arresting officer be dispensed with?

☐ Brought before the relevant judicial authority within 24 hours, ignoring Christmas Day, Good Friday and any Sunday.

☐ Does the Respondent know what breaches are alleged?

☐ Have these been committed to writing?

☐ Has he been warned of the possible consequences and invited to consider whether he wishes to seek legal advice and/or representation?

☐ Is adjournment required for representation?

☐ Is adjournment required for preparation?

☐ Is complainant present?

☐ Is adjournment required for complainant to attend?

☐ Must be dealt with within 28 days of arrest if adjourned (otherwise need to resort to notice to show cause) but can defer consideration of the penalty.

☐ The arrested person must be given not less than 2 days notice of the hearing

☐ If adjourned, what direction as to evidence required? [respondent cannot be compelled to serve his own evidence as opposed to evidence from other witnesses in advance]

☐ Remand in custody under Schedule 5 max 8 clear days. If not exceeding 3 clear days may commit him to the custody of a constable.[37]

---

[37] There are provisions about applications for bail in CPR Part 65.

☐ If remand on bail, may remand for more than 8 days if both parties consent. Can attach conditions. Can require recognizance.[38] But note absence of powers if he fails to surrender to bail. **Therefore impractical and unnecessary to grant bail – enough to release and adjourn.**

☐ S48 remands for medical examination and report. Max of 3 weeks if in custody and 4 weeks if on bail. Also power under s35 Mental Health Act 1983.

☐ Do bailiffs need to be on stand by in case of imprisonment?

☐ Evidence of breach.

☐ Ask him whether he wishes to adduce any further evidence.

☐ Criminal standard of proof.

☐ Is breach/contempt proved and finding recorded in writing?

☐ If breach proved, give him the opportunity to address the court as to penalty and to apologise.

☐ Maximum 2 years imprisonment.

☐ N79 completed.

☐ Penalty for each breach admitted or proved must be announced and recorded.

☐ Ensure that you say whether any periods of imprisonment are concurrent or consecutive

☐ Continuation or amendment of injunction

☐ Certainty as to any terms of suspension

☐ Approve and sign the order

☐ If immediate committal, completed order must be handed to contemnor

☐ In any other case, including suspended committal, the applicant is responsible for service unless the court orders otherwise.

---

[38] There are provisions about recognisances in CPR Part 65.

9. APPLICATION FOR COMMITTAL FOR BREACH OF INJUNCTION UNDER CHAPTER III OF PART V HOUSING ACT 1996

☐ Has a copy of the injunction been personally served?

☐ Or is service admitted or dispensed with?

☐ Does the relevant order contain a penal notice

☐ Application to commit by way of application notice or claim form. Has it been served? *[RSC Order 52 paragraph 4.2 – which applies to County Court as well – unless the court otherwise directs the hearing date of a committal application shall be not less than 14 days after service of the claim form or of the application notice, as the case may be, on the Respondent]*

☐ Has Defendant been warned of the possible consequences and invited to consider whether he wishes to seek legal advice and/or representation?

☐ Is adjournment required for representation?

☐ Is adjournment required for preparation?

☐ Is complainant present?

☐ Is adjournment required for complainant to attend?

☐ If adjourned, what direction as to evidence required? *[respondent cannot be compelled to serve his own evidence as opposed to evidence from other witnesses in advance]*

☐ Do bailiffs need to be on stand by in case of imprisonment?

☐ Evidence of breach.

☐ Ask him whether he wishes to adduce any further evidence.

☐ Criminal standard of proof.

☐ Is breach/contempt proved and finding recorded in writing?

☐ If breach proved, give him the opportunity to address the court as to penalty and to apologise.

☐ Maximum 2 years imprisonment.

☐ N79 completed.

☐ Penalty for each breach admitted or proved must be announced and recorded.

☐ Ensure that you say whether any periods of imprisonment are concurrent or consecutive

☐ Continuation or amendment of injunction

☐ Certainty as to any terms of suspension

☐ Approve and sign the order

☐ If immediate committal, completed order must be handed to contemnor

☐ In any other case, including suspended committal, the applicant is responsible for service unless the court orders otherwise.

The length of the sentence

Never less than 8 days.

Consider 14 days to 6 months as the usual bracket.

Maximum sentence is 2 years – this includes any activated suspended sentence and consecutive sentences.

10. ASBO AND ASBI CASE MANAGEMENT DIRECTIONS

(1) Pursuant to CPR 65.3(1) and CPR 8.9 (c) the claim is treated as allocated to the Multi-track. It may be tried by a District Judge. Allocation questionnaires and pre- trial checklists are dispensed with.

(2) List for trial on the first open date after . . . . t/e . . . . The trial shall take place in open court.

(3) Each party shall give to every other party standard disclosure of documents by serving a list with a disclosure statement by . . . . Any request to inspect or for a copy of a document must be made by . . . .

(4) No party may call a witness at trial without the permission of the trial judge unless a witness statement, verified by statement of truth, setting out his evidence, has been served by . . . . .This includes the evidence of the parties themselves.

(5) No expert evidence being necessary, no party has permission to call or rely on expert evidence.
   OR:- *(and only exceptionally)*
   The parties have permission to rely on the written evidence of a single joint expert in . . . . *[field]*. The expert's report must be limited to matters relating to . . . . *[issue]* and delivered to both parties by . . . . Pending any order as to costs, each party shall pay half of the expert's charges. If the parties are unable to agree any matter in relation to the choice of expert, or the joint instructions to be given, an application must be made urgently. Both parties must provide any facilities required by the expert for access or inspection promptly on request.

(6) The claimant must lodge at court at least 7 days before the trial,
   – an indexed bundle of documents (contained in a suitable binder), with each page clearly numbered,
   – a case summary (which should not exceed 500 words) and schedule of outstanding issues, referring where appropriate to the relevant documents,
   [– a trial template (subject to the approval of the trial Judge) which must include time for the Judge to consider, give judgment, and to deal with costs]
   The claimant must seek to agree the above with the other party(ies)

(7) The bundle must include a Scott Schedule itemising each material allegation upon which a finding of fact is sought by the parties in support of their position. The schedule must in respect of each allegation:-
   (a) Set out the contentions of each party;

(b)   Include a cross reference to the relevant paragraph[s] in the
      Particulars of Claim and/or Defence;
(c)   Identify any relevant witnesses, specifying the page numbers in the
      trial bundle containing the relevant parts of their statements;
(d)   Provide a column for use by the Judge.

The Scott Schedule is required whether or not the Defendant has
expressly put forward a defence or points of contention. The format and
content of the Scott Schedule should be agreed between the parties and/or
their legal representatives if possible.

(8)   The bundle must include drafts of the orders which the Claimant will seek
      on disposal of the claim. The Claimant must have at the hearing a Word
      copy of the draft order on disk or must have emailed such a copy to the
      court in advance of the hearing.

(9)   The parties shall file and exchange skeleton arguments no later than 3
      days before the trial.

(10) The claimant's solicitor must forthwith liaise with all other parties to
      determine details of the joint availability of all trial personnel for all
      parties within the trial window. If there are no, or only limited, dates of
      joint availability the reason for the non-availability of each party's trial
      personnel must be obtained. That solicitor must notify such availability to
      the court's Diary Manager (or case worker) by telephone number 0121
      681 3120, by no later than . . . . The hearing date will then be
      fixed.

11. DIRECTIONS ORDER IN ASBO CLAIM

In the Birmingham County Court   **Case Number [ ]**

BETWEEN

[ ]

<u>Claimant</u>

-and-

[ ]

<u>Defendant</u>

Before District Judge   on   200

Upon hearing [Counsel][the Solicitor] for the Claimant and
     [Counsel][the Solicitor] for the Defendant
     the Defendant in person
     the Defendant not attending
     without notice to the Defendant
     [others]

IT IS ORDERED that:

(1) In this order, the claim by the Claimant . . . . against the
     Defendant . . . . for possession of . . . . , and for associated
     remedies is referred to as 'the principal proceedings' and the application
     by the Claimant . . . . for an Anti Social Behaviour Order (an
     'ASBO') against the . . . . Defendant is referred to as 'the ASBO
     application'.

(2) . . . . is joined as . . . . Second Defendant so that the
     Claimant can make the ASBO application against him

(3) . . . . is joined as . . . . Second Claimant so that it can make
     the ASBO application against the . . . . Defendant

(4) The application to join . . . . as a party is adjourned to . . . .
     t/e . . . . The . . . . Claimant must serve that application
     and the ASBO application on the . . . . Defendant together with
     copies of all the statements of case and evidence filed to date and notice
     of the next hearing, not later than . . . . days before the hearing

(5)   [The application to join . . . . as a party is dismissed][. . . . . be removed as a party] on the ground that he is under 18 and the court has no jurisdiction to join him as a party to make an ASBO against him

(6)   The principal proceedings will be heard together with the ASBO application and the following directions apply (unless expressly stated otherwise) to both of them

(7)   Allocation Questionnaires are not required. The case is allocated to the [fast][multi-] track.

(8)   *(if allocated to MT)* The final hearing may be listed before a District Judge, [because the principal proceedings are for recovery of land][because a District Judge has jurisdiction to hear the principal proceedings and the matter is suitable for trial before a District Judge][if the Designated Civil Judge consents, but otherwise must be listed before a Circuit Judge]

(9)   [see separate form for interim ASBO]

(10) [case management directions form attached]

12. INTERIM ANTI-SOCIAL BEHAVIOUR INJUNCTION UNDER SECTIONS 153A, 153B, 153C, 153D AND/OR 153E HOUSING ACT 1996

INTERIM ANTI-SOCIAL BEHAVIOUR INJUNCTION **Under sections 153A, 153B, 153C, 153D and/or 153E Housing Act 1996**	

**INTERIM ANTI-SOCIAL BEHAVIOUR
INJUNCTION
Under sections 153A, 153B, 153C, 153D
and/or 153E Housing Act 1996**

To:
of:

IN THE BIRMINGHAM COUNTY COURT	
Claim no:	
Claimant	
Defendant	

IF YOU DO NOT OBEY THIS ORDER, YOU WILL BE GUILTY OF CONTEMPT OF COURT AND YOU MAY BE SENT TO PRISON

If you do not understand anything in this order, you should go to a Solicitor, Legal Advice Centre or a Citizens Advice Bureau.

Either party can apply to the court for this order to be varied or discharged. But you must obey the order unless it is varied or discharged by the court.

On Wednesday, 13 February 2008 the court considered an application for an injunction.

The court ordered that:

(Where marked * *delete or complete as appropriate)*

The court further ordered that:

a power of arrest made under [section 153C]* or [section 153D]* Housing Act 1996

applies to [all]* paragraph(s) [   ]* of the above order;

the order [and the power of arrest]* shall continue until   *at 4pm
unless it is varied or discharged by the court in the meantime;

the costs are reserved until the next hearing;

as this order has been made without you being given due notice, the court has fixed a
hearing at   on   at Birmingham Civil Justice Centre,
The Priory Court, 33 Bull Street, Birmingham B4 6DS when you will have an opportunity
to make representations in relation to the injunction.

Ordered by

On   Wednesday, 13 February 2008

Page 1 of 1

The court office at Birmingham Civil Justice Centre, The Priory Courts, 33 Bull Street, Birmingham B4 6DS is open between 10am and 4pm Monday to Friday. When corresponding with the court, please address forms or letters to the Court Manager and quote the claim number. Telephone: 0121-681-4441. Fax: 0121-681-3001/2.

13. ANTI-SOCIAL BEHAVIOUR INJUNCTION UNDER SECTIONS 153A, 153B, 153C, 153D AND/OR 153E HOUSING ACT 1996

ANTI-SOCIAL BEHAVIOUR INJUNCTION
Under sections 153A, 153B, 153C, 153D
and/or 153E Housing Act 1996

IN THE BIRMINGHAM COUNTY COURT	
Claim no:	
Claimant	
Defendant	

To:
of:

IF YOU DO NOT OBEY THIS ORDER, YOU WILL BE GUILTY OF CONTEMPT OF COURT AND YOU MAY BE SENT TO PRISON

If you do not understand anything in this order, you should go to a Solicitor, Legal Advice Centre or a Citizens Advice Bureau.

Either party can apply to the court for this order to be varied or discharged. But you must obey the order unless it is varied or discharged by the court.

On Wednesday, 13 February 2008 the court considered an application for an injunction.

The court ordered that:

(Where marked * *delete or complete as appropriate)*

The court further ordered that:

a power of arrest made [under section 153C]* *or* [section 153D]* Housing Act 1996 applies to [all]* paragraph(s) [   ]* of the above order;

the order [and the power of arrest]* shall continue [until   *at 4pm] *or* [until it is varied or discharged by the court]*.

The court further ordered that:*

Ordered by

On   Wednesday, 13 February 2008

Page 1 of 1

14. ANTI-SOCIAL BEHAVIOUR INJUNCTION – POWER OF ARREST UNDER SECTION 153C AND/OR 153D HOUSING ACT 1996

ANTI-SOCIAL BEHAVIOUR INJUNCTION - POWER OF ARREST
Under [section 153C]* *and/or* **[section 153D]* Housing Act 1996**

IN THE BIRMINGHAM COUNTY COURT Claim no:

	Claimant
	Defendant

(Here set out those provisions of the order to which this power of arrest is attached and no others)

(Where marked * *delete as appropriate)*

Power of Arrest

The court orders that a power of arrest under [section 153C]* *and/or* [section 153D]* Housing Act 1996 applies to the following paragraph(s) of an order made on Wednesday, 13 February 2008:

[*(In respect of a power of arrest under section 153C Housing Act 1996)* The court is satisfied that the relevant conduct consists of or includes the use or threatened use of violence and/or there is a significant risk of harm to a person mentioned in section 153A(4) of the said Act.]*

[*(In respect of a power of arrest under section under section 153D Housing Act 1996)* The court is satisfied that the relevant conduct includes the use or threatened use of violence and/or there is a significant risk of harm to any person.]*

A power of arrest is attached to the order whereby any constable may (under the power given by section 155 Housing Act 1996) arrest without warrant a person whom he has reasonable cause for suspecting to be in breach of any of the provisions set out in this order or otherwise in contempt of court in relation to such provision.

This Power of Arrest expires at 4pm on

Note to the Arresting Officer

Where a person is arrested under the power given by section 155 of the Housing Act 1996, the section requires that:
- A constable shall after making such an arrest forthwith inform the person on whose application the injunction was granted;
- Such person shall be brought before the relevant judge within 24 hours beginning at the time of his arrest
- And if the matter is not then disposed of forthwith, the judge may remand such person.

Nothing in section 155 authorises the detention of such person after the expiry of the period of 24 hours beginning at the time of his arrest, unless remanded by the court.

In reckoning any period of 24 hours for these purposes no account shall be taken of Christmas Day, Good Friday, or any Sunday.

Ordered by

On Wednesday, 13 February 2008

Page 1 of 2

The court office at Birmingham Civil Justice Centre, The Priory Courts, 33 Bull Street, Birmingham B4 6DS is open between 10am and 4pm Monday to Friday. When corresponding with the court, please address forms or letters to the Court Manager and quote the claim number. Telephone: 0121-681-4441. Fax: 0121-681-3001/2.

15. ANTI-SOCIAL BEHAVIOUR INJUNCTION – POWER OF ARREST UNDER SECTION 153C HOUSING ACT 1996

ANTI-SOCIAL BEHAVIOUR INJUNCTION - POWER OF ARREST
Under section 153C Housing Act 1996

IN THE BIRMINGHAM COUNTY COURT   Claim no:

	Claimant
	Defendant

(Here set out those provisions of the order to which this power of arrest is attached and no others)

The court orders that a power of arrest under section 153C Housing Act 1996 applies to the following paragraph(s) of an order made on Wednesday, 13 February 2008:

Power of Arrest

The court is satisfied that the relevant conduct consists of or includes the use or threatened use of violence and/or there is a significant risk of harm to a person mentioned in section 153A(4) of the said Act.

A power of arrest is attached to the order whereby any constable may (under the power given by section 155 Housing Act 1996) arrest without warrant a person whom he has reasonable cause for suspecting to be in breach of any of the provisions set out in this order or otherwise in contempt of court in relation to such provision.

This Power of Arrest expires at 4pm on

Note to the Arresting Officer

Where a person is arrested under the power given by section 155 of the Housing Act 1996, the section requires that:

- A constable shall after making such an arrest forthwith inform the person on whose application the injunction was granted;
- Such person shall be brought before the relevant judge within 24 hours beginning at the time of his arrest
- And if the matter is not then disposed of forthwith, the judge may remand such person.

Nothing in section 155 authorises the detention of such person after the expiry of the period of 24 hours beginning at the time of his arrest, unless remanded by the court.

In reckoning any period of 24 hours for these purposes no account shall be taken of Christmas Day, Good Friday, or any Sunday.

Ordered by

On   **Wednesday, 13 February 2008**

Page 1 of 1

16. ANTI-SOCIAL BEHAVIOUR INJUNCTION – POWER OF ARREST UNDER SECTION 153D HOUSING ACT 1996

ANTI-SOCIAL BEHAVIOUR INJUNCTION - POWER OF ARREST
Under section 153D Housing Act 1996

IN THE BIRMINGHAM COUNTY COURT   Claim no:

	Claimant
	Defendant

(Here set out those provisions of the order to which this power of arrest is attached and no others)

The court orders that a power of arrest under section 153D Housing Act 1996 applies to the following paragraph(s) of an order made on Wednesday, 13 February 2008:

Power of Arrest

The court is satisfied that the relevant conduct includes the use or threatened use of violence and/or there is a significant risk of harm to any person.

A power of arrest is attached to the order whereby any constable may (under the power given by section 155 Housing Act 1996) arrest without warrant a person whom he has reasonable cause for suspecting to be in breach of any of the provisions set out in this order or otherwise in contempt of court in relation to such provision.

This Power of Arrest expires at 4pm on

Note to the Arresting Officer

Where a person is arrested under the power given by section 155 of the Housing Act 1996, the section requires that:
- A constable shall after making such an arrest forthwith inform the person on whose application the injunction was granted;
- Such person shall be brought before the relevant judge within 24 hours beginning at the time of his arrest
- And if the matter is not then disposed of forthwith, the judge may remand such person.

Nothing in section 155 authorises the detention of such person after the expiry of the period of 24 hours beginning at the time of his arrest, unless remanded by the court.

In reckoning any period of 24 hours for these purposes no account shall be taken of Christmas Day, Good Friday, or any Sunday.

Ordered by

On   Wednesday, 13 February 2008

Page 1 of 1

Chapter 4

LOCAL GOVERNMENT ACT INJUNCTIONS

INTRODUCTION

4.1   Prior to the commencement of s 222 of the Local Government Act 1972 ('the 1972 Act') on 1 April 1974,[1] if a local authority wanted to act to restrain breaches of the criminal law affecting the residents of its area, it had to do so by an Attorney-General's relator action, seeking approval of the Attorney-General to act on his behalf – see *Prestatyn Urban District Council v Prestatyn Raceway Limited*.[2] *Solihull Metropolitan Borough Council v Maxfern Ltd*,[3] however, clarified that the effect of s 222 'is to enable the local authority to sue in its own name and without the intervention of the Attorney General in cases where prior to the Act it had been necessary to obtain the concurrence of the Attorney General'[4] in order to assert and protect public rights.

4.2   Injunctions under the 1972 Act include, but are not limited to, 'injunctions in aid of the criminal law' where prosecution would prove ineffective (see for example *Barking and Dagenham LBC v Jones*).[5] Established categories include injunctions to restrain a public nuisance, but there is a debate as to the extent to which a third category, namely, injunctions in the public interest or to uphold the law generally (where the local authority already has duties in respect of that area of law) exists – see *Birmingham City Council v Junior Cadogan and Others*, 7BM 72256, below.

4.3   If the injunction is sought in support of the criminal law, it is well established that a mere infringement or threat of infringement of the criminal law by itself will not be sufficient – there needs to be 'something more' and grant of such an injunction is an 'exceptional course',[6] Waller LJ said that

---

[1]   In respect of England and Wales; the section does not extend to Scotland.
[2]   See *Prestatyn Urban District Council v Prestatyn Raceway Limited* [1970] 1 WLR 33, [1969] 3 All ER 1573.
[3]   [1977] 2 All ER 177.
[4]   Ibid, at 181f, per Oliver J.
[5]   See, e g *Barking and Dagenham London Borough Council v Jones* (unreported) 30 July 1999, per Laws LJ.
[6]   See, e g *Guildford Borough Council v Hein* [2005] EWCA Civ 979, [2005] All ER (D) 393 (Jul) where it was said by Waller LJ that the 'something more' arose if 'in the circumstances, criminal proceedings are likely to prove ineffective to achieve the public interest purposes for which the legislation in question had been enacted': quoting Kerr LJ in *Portsmouth City Council v Richards* [1989] 1 CMLR 673; but see further discussion at **4.10**.

'something more' arose if 'in the circumstances, criminal proceedings are likely to prove ineffective to achieve the public interest purposes for which the legislation in question had been enacted ...' – quoting Kerr LJ in *Portsmouth City Council v Richards*[7] – but see further discussion below under 'Conditions' at **4.10**.

POTENTIAL CLAIMANTS

4.4   Claims may only be made by a 'local authority', the definition of which is set out in s 270 of the 1972 act as follows:

> 'a county council, a district council, a London Borough council or a parish council but, in relation to Wales, means a county council, county borough council or community council.'

That definition is expanded in this case to cover 'the Common Council and the London Fire and Emergency Planning Authority' (s 222(2)). In addition, s 265A adds the Broads Authority, and the Local Government Reorganisation (Miscellaneous Provisions) Order 1990 added waste regulation and disposal authorities under the Local Government Act 1985 together with the London Fire and Civil Defence authority. Joint authorities under Pt IV of the 1985 Act and urban development corporations are not included (as to the latter, see *London Docklands Development Corporation v Rank Hovis MacDougall*).[8]

POTENTIAL DEFENDANTS

4.5   The class of potential defendants is not limited by their legal status, and claims can be made against corporate bodies as well as against individuals – see for example *City of London Corporation v Bovis Construction Limited*[9] where an injunction was granted against Bovis as it was in control of a building site where there were persistent breaches of notices under the Control of Pollution Act, such breaches amounting to criminal offences. Due to delay in the criminal process, the local authority sought and obtained an injunction as there was an inference that breaches of the law would continue until effectively restrained by the law and that nothing short of an injunction would be effective.

Juveniles and those under a disability

4.6   As the primary means of enforcement of injunctions obtained under the Act are the sanctions for contempt of court, namely imprisonment, a fine or sequestration of assets, whilst it may be possible to seek an injunction against a person under the age of 18 if a litigation friend is appointed for the defendant

---

[7]   [1989] 1 CMLR 673.
[8]   (1985) 84 LGR 101.
[9]   [1992] 3 All ER 697, 49 Build LR 1.

(see CPR Part 21), in practice an injunction will be difficult to obtain due to the unlikelihood of enforcement. In the absence of special provisions, a young person aged less than 17 cannot be imprisoned for contempt, so that there would be no effective sanction for breach of the court's order unless the individual young person had capital, income or other property which could be used to exact a fine or which could be sequestrated. The court would wish to see evidence that this was the case before issuing an injunction.[10]

4.7   Similarly, in the case of defendants suffering from mental incapacity, it is necessary that the disabled person has sufficient understanding to know what he must not do and the possible consequences of breaching the order before an injunction will issue; otherwise, it could not be enforced as the court would not commit for contempt.[11]

4.8   Injunctions have been sought against:

- persons developing an unlawful caravan site in the green belt for occupation by gypsies;[12]

- an individual who persisted in chopping down trees on his land in breach of a tree preservation order;[13]

- numerous cases about Sunday trading, considered anti-social at the time;[14]

- an individual who carried on business for a number of years in breach of the Trade Descriptions Act 1968 and the Unsolicited Goods and Services Act 1971;[15]

- a young person who was suspected of drug dealing and associating with drug dealers causing a nuisance on a housing estate;[16]

- an individual who persistently engaged in breeding dogs without a licence, was neglectful of dogs and had previously been convicted of an offence of cruelty to animals;[17]

- individuals believed to be members of gangs engaging in violent criminal activity;[18]

---

[10]   *London Borough of Harrow v G* [2004] EWHC 17 (QB).
[11]   See *Wookey v Wookey* [1991] 3 All ER 365.
[12]   *Runnymede Borough Council v Ball* [1986] 1 WLR 353, [1986] 1 All ER 629; *Waverley Borough Council v Hilden* [1988] 1 WLR 246, [1988] 1 All ER 807.
[13]   *Kent County Council v Batchelor* [1979] 1 WLR 213, [1978] 3 All ER 980.
[14]   For example *Stoke on Trent City Council v B and Q Retail Ltd* [1984] AC 754.
[15]   *Barking and Dagenham London Borough Council v Jones* (unreported) 30 July 1999.
[16]   *Nottingham City Council v Zane* [2001] EWCA Civ 1248, [2002] 1 WLR 607.
[17]   *Guildford Borough Council v Hein* [2005] EWCA Civ 979, [2005] All ER (D) 393 (Jul).
[18]   *Birmingham City Council v Ranger and Watson* (Case 7BM72277) (unreported).

- non-tenants causing nuisance to local authority residents, including former cohabitees;

- unlicensed street traders;

- unlawful money lenders;

- prostitutes who habitually solicited in a particular area.

Plainly, the class of potential defendants is not closed.

PROCEDURE

4.9   Parts 23 and 25 of the CPR deal generally with the procedure to be adopted. Claims should be commenced under Part 7 CPR if the factual basis of the claim is likely to be disputed, Part 8 if it is not. For further details, see **5.24–5.40**, and the procedural checklist for Chapter 5.

Conditions to be satisfied before order is granted

4.10   Section 222 of the 1972 Act provides:

'(1) Where a local authority consider it expedient for the promotion or protection of the interests of the inhabitants of their area—

they may prosecute or defend or appear in any legal proceedings and, in the case of civil proceedings, may institute them in their own name ...'

This eliminates the need, as indicated above, in the case of the infringement of public rights, to sue on the relation of the Attorney-General and gives the local authority standing to take action where that is expedient for the promotion or protection of their inhabitants' interests. At common law, of course, a claimant can only sue for interference with private rights or for interference with public rights where he suffers special damage.[19]

4.11   Although nowadays often referred to as 'injunctions in aid of the criminal law', it is important to realise that s 222 injunctions are not *only* available in respect of actual breaches of the criminal law, but also, for example, to restrain commission of a public nuisance or in connection with an authority's duty to 'do all within its power to ensure through properly observed planning control the natural amenities of its area'.[20]

4.12   Similarly, in an appropriate case it is not necessary to wait until criminal proceedings have been tried and shown to have no effect before applying for

---

[19]   See, e g *dicta* of Lord Templeman in *Stoke on Trent City Council v B and Q (Retail) Limited* [1984] AC 754.
[20]   See Purchas LJ in *Runnymede Borough Council v Ball* [1986] 1 WLR 353, [1986] 1 All ER 629.

such an injunction, although that will be the general rule. In *Stoke on Trent City Council v B and Q Retail Ltd*[21] Lord Templeman in the House of Lords said that 'the council were entitled to take the view that the appellants would not be deterred by the maximum fine ... Delay whilst this was proved would have encouraged widespread breaches of the law'.

4.13 It is clear, however, that injunctions in aid of the criminal law are an exceptional remedy and the courts will exercise that jurisdiction with great caution, requiring 'something more' than simply evidence of criminal activity. Lord Templeman in *B and Q* explained that the courts should be reluctant to grant injunctions where the penalty for breach (including committal for contempt of court) may be much greater than the penalty that Parliament originally intended for the offence in question.

4.14 It does not seem to be the case that 'something more' is required in relation to injunctions to restrain commission of a public nuisance – see for example *Nottingham CC v Zain* below.

Interim Injunctions

4.15 Initially, varying views were expressed by judges as to the threshold which had to be crossed before an interim injunction would issue, especially in cases where the injunction was being granted to restrain the commission of a crime.

4.16 In *Portsmouth City Council v Richards*[22] Kerr LJ accepted (in the Court of Appeal) that there would need to be no arguable defence to the criminal charge in question (save for unresolved issues as to the validity of the criminal law itself) before an injunction would issue. Given that these are civil proceedings it is hard to see why that would be the case.

4.17 In *Kirklees Metropolitan Borough Council v Wickes Building Supplies*,[23] however, the House of Lords rejected an argument that before issue of an interlocutory injunction it was necessary that 'the defendant must plainly have no defence to a criminal prosecution'. Observing that such a proviso will often be satisfied in any event when the local authority applies for such an injunction, Lord Goff pointed out that the power to grant an injunction under s 37 of the Supreme Court Act 1981 is a discretionary power, which should not as a matter of principle be fettered by rules, stating:

> 'In my opinion, the existence of an alleged defence is a matter to be taken into account in the exercise of the court's discretion, when deciding whether it is just and convenient that interlocutory relief be granted ...'

---

21 [1984] AC 754.
22 [1989] CMLR 673, 87 LGR 757.
23 [1993] AC 227.

4.18   Elsewhere, for example in *Barking and Dagenham London Borough Council v Jones*[24] the Court of Appeal referred to the council having a 'good arguable case'.

4.19   In a public nuisance case, which is a civil tort as well as a crime, there is no reason why a variation on the usual principles applicable to prohibitory interlocutory injunctions cannot apply – that is the *American Cyanamid*[25] test save where the granting of an interlocutory injunction may mean the end of the case (see below). Even where the grant of the injunction may mean the end of the case, it is usually possible, if appropriate, to grant a short-term injunction on the usual basis whilst giving directions for a more lengthy interlocutory hearing to assess the merits of the claim and defence.

4.20   It is clear, however, that when an injunction is sought under s 222 in order to restrain criminal activity, 'something more' than evidence of a mere infringement (or threatened infringement) of the criminal law is required. The 'something more' test appears in the speech of Lord Templeman in the *B and Q* case. In that case it was clear that the store would continue to flout the Sunday trading laws unless effectively restrained, and that in that situation others would be encouraged to do so in order to compete, and this was sufficient to justify the grant of the injunction.

4.21   In *Runnymede Borough Council v Ball*[26] gypsies had bought land with a view to turning it into a caravan site. They disregarded numerous planning notices, thereby committing criminal offences, but the council opted to proceed for an injunction under s 222 and succeeded in obtaining one. The 'something more' here was the council's duty to enforce proper planning control for the benefit of its residents, coupled with the defendants' blatant disregard of the notices, to the extent that they were laying down hardcore and a sewerage system and thereby permanently altering the character of the land, which the local authority was there to protect for the benefit of its citizens.

4.22   In some cases the slowness of criminal procedure, rendering it ineffective to prevent the mischief the criminal law was enacted to prevent, has been the 'something more';[27] in others the 'something more' was the relatively low criminal fines in comparison to the profits to be made from the illegal activity.[28]

---

[24]   (Unreported) 30 July 1999, per Brooke LJ.

[25]   [1975] AC 396, [1975] 1 All ER 504.

[26]   [1986] 1 WLR 353, [1986] 1 All ER 629.

[27]   See discussions in *Barking and Dagenham London Borough Council v Jones* (unreported) 30 July 1999; and *Portsmouth City Council v Richards* [1989] CMLR 673, 87 LGR 757.

[28]   For example, the Sunday trading cases, or see *Barking and Dagenham London Borough Council v Jones* (unreported) 30 July 1999 (mis-describing goods to increase profit) or *Portsmouth City Council v Richards* [1989] CMLR 673, 87 LGR 757, where unlicensed sex shops continued to trade as usual despite relatively low fines imposed by magistrates' courts.

4.23 At one stage the courts thought that for there to be 'something more' there had to be evidence of 'deliberate and flagrant' flouting of the criminal law, but more recently it has become clear that this is only one example of the necessary additional element.

4.24 In *Guildford Borough Council v Hein*[29] in 2005, Waller LJ cited with approval the 'broad test' applied by Kerr LJ in the *Portsmouth* case (above):

'injunctions are only permissible if, in the particular circumstances, criminal proceedings are likely to prove ineffective to achieve the public interest purposes for which the legislation in question had been enacted . . .'

Two examples given are, first, where the criminal penalties are not sufficient to deter the unlawful activity or, secondly, emergency situations where it is necessary for the courts to intervene to prevent the continuation of 'an unlawful state of affairs or conduct which might result in irreversible unlawfulness unless an injunction were granted forthwith'. He also quoted Millett J in *Wychavon District Council v Midlands Enterprises (Special Events) Ltd*:[30]

'If they [the local authority] have good grounds for thinking that in any given case compliance with the law will not be secured by prosecution, they are entitled to apply for an injunction.'

4.25 In the same case Clarke LJ, agreeing, said 'It is not necessary for the claimant to establish that there has been a deliberate and flagrant flouting of the law ... as I see it, all depends on the facts of the particular case', and he, too, approved the *dicta* of Millet J in *Wychavon*, whilst reaffirming the exceptional nature of the relief.

4.26 It is therefore suggested that, except where the injunction effectively means the end of the case, a variation on the usual (*American Cyanamid*) test will apply, namely;

- Has the claimant shown there is a serious question to be tried?

- Would damages be an adequate remedy (unlikely to arise much in practice)?

- Where does the balance of justice/convenience lie (in other words, will the order do more harm than good – in this case the defendant's human rights may have to be weighed in the balance)?

- In a criminal case, is there 'something more' to justify the issue of the injunction?

---

[29] [2005] EWCA Civ 979, [2005] All ER (D) 393 (Jul).
[30] [1988] 1 CMLR 397.

- In a case where an injunction is sought to restrain the commission of a crime, where the defendant denies the offence and raises a defence, is it possible to assess the merits of the defence and, if so, is it just and convenient to grant the interlocutory injunction?[31]

- Is the applicant able to compensate the respondent for ensuing loss if it turns out that the order should not have been granted? In *Kirklees Metropolitan Borough Council v Wickes Building Supplies Limited*[32] the House of Lords held that there is a discretion not to require a cross-undertaking in damages from a local authority in such a case, and as a result this is rarely required.

- A further example of a situation where the *American Cyanamid* principles may not apply in this context is where Art 10 of the ECHR is engaged, ie the conduct of the defendant which it is sought to restrain involves his right to freedom of expression. This might arise where the authority is seeking to restrain a public nuisance involving noise from a protest, in which case the principles in *Cream Holdings v Banerjee* will apply.[33]

4.27 The authority must, of course, consider that the making of the application is 'expedient for the protection or promotion of the interests of the inhabitants of its area'. It will be difficult for the defendant to challenge this.[34] For example, in *Barking and Dagenham London Borough Council v Jones*[35] the authority was able to get an injunction even though none of Mr Jones' victims lived there because, first, his unlawfully run business was situated in its area and, secondly, as a consequence its trading standards department was under inordinate pressure dealing with his activities and requests from other authorities. However, if the defendant considers that the basis of s 222 has not been made out (eg because the authority has not applied its mind to whether the making of the application is expedient for the statutory purpose or its determination that it is contravenes *Wednesbury* principles) the proper course is to apply for judicial review of the decision to apply for an injunction and to apply for a stay of the injunction proceedings.[36] In *Waverley Borough Council v Hilden*[37] it was opined that if an original decision to seek an injunction was invalid, that invalidity could be cured by later ratification by the authority.

Final or perpetual injunctions

4.28 A perpetual injunction may be granted after final hearing, at which stage the authority must of course establish the basis of its claim on the balance of

---

[31] *Kirklees Metropolitan Borough Council v Wickes Building Supplies Limited* [1993] AC 227, per Goff LJ.

[32] [1993] AC 227.

[33] See Chapter 5, at **5.00**.

[34] *Waverley Borough Council v Hilden* [1988] 1 WLR 246, [1988] 1 All ER 807.

[35] (Unreported) 30 July 1999.

[36] See *Waverley Borough Council v Hilden* [1988] 1 WLR 246, [1988] 1 All ER 807, where a stay was refused because the judicial review had no prospect of success.

[37] Ibid.

probabilities and it must be just and convenient to make the order. Save for the 'threshold' test, the other comments set out above in relation to the granting of interim injunctions also apply here.

TERMS OF THE ORDER

4.29 Generally speaking the effect of the order will be to restrain specified prohibited conduct, although an order could be made in mandatory terms in an appropriate case and provided the appropriate conditions are met (see above).

Orders have been granted

4.30 Orders have been granted in the following situations:

- restraining the operation of unlicensed sex shops;[38]

- prohibiting noisy building work (other than in case of emergency)on Sundays and bank holidays and on other occasions outside restricted hours;[39]

- restraining the number and gender of dogs to be kept by a woman who persistently engaged in unlicensed dog breeding.[40] In this case it was felt that simply restraining the person from engaging in unlicensed dog breeding or causing harm to dogs was insufficient – it should be clear what the individual restrained can and cannot do;

- prohibiting the destruction of trees subject to a tree preservation order;[41]

- restraining the use of land owned by the defendants for the stationing of caravans or mobile homes or from causing or permitting such use of the land;[42]

- restraining the defendant from entering a housing estate where he was suspected of dealing in drugs;[43]

- prohibiting a prostitute from being present in a particular street or area at particular times of the day;

---

[38] *Portsmouth City Council v Richards* [1989] CMLR 673, 87 LGR 757.
[39] *City of London Corporation v Bovis Ltd* [1992] 3 All ER 697, 49 Build LR 1.
[40] *Guildford Borough Council v Hein* [2005] EWCA Civ 979, [2005] All ER (D) 393 (Jul).
[41] *Westminster City Council v Freeman* [1986] BTCC 435, [1985] NLJ 1232, CA.
[42] *Waverley Borough Council v Hilden* [1988] 1 WLR 246, [1988] 1 All ER 807.
[43] *Nottingham City Council v Zane* [2001] EWCA Civ 1248, [2002] 1 WLR 607.

- preventing named individuals from engaging in conduct likely to cause harassment, alarm or distress (here there is an obvious overlap with ASBIs and ASBOs, orders under the Protection from Harassment and Family Law Acts);

- preventing named individuals from congregating together and associating with each other in specified public places;

- excluding named individuals from specified areas where they are considered liable to commit crimes where the criminal law is ineffective to deal with this due to territorial 'gang' culture and intimidation.[44]

4.31 The last two examples are clearly not straightforward, although they represent a powerful weapon in cases where the criminal law may be ineffective due to fear of reprisals. Hearsay evidence from respected sources may have more effect in the civil court due to the lower standard of proof, and 'exclusion orders' can reduce crime in the 'gang's' area by removing key individuals who are unlikely to offend elsewhere as they will not enjoy the same 'protection'. It should be noted that the ability to use s 222 in these circumstances is now in some doubt following the decision in *Birmingham City Council v Junior Cadogan and Others* 7BM 72256, see above.

4.32 It is clear, however, that the courts can grant injunctions to stop a defendant doing things which would otherwise be lawful (such as visiting an area) where the main objective of the order would not be achieved simply by banning the unlawful conduct (subject of course to adequate proof of the defendant's participation in the unlawful conduct). A particular issue may arise where the defendant actually lives or works in the area from which he is to be excluded. This will require careful balancing of the individual's rights and liberties (such as his Art 8 ECHR rights) against the interests of the community as a whole. In some cases this has been achieved by the use of maps appended to the court's order, illustrating routes which the defendant is permitted to take within the 'exclusion zone' to get to his home, work, doctors' surgery, etc.

4.33 As noted above, the court has a discretion not to require an undertaking in damages from the local authority as a term of the order.

Power of arrest

4.34 Since 2004, initially by virtue of s 91 of the Anti-Social Behaviour Act 2003, it has been possible in certain circumstances to attach a power of arrest to an injunction granted under s 222. Section 91 has now been superseded (from 6 April 2007) by s 27 of the Police and Justice Act 2006.

4.35 Section 27 provides that, where a local authority is party to an action by virtue of s 222, if the court grants an injunction which prohibits conduct that is

---

[44] See, e g *Birmingham City Council v Ranger and Watson* (Case 7BM72277) (unreported).

capable of causing nuisance or annoyance to any person, it may attach a power of arrest to any provision of the injunction if the local authority applies to the court for a power of arrest and the court considers that:

- the prohibited conduct consists of or includes the use or threatened use of violence; or

- there is a significant risk of harm to any person who may be caused nuisance or annoyance by the prohibited conduct.
  Here 'harm' includes 'serious ill treatment or abuse (whether physical or not)' (s 27(12)).

ENFORCEMENT

4.36 If no power of arrest has been attached to the initial order, and the grounds in s 27 of the 2006 Act are made out, application for the attachment of such a power may prove effective.

4.37 Section 27 now provides power for the court to remand an arrested individual if the matter is not disposed of when he is first brought before the court, which must be within 24 hours of the arrest. Sections 27(9) and (11) allow for a defendant to be remanded whist medical examination and report is made, or whilst a report on the accused's mental condition is obtained. Otherwise, enforcement will be by committal for contempt of court.

COSTS

4.38 Where a local authority fails to obtain an injunction, costs will not necessarily follow the event. In *Bradford Metropolitan District Council v Booth*[45] it was held that where the authority has acted 'in the reasonable and proper exercise of its public duty' it should not necessarily be penalised in costs where it does not obtain the relief it seeks. The court must consider the overriding objective, and should balance the financial prejudice to the individual successful defendant in not obtaining his costs against the possible deterrent effect to local authorities in respect of taking action to promote and protect the local community if they have to pay substantial amounts in costs. This reasoning is similar to that expressed in the *Wickes* case (above) when the House of Lords held that there was a discretion not to seek a cross-undertaking in damages which should be exercised where the authorities would not otherwise take action to restrain unlawful activity and that activity would, as a result, flourish unrestrained.

---

[45] (2001) 3 LGLR 124.

CHECKLISTS, FORMS AND PRECEDENTS

4.39 Checklists, forms and precedents relating to Local Government Act injunctions are reproduced below.

1. SECTION 222, LOCAL GOVERNMENT ACT: INJUNCTION GROUNDS CHECKLIST

- Is applicant a 'local authority' within meaning of section 222?
- Does the authority consider it expedient to apply for an injunction in order to promote or protect the interests of the inhabitants of its area?
- If the application concerns a breach of the criminal law, is there 'something more' which would justify application for an injunction rather than letting the criminal procedure run its course?
- If not, does the conduct sought to be restrained amount to a public nuisance (or, arguably, breach of another area of the civil law in respect of which the authority has duties)?
- Has Parliament provided a more appropriate remedy?
- Is the conduct sought to be restrained unlawful, and/or is it necessary to restrain/curtail it in order to prevent unlawful conduct?

2. SECTION 222, LOCAL GOVERNMENT ACT: TEST FOR GRANT OF INTERIM INJUNCTION CHECKLIST

Will injunction effectively end case?

- If so, short term injunction may be granted pending hearing where probable merits can be assessed;
- If not, is article 10 ECHR (freedom of expression) engaged?
- If so, is it likely that C will obtain order restraining publication at final hearing (s 12(3) HRA 1998)?
- If article 10 is not engaged (or s 12(3) HRA 1998 is satisfied), is there a serious question to be tried? In criminal cases this may involve attempting to assess the merits of any defence.
- If injunction relates to breach of the criminal law, is there 'something more' to justify issue of injunction rather than letting criminal process run its course?
- If not, has Parliament already provided a more appropriate remedy?
- (If appropriate) would damages be an adequate remedy?
- Where does the balance of justice/convenience lie (that is, will the order do more harm than good)? Is it likely that the court will exercise its discretion to require an undertaking in damages and if so, can C satisfy such an undertaking?

3. APPLICATION FOR INJUNCTION

Application for Injunction

(General Form)

(see form N16A)

Name of Court Claim No

CRANFORD COUNTY COURT

Claimant's Name and ref.

Cranford Metropolitan Borough Council

Defendant's Name and ref.

Darren Le Bon (1)

Cody Taylor (2)

xBy application in pending proceedings

x Under statutory provision: section 222 Local Government Act 1972

This application raises issues under the Human Rights Act 1998 (Yes)

The Claimant Cranford Metropolitan Borough Council

Applies to the court for an injunction order in the following terms:

The Defendants Darren Le Bon and Cody Taylor

Be forbidden from entering the Crow's Nest Estate, or within a 2 mile radius of Crow's Nest Community Centre as identified on the map attached to this application

And that the Defendants pay the costs of this application

The grounds of this application are set out in the written evidence of Peter C Dixon, PC Stamp and Sergeant Clegg signed on

This written evidence is served with this application.

This application is to be served upon Darren Le Bon and Cody Taylor [address[es]]

This application is filed by [name of solicitors]
(the solicitors for) the Claimant

Whose address for service is

Signed   Dated

To

Of

This application will be heard by the

Judge

At

**On . . . . . . the day of 20
at . . . . . . o'clock**

If you do not attend at the time shown the court may make an injunction order in your absence

If you do not fully understand this application you should go to a Solicitor, Legal Advice Centre or a Citizens' Advice Bureau

4. CLAIM FORM

Claim Form   **In the CRANFORD COUNTY COURT**

Claim No

Issue date

**Claimant: Cranford Metropolitan
Borough Council
Council House
Ringway
Cranford
DX
Fax**

Defendants : Darren Le Bon (1)

Cody Taylor (2)

Brief details of Claim:

The Claimants claim an injunction, acting under section 222 of the Local Government Act 1972, in order to promote and protect the interests of the inhabitants of their area (specifically inhabitants of the Crow's Nest Estate, Cranford CF2) by excluding the defendants from that area or within a 2 mile radius of the Crow's Nest community centre as shown on the attached map. The claimant believes that the activities of the defendants have caused or contributed to an increase in drug related crime and disorder in the area.

Value (not applicable)

Defendant's name and address:

Darren Le Bon (1)   Amount claimed

Cody Taylor (2)   Court fee

26 Durberville Tower   Solicitor's costs

Hay Lane   Total amount

Rivermead

Does your claim include any issues   yes
under the Human Rights Act 1998

Particulars of Claim (attached)

Statement of Truth

The Claimant believes that the facts
stated in these particulars of claim
are true.

I am duly authorised by the claimant
to sign this statement

Full name

Name of Claimant's solicitor's firm

Signed   position or office held

                                            Claimant's solicitor

IN THE CRANFORD COUNTY   **CLAIM NO**
COURT

BETWEEN:

CRANFORD METROPOLITAN BOROUGH COUNCIL

<u>Claimant</u>

-and-

DARREN LE BON (1)

CODY TAYLOR (2)

<u>Defendants</u>

Particulars of claim

1 The claimant is a local authority within the meaning of section 222 of the Local Government Act 1972.

2 The Defendants are the son and nephew respectively of Vincent le Bon, formerly the claimant's tenant at 32 Rookery Road, Crow's Nest Estate , Cranford CF2 3SL. Until 12th October 2007 they lived at that address also.

3 Vincent Le Bon was convicted at Cranford Crown Court on 26th June 2007 of possession of heroin and cocaine with intent to supply and of living off immoral earnings. He is currently serving a 7 year prison sentence and on 13th September 2007 the claimant obtained a possession order in respect of 32 Rookery Road. The residents of that property (including the defendants) were evicted on 12th October 2007 and now the defendants reside at 26 Durberville Tower, Hay Lane, Rivermead, approximately 5 miles from the Crow's Nest Estate.

4 Since in or about January 2008, the Defendants have been returning to the Crow's Nest estate, on a daily basis.

5 Since they started to return, the incidence of drug related offences at the crow's nest estate has risen by 25%.

6 Residents at the estate have complained of an increase in gang fighting, robberies, muggings and burglaries since January 2008, and that such activities are threatening their ability to live peacefully on the estate.

7 The defendants have been found, on numerous occasions, to be loitering near scenes of gang violence.

8 The first defendant has three convictions for possession of class A drugs, the 2nd Defendant has four such convictions.

9 Both have been convicted of offences of possession of class A drugs with intent to supply, most recently in January 2007. The 1st Defendant was released from prison in relation to that conviction in March 2007, the 2nd Defendant in June 2007. Both have been charged with intent to supply class A drugs on 3 occasions in the last 4 months but in each case the prosecutions have been discontinued due to the unwillingness of witnesses to give evidence due to fear of the defendants.

10 On 10th January 2008 and again on 21st January 2008, large quantities of heroin and cocaine were found discarded near to where police officers had stopped the defendants.

11 The defendants claim to visit the Crow's Nest estate for the purposes of

music practise but do not in fact practise their instruments when visiting the estate. The purpose of their visits is to participate in unlawful drug dealing and drug related violence and other crimes.

12   In the circumstances, the defendants' visits to the estate constitute a public nuisance also.

13   The defendants intend to continue their unlawful activities unless restrained by an order of the court.
      AND the Claimant claims:
      (1)   an injunction restraining the defendants from entering upon the Crow's Nest estate or within a 2 mile radius of the Crow's Nest Community Centre as shown on the attached map;
      (2)   Costs

DATED

5. WITNESS STATEMENT IN SUPPORT OF CLAIM FOR INTERIM INJUNCTION

IN THE CRANFORD COUNTY COURT	**Claimant**
CLAIM NO.	**PC Dixon**
	1st
	Dated

BETWEEN:

CRANFORD METROPOLITAN BOROUGH COUNCIL

<u>Claimant</u>

-and-

DARREN LE BON (1)

CODY TAYLOR (2)

<u>Defendants</u>

Witness statement in support of claim for interim injunction

I, Peter Chopin Dixon of Council House, Ringway, Cranford CF1 3XZ, Chief Officer of Housing, Development and Communities at the Claimant Council, STATE as follows:

1. I make this statement from my own knowledge save where otherwise indicated.

2. The claimant is the owner and landlord of the Crow's Nest housing estate, Cranford. The Crow's Nest has a high level of youth unemployment (46% of those aged between 16 and 25 and who are not in full or part time education are unemployed). In addition there is a significant problem of drug dealing and addiction on the estate.

3. This in turn leads to problems of public order and of the safety of the residents of the estate.

4. Acts of criminal damage, muggings, and burglary are common place and I refer to the statement of community policeman PC Stamp in support of this statement. In addition there is a real and rising problem of violent conflict due to disputes between rival gangs of drug dealers and I refer again to the statement of PC Stamp in this regard.

5. Recently, my department has sought to tackle this problem by evicting the families of known drug dealers and this has met with a degree of success.

6. The Defendants are the son and nephew of Vincent Le Bon, a convicted dealer in class "A" drugs. The 2nd defendant lives with the le Bon family (including the 1st Defendant and both defendants claim to be members of a local pop group known as "Nurad Nurad". Vincent Le Bon was the tenant of a property on the Crow's Nest estate and the claimant obtained an eviction order against him six months ago after his most recent convictions for drug dealing and living off immoral earnings.

7. Subsequent to the eviction, and the Le Bon family moving to a relatively rural location, there was a noticeable reduction in drug related crime and in the availability of class A drugs in the Crow's Nest area (see statement of PC Stamp).

8. In the last month, however, there has been a noticeable rise in both the availability of drugs and the incidence of drug related crime. Sources have told police officers that the supplies are being brought in and sold by the two defendants who have begun to return to the estate on a daily basis, ostensibly to practise with their band at the local community centre. In addition, the same sources (who are too afraid of the defendants to give evidence themselves) have told police officers that it is the defendants who are encouraging youths to attack other drug dealers on the estate in an effort to drive them out. This has

lead to a proliferation of violence and has endangered residents who are completely unconnected with the drug dealers and their gangs (again, see statement of PC Stamp and Sergeant Boon).

9. The 1st defendant has three convictions for possession of class A drugs, the 2nd defendant has four such convictions (see statement of PC Stamp). Each of them has convictions for possession of drugs with intent to supply and most recently they were convicted of such a crime (acting together) in January 2007. The 1st defendant was released in March 2007, the 2nd in June 2007. Each has convictions for violent assaults. I am told by Sergeant Clegg that each of them has been charged on at least three occasions in the last 4 months with the supply of class A drugs on the Crow's Nest estate, but the prosecutions have had to be abandoned on each occasion due the unwillingness of witnesses to testify against them for fear of repercussions.

10. On five occasions in the last month, the defendants have been found by the police in the vicinity of violent disorders. Searches of the defendants for drugs have produced nothing but on two occasions packages of cocaine and heroin have subsequently been found "dumped" near to where the defendants were standing when stopped by the police.

11. The defendants no longer live on the estate but in Rivermead, 5 miles away. I am told by PC Stamp that the pop group to which they claim to belong and which provides their stated reason for visits to the estate has never performed at any public engagement, and Mr Steptoe, caretaker of the community centre, tells me that although the practice room is hired for two hours at a time, the defendants and their fellow band members never stay for longer than 15 minutes before leaving to wander round the estate. He has never heard any music issuing from the room nor seen any instruments, although the defendants enter and leave the room carrying large instrument bags .

12. In those circumstances the Claimant seeks an injunction until trial, excluding the defendants from the Crow's nest estate or within a radius of 2 miles of the Crow's Nest Community Centre, as identified on the attached map, which I now refer to and which is attached hereto marked "PCD1", in order to prevent the continuation of public disorder and nuisance caused or contributed to by the activities of the defendants.

I believe that the facts stated in this witness statement are true.

Signed:

Dated:

6. DRAFT ORDER

Injunction Order   **IN THE CRANFORD COUNTY COURT**

(Local Government Act 1972)   **CLAIM NO**

BETWEEN:

CRANFORD METROPOLITAN BOROUGH COUNCIL

Claimant   Claimant's ref

-and-

DARREN LE BON (1)
CODY TAYLOR (2)

Defendants   Defendants ref

Defendants   Issued on

To   Darren Le Bon

And   Cody Taylor

Of   26 Durberville Tower

                                      Hay Lane

                                      Rivermead

Draft order

If you do not obey this order you will be guilty of contempt of court and you may be fined or sent to prison or you may be guilty of a criminal offence for which you may be fined or sent to prison or both

On the . . . . . . of . . . . 20 . . . . . . the court considered an application for an injunction

The court ordered that Darren Le Bon and Cody Taylor

Are forbidden from entering Crow's Nest estate, Cranford or within a 2 mile radius of Crow's Nest Community Centre as shown on the map attached to this order.

This order shall remain in force until the . . . . . . of . . . . 20 . . . . . . at . . . . . . o'clock unless before then it is revoked by a further order of the court

And it is ordered that the defendants shall serve any evidence in reply to the evidence served by the claimant by . . . . . . pm on 20 . . . . . .

It is further ordered that the costs of this application be reserved

Notice of further hearing

The court will reconsider the application and whether the order should continue at a further hearing at

On . . . . the day of . . . . 20 . . . . . . at . . . . . . o'clock

If you do not attend at the time shown the court may make an injunction order in your absence.

If you do not understand anything in this order you should go to a Solicitor, Legal advice Centre or a Citizens' advice Bureau

The court office at

Is open between 10am and 4pm Monday to Friday. When corresponding with the court, please address forms or letters to the Court manager and quote the claim number

Chapter 5

PROTECTION FROM HARASSMENT

INTRODUCTION

5.1   The Protection from Harassment Act 1997 came into force on 16 June 1997. It was inspired by, and a direct political response to, a number of high profile 'stalking' cases where it seemed that the protection provided by law had been inadequate. It provides both civil and criminal remedies, although only civil injunctions are dealt with here. The Act was amended by adding provision for powers of arrest for breach of an injunction in September 1998.

5.2   Section 1 prohibits harassment in two situations:

(1)   harassment of another individual that the persecutor knows or ought to know amounts to harassment of the other (s 1(1));

(2)   harassment of two or more persons, by which the persecutor intends to persuade any person (including a third party not directly subjected to harassment) not to do something he is entitled or required to do, or to do something he is not under any obligation to do (s 1(1A)). Again, the circumstances must be such that the persecutor knows or ought to know that his course of conduct involves harassment of the others.

In each case, a person will be taken to know that his course of conduct amounts to or involves harassment if a reasonable person in possession of the same information would think so ('the mental element').[1] It does not matter whether the harasser is personally incapable of realising that his acts amount to or involve harassment due to a mental illness or disorder.[2] It is, however, at least arguable that no injunction will issue if the defendant does not have the mental capacity to understand the nature of the order and that he is required to obey it, because in such a situation there will be no sanction for contempt.[3]

5.3   The first type of prohibited conduct typically covers stalking, disputes between neighbours or between colleagues in the workplace; the second type covers campaigns by individuals or groups to put unlawful pressure on others, e g the Stop Huntingdon Life Sciences campaign and others referred to in the cases dealt with below.

---

[1]   *Hipgrave v Jones* [2004] EWHC 2901(QB), [2005] 2 FLR 174.
[2]   *R v Colohan* [2001] EWCA Crim 1251, [2001] 2 FLR 757.
[3]   See *Wookey v Wookey* [1991] 3 All ER 365.

5.4   Defences are provided under s 1(3) if the harasser shows:

(a)   that the course of conduct was pursued for the purpose of preventing or detecting crime;

(b)   that it was pursued under statutory authority or obligation;

(c)   that in the particular circumstances of the case, pursuit of the conduct was reasonable.

5.5   In *Howlett v Holding*[4] it was held that the exception in para (a) above was framed with the law enforcement agencies, and not private individuals or vigilantes, in mind. Paragraph (b) might typically apply to local or other public authorities who have a regulatory function. In *DPP v Selvanayagam*[5] the Court of Appeal held that it was hard to conceive that conduct which amounted to breach of an injunction could ever be 'reasonable', although Roch LJ gave the extreme example of breaching an injunction to rescue someone from imminent danger as possibly passing that threshold.

5.6   Sections 3 and 3A of the Act create a civil remedy for the victim of any actual or apprehended breach of s 1, which by inference includes the right to apply for an injunction restraining the defendant from pursuing any conduct which amounts to harassment (ss 3(3) and 3A) and, if the claimant considers that the defendant has breached such an injunction, he can apply for a warrant for the arrest of the defendant on oath (s 3(3)–(5)). Breach of an injunction granted under the Act without reasonable excuse is also a criminal offence which gives the police powers of warning and arrest which are not present when a mere undertaking is given.[6] This is therefore one situation where giving an undertaking does not have the same effect as obtaining an injunction.

5.7   As late as the year 2000, it was held in the case of *Tuppen v Microsoft*[7] that the act was directed at 'stalking, anti-social behaviour by neighbours and racial harassment' and not, for example, the alleged oppressive conduct of litigation. This approach was based to a substantial degree on comments made by the then Home Secretary on the second reading of the Protection from Harassment Bill. Since 2000, however, the law has developed to such an extent that one has to question whether the *Tuppen* approach is still correct. In *Thomas v News Group Newspapers Ltd*,[8] for example, Lord Phillips MR in the Court of Appeal agreed with the county court judge that the meaning of 'harassment' was sufficiently clear that it was not necessary to look at what had been said in Parliament under the principle in *Pepper v Hart*[9] and that the

---

4   (2006) *The Times*, February 8.
5   (1999) *The Times*, June 23.
6   See *Oxford University v Broughton and Others* [2006] EWCA Civ 1305; and s 24(1) of the Police and Criminal Evidence Act 1984, as amended.
7   (2000) *The Times*, November 15.
8   [2001] EWCA Civ 1233.
9   [1993] AC 593.

definition clearly went beyond the narrow categories of stalking and neighbour disputes. Subsequently, and as we shall see below, the Act has been interpreted widely and held to cover, for example, workplace bullying,[10] activity by animal rights activists,[11] complaints about a solicitor made to his partners and published on the internet[12] and a campaign by local businessman to discredit a councillor who opposed a planning application his company had made.[13] In *Majrowski v Guy's and St Thomas's NHS Trust*[14] Lord Nicholls stated of the 1997 Act, 'the purpose of the statute is to protect victims of harassment whatever form the harassment takes, wherever it occurs and whatever its motivation'. A recent example involves individuals obtaining injunctions against a bank which was pursuing them when they fell behind on repayment of a loan.[15] The Act, however, must not be given such a wide interpretation that it restricts legitimate freedom of expression/freedom of assembly under Arts 10 and 11 of the European Convention on Human Rights (see below).

5.8 The Act is sometimes also a useful alternative in domestic violence cases, since the process is relatively less formal than under the Family Law Act and given the relatively wide definition of 'harassment' which has been adopted.[16]

POTENTIAL CLAIMANTS

5.9 It seems clear that only individuals and not corporate bodies may be claimants under the Act.[17] This is because, under s 7(2), references to harassment include causing alarm or distress to a person. It was pointed out by Owen LJ[18] that a corporate body cannot be caused alarm or distress. Nor is it possible for a local authority to obtain such an injunction.[19]

5.10 It is entirely permissible, however, for individuals to bring applications on behalf of those who share the same interest in not being harassed, for example fellow employees in the above case, using CPR, r 19.6, and it has become commonplace in such situations for a director to represent the company's workforce. In *Huntingdon Life Sciences v Stop Huntingdon Animal*

---

[10]   See *Majrowski v Guy's and St Thomas's NHS Trust; Green v DB Group Services (UK) Ltd* [2006] EWHC 1898 (QB), [2006] IRLR 764.

[11]   See, e g *Emerson Developments Ltd v Avery* [2004] EWHC 194 (QB); *Hall v Save Newchurch Guinea Pigs (Campaign)* [2005] EWHC 372 (QB), (2005) *The Times*, April 7.

[12]   *Cray v Hancock* [2005] All ER (D) 66 Nov.

[13]   *Howlett v Holding* (2006) The Times, February 8.

[14]   [2006] IRLR 695, at [18].

[15]   (2007)The Times, September 25, reporting that an injunction had been granted under the Act against the Halifax Bank after a customer, who had become ill with lung cancer and had got behind with repayments, received over 750 telephone calls from bank staff about the matter over a 10-month period.

[16]   See, e g *Pratt v DPP* [2001] EWHC Admin 483, dealt with below.

[17]   See *Daiichi UK Ltd v Stop Huntingdon Animal Cruelty* [2003] EWHC 2337 (QB), [2004] 1 WLR 1503.

[18]   Ibid, at [13].

[19]   *Thameside Metropolitan Borough Council v M (Injunctive Relief; County Courts; Jurisdiction)* [2001] Fam Law 873.

Cruelty[20] there was said to be 'substantial evidence' that a number of employees had been subjected to 'assault, intimidation and individual harassment' at work or at or near their private addresses by groups or individuals who were intent on causing the employing company to cease its animal experimentation activities, which were lawful. The workforce had agreed that the managing director could apply for an injunction on their behalf. It was said that r 19.6 should be interpreted so as to permit representative proceedings to take place not 'as a rigid matter of principle' but as 'a flexible tool of convenience in the administration of justice'.

5.11   As indicated above, potential claimants under the Act come in many guises. These have included employees such as those above where the harassment is targeted at causing the employer to cease its activities (or the employees of a customer of such an establishment).[21] In *Hall v Save Newchurch Guinea Pigs (Campaign)*[22] a local councillor brought a representative action under CPR, r 19.6 on behalf of the inhabitants of the two parishes that he represented. These areas included or were close to farms where guinea pigs were bred for medical research and which the defendants were attempting to close down, using tactics that it was said affected the whole community. He was entitled to represent those in the parishes he represented, but not those in the surrounding five areas, partly because, as the judge pointed out, if the injunctive relief was effective in reducing activity directed at those principally affected, the whole community would benefit.

5.12   Perhaps more predictably, in *Kellett v DPP*[23] the Act was held to apply where the defendant, who had been involved in a lengthy history of litigation with the victim, including boundary disputes, contacted her employer on more than one occasion claiming that the victim was at home when she should have been working and was therefore acting in a fraudulent manner and ought to be sacked. This was a criminal case but the same facts could have supported an injunction application if necessary. Similarly, in *Howlett v Holding* (above) Eady J granted Mrs Howlett an injunction forbidding Mr Holding from causing aircraft to fly past with banners describing Mrs Howlett in derogatory terms or from putting her under surveillance by a private detective agency with the apparent purpose of showing that she was a benefits cheat. Mrs Howlett was the local councillor who had spoken out against a planning application presented by a company with which Mr Holding was involved.

5.13   More unusually, in *Thomas v News Group Newspapers* (above) Ms Thomas was a clerk employed by the Metropolitan Police. She was a witness to an incident following which two police sergeants were demoted after making derogatory remarks about a Somali asylum seeker. *The Sun* newspaper

---

[20]   [2003] All ER (D) 280 (Jun).

[21]   See, for other examples, *Daiichi UK Ltd v Stop Huntingdon Animal Cruelty* [2003] EWHC 2337 (QB), [2004] 1 WLR 1503; *EDO MBM Technology Limited v Campaign to Smash EDO and Others* [2006] EWHC 598 (QB); *Emerson Developments v Avery* [2004] EWHC 194 (QB).

[22]   [2005] EWHC 372 (QB), (2005) *The Times*, April 7.

[23]   [2001] EWHC Admin 107, [2001] All ER (D) 124 (Feb).

picked up the story and ran two articles about it together with publication of a related 'letters' page. The first article published her name and place of work and the fact that she was black. It made no mention of the fact that a white witness had also complained. Ms Thomas received hate mail and was afraid to go to work as a result. Whilst it has always been clear that the Act, and hence the remedy of injunction, is available to individuals who are the victims of a course of conduct involving racial abuse (and presumably other kinds of discriminatory abuse) from others, the publishers at first argued that it was not intended to cover those subject to newspaper articles. By the time the case reached the Court of Appeal, however, the parties agreed that the publication of press articles calculated to incite racial hatred of an individual (and in respect of which the other conditions in the Act apply) were capable of falling within the provisions of the 1997 Act. It was held that Ms Thomas had an arguable case, and that Art 10 of the ECHR was not there to permit the press to publish material which ran contrary to the aims of the convention (see **5.64** et seq).

5.14 As indicated above, victims of domestic violence and stalking may be covered by the Act provided the definition of 'harassment' is made out and a course of conduct is established.[24]

5.15 The cases of *Majrowski* (above) and *Green v DB Group Services (UK) Ltd*[25] make it clear that *workplace bullying* may fall within the definition of harassment so that in a relevant case an employee may make a claim for an injunction. Mr Majrowski complained that his line manager had pursued a course of conduct against him over a number of years which amounted to singling him out for unpleasant and undermining treatment. Similarly, Ms Green experienced serial bullying from a group of four female colleagues which was directed at her and intended to unnerve and obstruct her, followed by conduct from a male peer which involved interfering with her work, undermining her in both internal and external meetings and pretending to be her boss whilst dealing with a client. This culminated in Ms Green suffering a nervous breakdown and succeeding in her claims on the basis both of negligence and the 1997 Act. Whilst these are claims for damages, it can be seen that in an extreme situation where an employer is persistently failing to deal with a situation of bullying, an application for an injunction (or the threat of such) may be effective.

5.16 In *Majrowski* the House of Lords considered the situation of a customer harassed by an employee and observed that the employer could also be liable in that situation. Vicarious liability is also likely to extend to harassment by the defendant's employees targeted at ex colleagues or former customers, provided the harasser acts within the course of his employment, for example by repeatedly issuing malicious and untrue job references.

---

[24] See *Lau v DPP* [2000] 1 FLR 799 and *Pratt v DPP* [2001] EWHC Admin 483 for two cases which fall either side of the line. These are both criminal cases but the facts are equally relevant to injunction claims.

[25] [2006] EWHC 1898 (QB), [2006] IRLR 764.

5.17 Clearly, the categories of potential claimants are not closed, as is seen by the latest examples of bank customers harassed by their lenders (above).

Potential defendants

5.18 Whilst corporate entities cannot make claims under the Act (see **5.9**) it is clear that both incorporated and unincorporated bodies can be defendants to such claims. In *Daiichi UK Ltd v Stop Huntingdon Animal Cruelty*[26] the first defendant ('SHAC') was an 'unincorporated association whose stated objective was closure of laboratories run by a company not party to the actions [Huntingdon Life Sciences]'. The Court of Appeal held that there was sufficient evidence to establish that SHAC (and the other defendants who were unincorporated associations) existed as groups and that they were part of an alleged campaign against the employees of the targeted companies. In those circumstances, SHAC and a number of other similar groups of animal rights activists were sufficiently identifiable as groups to be joined as defendants. The difficulty of identifying who was to be bound by an order against SHAC was overcome by directing the order at 'protestors', who were defined as any of the defendants acting by themselves, their servants or agents and any other person who was acting in consort with the defendants and who had notice of the terms of the order.[27]

5.19 Owen LJ indicated (para 19), in a stance later upheld in *Majrowski* in the House of Lords, that a corporate body could be a defendant, not least because such a body could be vicariously liable for harassment.

5.20 Similarly, *Majrowski* itself confirmed that an employer (whatever its legal personality) could be vicariously liable for acts of harassment carried out by an employee within the scope of his employment and is therefore a proper defendant. This was confirmed by a reference in s 10 of the Act to an employer's potential liability; it was immaterial that the provision in question applied to Scotland as there was no reason to suppose that employers were to be treated differently in other parts of the United Kingdom. Lord Nicholls held (para 16) that vicarious liability arises unless a statutory provision expressly or impliedly excludes liability, and the general rule is that an employer is liable for wrongs committed by employees in the course of their employment. In determining what actions lie within the scope of employment, the court applied the test in *Lister v Hesley Hall School*[28] – that is the closeness of the connection between the offending conduct and the nature and circumstances of the employment. This is a 'new test of fairness and justice' which depends on the 'sufficiency of the connection between the breach of duty and the employment' and/or whether the risk of breach was reasonably incidental to the employment. Employers can be liable for acts of harassment by employees towards other employees or towards clients or customers.

---

[26] [2003] EWHC 2337 (QB), [2004] 1 WLR 1503.
[27] See **Precedent 9**.
[28] [2001] UKHL 22, [2002] 1 AC 215.

5.21 Potential defendants are as varied as potential claimants (see **5.9–5.17**). Examples include former partners who embark on a course of conduct amounting to harassment,[29] disgruntled businessmen targeting local councillors,[30] malicious neighbours,[31] those involved in unlawful protest[32] and national newspapers[33] and, as suggested above, banks and other lenders who use excessive means to bombard customers with daily calls about debts.

Accessories

5.22 Under s 7(3A), if an individual (A) *aids, abets, counsels or procures* another (B) to carry out conduct which is or becomes part of a course of harassing conduct by B, that conduct is to be treated as if carried out by A as well as by B. In addition, A's knowledge and purpose, and what he ought to have known, are taken to be what was contemplated or reasonably foreseeable at the time of the aiding, abetting, counselling or procuring (rather than at the time of the conduct itself). Thus, in cases under s 1(1), A would have to commit another act, or alternatively aid, abet, counsel or procure another act against the victim, which was part or deemed to be part of a course of conduct by him in order to fall within the Act, but under s1(1A) only one act would be necessary (see **5.2**).

Juveniles

5.23 Whilst, subject to the rules for the appointment of a litigation friend (CPR Part 21) it should be possible to seek an injunction under the 1997 Act for an individual aged under 18, there are real difficulties in obtaining an injunction against a juvenile *defendant*. In the case of *London Borough of Harrow v G*[34] the Court of Appeal upheld the principles in *Wookey v Wookey*[35] to the effect that an injunction will not issue in vain – i.e. it must have some 'teeth' and be capable of enforcement. Individuals aged under 17 cannot generally be imprisoned for contempt so that unless some other remedy is available, the court would have to be persuaded by evidence that the young person had some income or capital and so could be made subject to a fine or sequestration of assets. In *London Borough of Harrow v G* it was held that the existence in that case of a power of arrest did not alter the position since after arrest it must be possible to enforce the injunction). Section 3(6) (see **5.90–5.95**) probably does not alter this position as it does not extend the offence to those under the age of 17 nor provide for sanctions applicable to minors.

---

[29] See, e g *Robinson v Murray* [2005] EWCA Civ 935, (2005) *The Times*, August 19.
[30] *Howlett v Holding* (2006) The Times, February 8.
[31] *Kellett v DPP* [2001] EWHC Admin 107, [2001] All ER (D) 124 (Feb).
[32] For example *Hall v Save Newchurch Guinea Pigs (Campaign)* [2005] EWHC 372 (QB), (2005) The Times, April 7.
[33] See *Thomas v News Group Newspapers Ltd* [2001] EWCA Civ 1233.
[34] [2004] EWHC 17(QB).
[35] [1991] 3 All ER 365.

Procedure for claim/application

Application for injunction after claim

5.24   CPR, r 65.28 provides that proceedings under s 3 of the 1997 Act are to be subject to the Part 8 procedure for claims. If commenced in the High Court, proceedings must be started in the Queen's Bench Division; if in the county court, either in the court for the district in which the defendant resides or carries on business or where the claimant resides or carries on business. Both circuit and district judges have jurisdiction to grant injunctions under the Act in the county court (CPR PD2B, para 8.1).

5.25   Where a claim has been commenced, an application backed by evidence will generally be required. There is no standard form in the High Court, but application Form N16A should be used in the county court. Part 23 and CPR PD25 generally set out the application procedures.

5.26   In urgent cases, the court may dispense with an application notice (CPR, r 23.3) but this will usually only be in cases of exceptional urgency, when that course best serves the overriding objective and in other restricted circumstances (CPR PD23, para 3).

5.27   The court also has the power to grant an injunction without notice to the respondent (CPR, r 25.3), and even by telephone (CPR PD25, paras 4.1 and 4.5 set out the procedure in the Royal Court of Justice in such cases), where it appears to the court there are good reasons for not giving notice (e g if there are grounds for considering that violence will escalate or irreversible steps taken if notice is served). Even then, unless secrecy is essential, informal steps should be taken to inform the respondent (CPR PD25, para 4.3).

5.28   Even in urgent cases, an application notice, evidence in support and a draft order should be filed in court at least 2 hours before the hearing wherever possible.

5.29   If there is no application notice, a draft order should be supplied at the hearing wherever possible (CPR PD25, para 4.3).

5.30   The general rule, however, is that in the absence of such circumstances the application should be on notice (CPR, r 23.4). It is trite law that, on an application made without notice, the claimant has a duty of full and fair disclosure of all material facts, including those which undermine the claim.[36]

5.31   If the court grants or dismisses an application where a copy of the notice has *not* previously been served, the applicant will have to undertake to file the notice and pay the fee the same or the next working day (CPR PD25, para 5.1).

---

[36]   See *Brink's Mat Limited v Elcombe* [1988] 1WLR 1350, CA.

5.32 The notice and any supporting evidence must be served with the court's order upon the parties and anyone else against whom the order was sought or made unless the court directs otherwise, and the order must contain a statement that the person who is served with the order has the right to apply to set it aside or vary it. Such an application must be made within 7 days of service (CPR, rr 23.9 and 23.10).

5.33 The claimant must undertake to serve these documents as soon as practicable after the hearing (CPR PD25, para 5.1(2)).

5.34 If the injunction is granted without notice, the order will provide for a rapid return date so that the defendant can make his case and the application be considered further (CPR PD25, para 5.1(3)).

5.35 Where there is an application notice, and the application is being made on notice, as will generally be the case, it must state what order is applied for and (briefly) why it is being sought together with the date, time and place of hearing (CPR, r 23.6; CPR PD25, para 2.1). It should be verified by a statement of truth if being relied upon as evidence.

5.36 If the court is serving the application there should be sufficient copies of the application and supporting evidence for each respondent.

5.37 Generally speaking, 3 clear days' notice will be required (CPR, r 23.7) although the court has power to abridge time. Applications should be served as soon as practicable and it is good practice to let the proposed respondent know of the application as early as possible unless an application without any notice is justified on the facts.

5.38 An application must always be supported by evidence unless the court orders otherwise, and if made without notice the evidence must explain why notice has not been given (CPR, r 25.3(2) and (3)). A draft order (together with disc) should be supplied where possible

5.39 An application notice or statement of case verified by a statement of truth under CPR Part 22 can be sufficient evidence by itself or coupled with a witness statement so verified (CPR PD25, para 3.2) and the evidence should set out the facts on which the applicant relies. Part 32 deals with the requirements for other types of supporting evidence.

Injunction before claim commenced

5.40 Under CPR, r 7.2, claims are not commenced until the court issues a claim form. If the matter is urgent, however, or it is otherwise desirable to do so in the interests of justice, the court may grant an interim injunction before the claim is made (CPR, r 25.2(b)). In such circumstances the claimant will have to undertake to issue the claim immediately or the court may give directions for commencement of the claim. Wherever possible, the claim form should be issued with the injunction order (CPR PD25, para 4.4) and the order should be headed with the parties names followed by 'Claimant and Defendant in an intended action'. The other rules for applying without an application notice or without notice are as set out above.

Injunction granted following hearinglin presence of the parties

5.41 An interim injunction can be stated to have effect until trial or further order in such circumstances.

Final injunction

5.42 If the case proceeds to a final hearing, a final injunction could be awarded as well as damages for the statutory tort of harassment.

Conditions to be satisfied before Injunction granted

Threshold test for interim injunctions

5.43 In *Emerson Developments Ltd v Avery and Others*[37] counsel for the defendants accepted that in general terms the test as to the grant of an interim injunction will be that applied in *American Cyanamid v Ethicon,*[38] namely:

(1)   Is there a serious question to be tried?

(2)   If so, are damages an adequate remedy? (if so, no injunction).

(3)   If not, where does the balance of convenience/justice lie? (if with the defendant, no injunction).

(4)   Although usually the court asks whether the claimant is able to compensate the defendant if it is later judged that the injunction should not have been granted, it is unlikely to do so in cases under the 1997 Act where the defendant is being restrained from carrying out unlawful conduct.

5.44 It was successfully argued in *Emerson*, however, that in cases where Art 10 of the ECHR is engaged (freedom of expression), s 12(3) of the Human Rights Act 1998 requires that the court must be satisfied on the evidence that the claimants are likely to establish that publication of the material in question (by whatever means) would not be allowed at final hearing before going on to consider points 2–4 above. In *Cream Holdings v Banerjee*[39] Lord Nicholls in the House of Lords stated that the court should not grant an injunction unless satisfied that 'the applicant's prospects of success at trial are sufficiently favourable to justify such an order being made in the particular circumstances

---

[37]   [2004] EWHC 194 (QB).
[38]   [1975] AC 396, [1975] 1 All ER 504, HL.
[39]   [2004] UKHL 44, [2005] 1 AC 253.

of the case'. This would involve, for example, the court weighing the likely damage to the claimant if the injunction is not granted against the cogency of the evidence of actual or threatened harassment and the damage to the defendant if it is. Lord Nicholls went on to say (at paras 22–23) that in general, courts should be 'exceedingly slow' in such cases to make an order where the applicant has not satisfied the court that it is 'more likely than not' that he will succeed at trial. Circumstances where a court might award an order where the probability test is not satisfied include those where the potential adverse consequences of not issuing are particularly grave or an injunction is required for a short period to enable the court to give more detailed consideration to the issue.

5.45 Cases where Art 10 is engaged and thus the 'likelihood of success' becomes a factor include most cases where the alleged harasser is seeking to communicate his views about the victim to third parties, but not generally in cases where the harassing conduct or speech is directed to the victim alone. The higher threshold is likely to apply to protest cases such as *Emerson* and cases involving newspaper campaigns or series of articles,[40] but also any other case where publication by any means of the alleged harasser's opinion is involved, such as *Howlett v Holding* (above). On the conditions to be satisfied where Arts 10 and 11 are engaged, see **5.64–5.76**.

Standard of proof

5.46 This remains the civil standard. However, in *Hipgrave v Jones*[41] a distinction was drawn between anti social behaviour orders (designed to protect the community, where the criminal standard of proof applies) and proceedings under this Act, designed to protect individuals. In a helpful summary of the case law, however, Tugendhat J applied the well-known guidance of Lord Nicholls in *Re H and Others (Minors) (Sexual Abuse: Standard of Proof)*:[42]

> 'The balance of probability standard means that a court is satisfied an event occurred if the court considers that, on the evidence, the occurrence of the event was more likely than not ... the court will have in mind as a factor ... that the more serious the allegation, the less likely it is that the event occurred, and hence, the stronger should be the evidence before the court concludes that the allegation is established on the balance of probability ... this does not mean that where a serious allegation is in issue the standard of proof required is higher. It means only that the inherent probability or improbability of an event is in itself a matter to be taken into account when weighing the probabilities and deciding whether, on balance, the event occurred.'

---

[40] See *Thomas v News Group Newspapers Ltd* [2001] EWCA Civ 1233.
[41] [2004] EWHC 2901 QB, [2005] 2 FLR 174.
[42] [1996] AC 563, at 596–597, [1996] 1 FLR 80 at 95.

5.47 In *Oxford University v Broughton and others*[43] there was discussion of this type of injunction having a 'public order' function also, but there was no consideration of what effect (if any) this would have on the standard of proof.

Unlawful conduct

5.48 Section 1(1) renders it unlawful for a person to pursue a course of conduct which amounts to harassment of another and which he knows or ought to know amounts to harassment of that other. Equally, under s 1A it is unlawful to pursue a course of conduct against two or more persons, which he knows or ought to know involves harassment of those persons and by which he intends to persuade any person (whether or not the subject of harassment) (i) not to do something he is entitled or required to do or (ii) to do something he is not under any obligation to do.

'A course of conduct'

5.49 Section 7(3) of the Act provides that in the case of conduct directed towards a single person, there must be conduct on at least two occasions towards that person, and in the case of conduct in relation to two or more persons under s 1(1A), there must be conduct on at least one occasion to each of those persons. In *Lau v DPP*[44] two incidents 4 months apart were held not to constitute a course of conduct. Schiemann LJ commented that whilst two incidents are sufficient, the fewer incidents there are and the more widely spread, the less likely it is that a course of conduct will be established, although all will depend on the circumstances – for instance, a threat to carry out a particular act on someone's birthday or at Christmas every year may suffice. In *Pratt v DPP*,[45] two incidents four months apart were sufficient as the incidents were sufficiently connected 'in type and context' to justify the conclusion that they were a course of conduct (here, both incidents occurred whilst a separated couple were 'unhappily living together under the same roof' and this was held to be a sufficient nexus).

5.50 'Conduct' includes speech (s 7(4)).

5.51 Under s 1(1A), however, where two or more persons are being harassed with the requisite purpose, it is only necessary for each victim to be harassed on one occasion (s 7(3)(b)).

'Harassment'

5.52 Under s 7(2) it is made clear that references to harassing a person 'include alarming the person or causing the person distress' but there is no

---

[43]   [2006] EWCA Civ 1305.
[44]   [2000] 1 FLR 799.
[45]   [2001] EWHC Admin 483.

specific definition of harassment. For example in *Thomas v News Group Newspapers Ltd*[46] Lord Phillips MR stated (para 24) that whilst:

> 'harassment must not be given an interpretation which restricts the right of freedom of expression save insofar as necessary to give effect to the legitimate aim' (of protecting individuals from unlawful harassment) the Act 'does not attempt to define the type of conduct that is capable of constituting 'harassment' ... harassment is however a word which has a meaning which is generally understood ... it describes conduct which is targeted at an individual which is calculated to produce the consequences described in section 7 and which is oppressive and unreasonable ...'

This passage has been quoted extensively and applied in eg *Majrowski v Guy's and St Thomas's NHS Trust*[47] and *Green v DB Group Services (UK) Ltd.*[48]

5.53 In the context of the publication of material in the press which criticises an individual, he pointed out that a 'pleading which does no more than allege that a newspaper article has forseeably caused distress' will be susceptible to strike out (and insufficient to justify the award of an injunction – see **5.43**). In other words, simply causing alarm or distress (even intentionally) will not necessarily be enough unless the conduct is objectively (see **5.57**) viewed as 'unreasonable' or oppressive. In the context of newspaper articles, and other cases where the freedoms of expression and assembly are involved, however, it is not the opinions of the writer or speaker that are to be subjected the reasonableness test but a balance has to be struck between the relevant freedoms and the statutory right not to be subjected to harassment (see more at **5.64** et seq).

5.54 More recently, in *Majrowski* (above) in the House of Lords, Lord Nicholls had this to say (para 30):

> '... courts will have in mind that irritations, annoyances, even a measure of upset, arise at times in everybody's day to day dealings with other people. Courts are well able to recognise the boundary between conduct which is unattractive, even unreasonable, and conduct which is unacceptable. To cross the boundary from the regrettable to the unacceptable, the gravity of the misconduct must be of a gravity which would sustain criminal liability under section 2.'

These principles were recently reaffirmed in *Conn v Sunderland City Council*[49] in which it was held that there was no 'harassment' where a threat by the claimant's foreman to smash a window with his fists and report the claimant and two colleagues to personnel, in circumstances where the colleagues did not take the threat seriously, was held to lack the necessary element of gravity to be capable of attracting a criminal sanction and hence not capable of forming part of a course of conduct of harassment.

---

[46]   [2001] EWCA Civ 1233.
[47]   [2006] IRLR 695.
[48]   [2006] EWHC 1898 (QB), [2006] IRLR 764.
[49]   [2007] All ER (D) 99 (Nov)

5.55 So far the courts have held the following to be capable of constituting harassment: abuse, assault and threats[50] alleging on more than one occasion (and without any proper basis) that a neighbour is fraudulently receiving her wages by being at home without good reason during working time;[51] threatening letters and phone calls; sending letters maliciously alleging that individuals are paedophiles or sex offenders; causing criminal damage; fire bombings; carrying out intimidating home visits;[52] deliberately ignoring a colleague, excluding her from conversations, laughing when she walked past, making crude remarks about her, failing to put through calls and hiding her post;[53] assaulting an ex-partner and throwing water over her;[54] posting defamatory remarks about a solicitor on a website;[55] and paying computer hackers £150 to assist in sabotaging an ex-lover's emails (so as to alter emails sent by him or make it appear as if he had sent emails he had not).[56] In the last case a suggestion from the respondent's counsel, apparently accepted by the court, was that publishing the truth about someone may amount to harassment – for example, the correct address or telephone number of a well-known or infamous individual.

5.56 Under s(1A) (harassment of two or more persons) the harasser's intention must be to persuade a person (in this context, an individual with legal personality is included) (whether or not one of the victims of the harassment) either (i) not to do something that person is entitled or required to do, or (ii) to do something that he is not under any obligation to do. The reported cases tend to be those in which protestors were trying to stop a business from carrying out work which, although lawful, the protestors disapprove of, or where protestors are trying to stop building work going ahead.[57]

Objective test of harassment

5.57 As noted at **5.2**, s 1(2) provides that a person ought to know that his course of conduct amounts to or involves harassment of another if a reasonable person in possession of the same information would think so. This has been referred to as 'the mental element'.[58]

---

[50]   For example, *Hipgrave v Jones* [2004] EWHC 2901(QB), [2005] 2 FLR 174.

[51]   *Kellett v DPP* [2001] EWHC Admin 107, [2001] All ER (D) 124 (Feb) – the neighbour appeared unaware that the victim was exercising her contractual right to flexi-time!

[52]   *Daiichi UK Ltd v Stop Huntingdon Animal Cruelty* [2003] EWHC 2337 (QB), [2004] 1 WLR 1503.

[53]   *Green v DB Group Services (UK) Ltd* [2006] EWHC 1898 (QB), [2006] IRLR 764.

[54]   *Pratt v DPP* [2001] EWHC Admin 483.

[55]   *Cray v Hancock* [2005] All ER (D) 66 Nov.

[56]   *R v Debnath* [2005] EWCA Crim 3472, [2006] Cr App Rep (S) 169).

[57]   See the cases involving *Daiichi UK Ltd v Stop Huntingdon Animal Cruelty* [2003] EWHC 2337 (QB), [2004] 1 WLR 1503 and *Oxford University v Broughton and Others* [2006] EWCA Civ 1305 mentioned above for examples.

[58]   See *Hipgrave v Jones* [2004] EWHC 2901(QB), [2005] 2 FLR 174.

5.58 In *Kellett v DPP*[59] the neighbour had, when contacting the victim's employer to complain of her allegedly fraudulent conduct, asked that the victim should not be informed of his calls as it might cause her to stop the conduct he complained of and thus avoid detection. He argued that a reasonable person in his position would not consider his course of conduct to be harassment but this was rejected, on the basis that it was his intention to cause problems between the victim and her employer, and that he had no good cause for thinking that she was acting fraudulently as he was alleging. It did not matter that he had not told the claimant himself of his calls or that he had asked that her employer did not reveal the source; it was the effect of his conduct on the victim that had to be considered.

5.59 In the case of secondary parties (those who aid, abet, counsel or procure) the test of what was known or ought to have been known is judged according to what was contemplated or reasonably foreseeable at the time of the aiding, abetting, counselling or procuring. Those vicariously liable will be deemed to have the knowledge of those for whom they are legally responsible.

Exceptions

5.60 Although these will rarely be determinative at injunction stage, it may be necessary to consider whether the exceptions in s 1(3) apply where the defendant says that the claimant has no serious question to be tried or that, in a case where Art 10 is engaged, the claimant is unlikely to succeed.

5.61 As noted above, s 1(3)(a) permits the conduct in question if the defendant shows that it was 'pursued for the purpose of preventing or detecting crime'. As we have seen, in *Howlett v Holding* (above) it was accepted that this is intended to apply to the law enforcement agencies, not private individuals who suspect criminal activity – presumably if they have real concerns they should let the appropriate agency know rather than take matters up themselves.

5.62 Similarly, s 1(3)(b) exempts conduct where the defendant shows 'that it was pursued under any enactment or rule of law or to comply with any condition or requirement imposed by any person under any enactment'. This might typically cover regulatory activity by local authorities or, for example, action by bailiffs which an individual might find harassing but which is permitted by law.

5.63 The last exception is under s 1(3)(c), where the defendant shows 'that in the particular circumstances' of the case the pursuit of the course of conduct was 'reasonable'. Although seemingly wide, this exception does not figure much in the reported cases, but was rejected in the case of *Kellett* (above) – the neighbour should have made sure of his facts before contacting the victim's employer alleging fraud; and as mentioned above in *DPP v Selvanayagam*[60] the

---

[59]   [2001] EWHC Admin 107, [2001] All ER (D) 124 (Feb).
[60]   (1999) *The Times*, June 23.

Court of Appeal made it clear that only in exceptional circumstances would breach of an injunction be 'reasonable' conduct. If the terms of an injunction become inappropriate, the correct course is to apply to discharge them, not flout them.

Balancing the claimant's right not to be harassed against the defendant's right to freedom of expression and assembly

5.64   The 1997 Act gives individuals the right to protection from harassment, but sometimes that right needs to be balanced against the rights and freedoms of others. In particular, in a number of cases claimants have been faced with arguments that their right to protection interferes with the defendant's right under the ECHR, Art 10 to freedom of expression, and in some instances the right to freedom of assembly and association (Art 11).

5.65   Article 10 provides as follows:

> '(1) Everyone has the right to freedom of expression. This right shall include freedom to hold opinions and to receive and impart information and ideas without interference by public authority and regardless of frontiers. This Article shall not prevent States from requiring the licensing of broadcasting, television or cinema enterprises.

> The exercise of these freedoms, since it carries with it duties and responsibilities, may be subject to such formalities, conditions, restrictions or penalties as are prescribed by law and are necessary in a democratic society, in the interests of national security, territorial integrity or public safety, for the prevention of disorder or crime, for the protection of health or morals, for the protection of the reputation or rights of others, for preventing the disclosure of information received in confidence, or for maintaining the authority and impartiality of the judiciary.'

Apart from s 6, which renders it unlawful for any public authority, including a court, to act in a way which is incompatible with a Convention right, s 12 of the Human Rights Act 1998 is also relevant. It states:

> '(1)   This section applies if a court is considering whether to grant any relief which, if granted, might affect the exercise of the Convention right to freedom of expression.
> (2)   If the person against whom the application for relief is made ("the respondent") is neither present nor represented, no such relief is to be granted unless the court is satisfied—
>   (a)   that the applicant has taken all practicable steps to notify the respondent; or
>   (b)   that there are compelling reasons why the respondent should not be notified.
> (3)   No such relief is to be granted so as to restrain publication before trial unless the court is satisfied that the applicant is likely to establish that publication should not be allowed.

(4) The court must have particular regard to the importance of the Convention right to freedom of expression and, where proceedings relate to material which the respondent claims, or which appears to the court, to be journalistic, literary or artistic material *(or to conduct connected with such material)* to—
  (a) the extent to which—
    (i) the material has, or is about to, become available to the public; or
    (ii) it is, or would be, in the public interest for the material to be published;
  (b) any relevant privacy code.
(5) In this section ... "relief" includes any remedy or order (other than in criminal proceedings.' (emphasis added)

5.66 Whilst s 12(4) will generally apply only to the comparatively rare cases of harassment by publication in the press or by artistic or literary material, Art 10 clearly has a wider relevance to Protection from Harassment Act 1997 claims where the alleged harasser is publishing his views about an individual or situation. 'Publication' has been given a wide meaning in relation to freedom of expression and could include most circumstances where the alleged harasser conducts the harassment by expressing views about the alleged victim to third parties – for example in *Cray v Hancock*[61] by alleging to a solicitor's partners that he was greedy and incompetent.

5.67 Similarly, Art 11, which provides as follows, is clearly relevant in protest type claims:

'(1) Everyone has the right to freedom of peaceful assembly and to freedom of association with others, including the right to form and to join trade unions for the protection of his interests.
(2) No restrictions shall be placed on the exercise of these rights other than such as are prescribed by law and are necessary in a democratic society in the interests of national security or public safety, for the prevention of disorder or crimes, for the protection of health or morals or for the protection of the rights and freedoms of others. This article shall not prevent the imposition of lawful restrictions on the exercise of these rights by members of the armed forces, of the police or of the administration of the state.'

The courts have been grappling with the tension between the alleged victim's right not to be harassed and the alleged harasser's right to protest peacefully since even before the Human Rights Act 1998 came into force. In *Huntingdon Life Sciences Ltd v Curlio*,[62] Eady J pointed out that the Act was not intended to restrict those who were exercising their right to peaceful protest about a matter of public interest, and the British Union for the Abolition of Vivisection was dismissed from the proceedings.

---

[61] [2005] All ER (D) 66 Nov.
[62] (1997) *The Times*, December 11.

5.68 Subsequently, after the introduction of the 1998 Act, the debate became more focussed. In *Thomas v News Group Limited*[63] counsel for the newspaper argued that the reasonableness of a view expressed in a newspaper should not be judged by the courts. Whilst accepting that this was the case, and that the right to freedom of expression extends to the publication of opinions that 'offend, shock or disturb', Lord Phillips commented (para 21) that the:

> 'Article 10 freedom is subject to exceptions which must be construed strictly and the need for any restrictions must be established convincingly ... the test of "necessity" in a democratic society requires the court to determine if the "interference" corresponds to a "pressing social need", and if so, whether the means adopted to restrict freedom of expression are "proportionate to the legitimate aim" and whether the reasons for justification are relevant and sufficient.'

5.69 Harassment must not, therefore, be given an interpretation which restricts the right of freedom of expression save insofar as necessary to give effect to the 'legitimate aim' of protecting the claimant from harassment. This does not mean that the alleged harasser's Art 10 or 11 rights are to be given precedence over the claimant's Art 8 right to respect for his private and family life[64] and it is noticeable that the courts will pay more heed to Art 10 rights where the subject matter is publication by the media and the public interest is involved than where an individual merely seeks to make his views known about the alleged victim.[65]

5.70 As we have already seen, however, where the alleged 'harassment' involves the publication by whatever means of views about the victim, and hence s 12(3) applies, a higher threshold must be passed before an injunction can be considered (see **5.44**).

5.71 In *Thomas*, the Master of the Rolls stated 'before press publications are capable of constituting harassment, they must be attended by some exceptional circumstances which justify the sanctions and the restriction of freedom of expression involved [in remedies for harassment]' (para 35). Whilst it was common ground that such circumstances were rare, it was also agreed that the publication of articles calculated to incite racial hatred of an individual are examples of conduct capable of amounting to harassment under the 1997 Act, since the right of freedom of expression does not extend to protect remarks directed against the Convention's underlying values. Lord Phillips concluded that 'the test requires the publisher to consider whether a proposed series of articles, which is likely to cause distress to an individual, will constitute an abuse of the freedom of the press which the pressing social needs of a democratic society require should be curbed'. His view that Art 10 does not

---

[63] [2001] EWCA Civ 1233.
[64] *In re S (A Child) (Identification: Restrictions on Publication)* [2004] UKHL 47, [2004] 3 WLR 1129.
[65] See, e g *Howlett v Holding* (2006) *The Times*, February 8.

protect publication of information which undermines the core values of the Convention on Human Rights has, however, come in for some criticism.[66]

5.72 The later cases concentrate on balancing the alleged victim's right to protection against the alleged harasser's Art 10 and Art 11 rights. In *Huntingdon Life Sciences Ltd v Stop Huntingdon Animal Cruelty*[67] in 2003 it was stressed that the starting point at common law is that unless the defendant's conduct is shown to be unlawful, there is at first sight no reason to prevent it. Gibbs J (para 48) stated:

> 'This approach is qualified to the extent that otherwise lawful conduct may be prohibited as far as necessary to protect a victim or likely victim of wrongdoing. The convention, on the other hand, asserts as positive rights, freedom of expression ... and freedom of personal assembly or association. Again, however, these freedoms may, under the Convention itself, be curtailed to prevent disorder or crime, for example to protect the rights of others. Thus whilst the language and context are not exactly the same, the resulting balancing exercise is remarkably similar.'

He went on to find that the balance fell heavily on the side of granting the injunction since there was clear evidence of the defendants having already broken the law and been convicted, or had encouraged breaches of the law.

5.73 In *Daiichi UK Ltd v Stop Huntingdon Animal Cruelty*[68] it was stated that the restriction on the defendants' rights should be no more than was necessary to protect the claimant's rights, although it was again stressed that the Convention rights are qualified rights. In this context, this concern has so far seemed to weigh more heavily when considering the terms of any injunction rather than whether it should be granted.

5.74 In the case of *In re S*[69] Steyn LJ addressed the correct approach where a claimant's Art 8 rights appear to conflict with Art 10 rights. He held that neither right took precedence – rather, the correct approach is to focus on the comparative importance of the specific rights claimed in the particular case, with the justifications for interfering with or restricting each right being brought into account and the proportionality test being applied to each.

5.75 In *R v Debnath*[70] the defendant was appealing from a criminal restraining order which prohibited her, amongst other things, from publishing any information concerning the claimant and his fiancée, whether or not true. The defendant had conducted a campaign against the victim, a former work colleague, after having a one-night stand with him. She believed he had given her a sexually transmitted disease, although she had never actually had that disease. The campaign ranged from criminal damage to his car, registering him

---

[66]　See Lester and Pannick, *Human Rights Law and Practice*, 2nd edn, para 4.10.18.
[67]　[2003] All ER (D) 280 (Jun).
[68]　[2003] EWHC 2337 (QB), [2004] 1 WLR 1503.
[69]　[2005] 1 AC 593, HL.
[70]　[2005] EWCA Crim 3472.

on gay contact websites, falsely complaining to his employers that he was harassing her and tampering with his emails and those of his fiancée.

5.76 On appeal, the defendant argued that the wide terms of the injunction infringed her Art 10 rights to publish the truth. The prosecution argued that the defendant's rights had to be balanced against the victim's rights, including his right and that of his fiancée to private and family life under Art 8. The Court of Appeal held that in the circumstances, the order was justified, particularly as the defendant seemed incapable of distinguishing truth from fiction and continued her campaign even when on remand. Cresswell J stated, 'In our judgment the restraining order is (a) prescribed by law [under the 1997 Act], (b) to further a legitimate aim [protection of the victim from harassment]; (c) necessary in a democratic society; and (d) proportionate'. This test was based on the case of *R v Shayler*.[71]

5.77 In *Howlett v Holding* (above) Mr Holding was restrained from causing aircraft to fly 'abusive and derogatory' banners and to drop damaging leaflets about Mrs Howlett. The court held that Mr Holding's Art 10 right to freedom of expression did not have automatic precedence over Mrs Howlett's Art 8 right to 'physical and psychological integrity'. Mrs Howlett's anguish was seen to be out of proportion to the value attached to his right of free speech in this case.

TERMS OF THE ORDER

Interim injunctions

Prohibited activity

5.78 Although, as indicated in *Thomas v News Group Limited*, 'harassment' is a term which should be generally understood, if a particular form of harassment has been carried out or been threatened it is generally speaking better to spell this out to avoid later misunderstanding, for example 'X is prohibited from harassing Y, whether by contacting her or her partner Z or her employer by telephone, letter, email, text message or otherwise'.

5.79 The terms of an injunction may be so wide as to interfere with otherwise lawful activity.[72] Although this case predates the Act, it is of general application and has been applied in many cases under the 1997 Act.[73] In *Burris v Azadani*,[74] Bingham MR pointed out that save in restricted circumstances, the county court's jurisdiction to grant injunctions is the same as that of the High Court under s 37 of the Supreme Court Act 1981, namely (and subject to the existence of an arguable cause of action to support the grant) 'in all cases in

---

[71]   [2002] UKHL 11, [2003] 1 AC 247, at [23].
[72]   See *Burris v Azadani* [1995] 1 WLR 1372, CA.
[73]   For example, *Hall v Save Newchurch Guinea Pigs (Campaign)* [2005] EWHC 372 (QB), (2005) *The Times*, April 7.
[74]   [1995] 1 WLR 1372 CA.

which it appears to the court to be just and equitable to do so'. Pointing out that an interlocutory injunction can be granted in cases where commission of a tort is likely (and here, s 3 makes it clear that a remedy is available in cases of apprehended as well as actual harassment), he stated:

> '... it would not seem to me to be a valid objection to the making of an exclusion order that the conduct to be restrained is not in itself tortuous or otherwise unlawful if such an order is reasonably regarded as necessary for the protection of [the claimant's] legitimate interests ... the defendant's liberty is to be respected up to the point at which his conduct infringes or threatens to infringe the claimant's rights ...'

5.80 In the *Burris* case, this meant that an order could be made excluding the defendant from a 250-yard radius of the home of the claimant, whom he was stalking.

5.81 *Exclusion zone* orders have thus been made in a number of cases under the Act, in cases involving large-scale protests as well as protection of individuals.[75]

5.82 Other restrictions on otherwise lawful activity which have been upheld include: a ban on publishing any information regarding the victim and his fiancé, whether or not true, and a ban on contacting them at all;[76] the banning of protest meetings save on particular days and particular times;[77] a ban on the use of noise amplification equipment during protests save at specified days and times; and a ban on photographing or videotaping defined visitors to a site where construction of a research laboratory was taking place.[78]

5.83 The courts have been keen to stress, however, that such restrictions on lawful activity should not be granted too readily, and only so far as necessary to protect the claimant's rights. Although this is a difficult balance to strike, 'Respect for the freedom of the aggressor should never lead the court to deny necessary protection to the victim'.

5.84 Thus, in *Hall v Save Newchurch Guinea Pigs*[79] the High Court refused to impose an exclusion zone covering 200 square kilometres before the current 100-yard exclusion zone and other orders had been put to the test, Owen J stressing that any relief had to be no wider than necessary and pointing out that the claimants could always apply to vary the order and extend the exclusion zone if the protection proved inadequate. In *R v Debnath*[80] the order not to publish any material (including true material) was described as 'exceptional' but justified on the basis that the defendant was intent on

---

[75] For example *Oxford University v Broughton and Others* [2006] EWCA Civ 1305.
[76] *R v Debnath* [2005] EWCA Crim 3472, [2006] Cr App Rep (S) 169.
[77] For example *Hall v Save Newchurch Guinea Pigs* [2005] EWHC 372.
[78] *Oxford University v Broughton and Others* [2006] EWCA Civ 1305.
[79] [2005] EWHC 372.
[80] [2005] EWCA Crim 3472, [2006] Cr App Rep (S) 169.

harassing the victim and his fiancé, seemed incapable of distinguishing truth from lies and that publishing true facts such as a victim's home address may amount to harassment.[81]

5.85 Many examples of the type of conduct which may amount to harassment and thus prohibited by injunction are described above.

Protected persons

5.86 Injunctions may extend beyond the named claimants when this is necessary to protect their legitimate interests in not being harassed or where the claimant is a representative claimant. In some orders, a definition of 'protected persons' may be appropriate (eg the cases where attempts are being made by protestors to close down businesses, noted above) and an example of such a clause is given in the Precedents at the end of this chapter..

Persons restrained

5.87 Whilst it is commonplace to restrain the defendant and any 'servant or agent' acting for him, in some cases an even wider range of persons can be restrained where this is necessary to protect the claimant from harassment. Examples of such situations include instances of vicarious liability against an employer of the harasser, or where the defendant is a representative defendant, for example an unincorporated campaigning group as in the *Huntingdon Life Sciences* cases. In the last type of situation, the injunction can extend to those 'acting in concert' with the named defendant, and a definition clause covering, for example, 'protestors' may be useful. An example is again given in the Precedents at the end of this chapter.

Other terms

5.88 Where an application is made in an urgent situation without issuing a claim form or application notice it is usual for the order to record undertakings by the claimant to take the relevant steps that have been omitted immediately or on the next working day, and directions can be given to progress the action. It is usual also to incorporate a penal notice, even though breach of an injunction amounts to a criminal offence under s 3(6). If an interim injunction is granted after a hearing on notice or by consent, it may be expressed to continue 'until trial or further order'.

---

[81] As in *Silverton v Gravett* 2001 WL 1535358 QBD (19 October 2001) where animal rights activists were said to employ a tactic of publishing the home addresses of the owners of businesses selling animal furs and recommending approaching the owners at their homes as an effective means towards the end of forcing the businesses to close down.

FINAL INJUNCTIONS

5.89 A final injunction may be granted after trial of the action in addition to any award of damages. In such a case, where it is sought to restrain conduct which would otherwise be lawful (for example by imposing an exclusion zone) it is wise to incorporate a 'liberty to apply' provision in case circumstances change (eg if the claimant moves away there may be no need to restrain the defendant from entering the exclusion zone).

ENFORCEMENT

5.90 Under s 3(6), where the High Court or county court has granted an injunction under the Act, and without reasonable excuse the defendant does anything he is prohibited from doing by the injunction, he is guilty of a criminal offence, punishable by up to 5 years' imprisonment or a fine on indictment and for up to 6 months or a fine not exceeding the statutory maximum on summary conviction.

5.91 This means that the police have powers to warn or arrest anyone they have reasonable grounds for suspecting of breaching an injunction under the Act.

5.92 If the police exercise their powers of arrest and the arrestee is convicted under s 3(6), the same conduct is not punishable as contempt of court, and similarly if the conduct is punished as a contempt of court, it cannot also be the subject of a criminal conviction (s 3(8)).

5.93 Alternatively, if the police do not exercise their powers, the victim can apply under s 3(3) for a warrant for the arrest of the defendant. Where the injunction was granted by the High Court, the application must be made to that court, if by the county court to a judge or district judge of any county court.

5.94 The application must be substantiated on oath and, if the judge or district judge has reasonable grounds for believing that there has been a breach of the injunction, the warrant may be issued. In the county court, application is on Form N139 and the warrant is in Form N140.

5.95 Alternatively, the claimant can apply to commit the respondent for contempt of court, the procedure for which is dealt with elsewhere in this work. Arrest followed by criminal conviction may seem a more effective remedy, however.

COSTS

5.96   Often, public funding will be involved in these cases, or the parties will have restricted means, which can make discussion of costs academic.

5.97   In cases where the parties are not publicly funded or impecunious, however, whether costs are awarded to a successful party generally depends on whether an interim or final injunction is being granted.

5.98   In the case of interim injunctions, due to the nature of the exercise being carried out by the court, the usual order will be costs in the case or costs reserved, unless a particular feature of the case (for example the decision on the injunction is likely to put an end to the matter) suggests otherwise. In cases involving Art 10 of the ECHR, when the claimant has to establish that he is more likely than not to succeed, however, it may be easier for the court to take a view on the merits and award costs at the interlocutory stage.

5.99   In the case of final injunctions, however, as in any other action the successful party will generally recover costs, subject to arguments based on the individual circumstances of the case.

CHECKLISTS AND PRECEDENTS

5.100 Checklists and precedents relating to Protection from Harassment Act injunctions are reproduced below.

1. CHECKLIST: PROTECTION FROM HARASSMENT: ELEMENTS OF STATUTORY TORT

- Harassment of another individual; or

- Harassment of two or more persons, intended by harasser to persuade any person (including third party not directly subject to harassment) not to do something he is entitled or required to do, or to do something he is not under an obligation to do;

AND

- Is harassee an individual?

- Does harasser know (or ought he to know) that conduct amounts to harassment? ie would a reasonable person in possession of the same information think so?

- Is there a course of conduct? ie on at least two occasions under 1 above, and at least one occasion against each person harassed under 2 above.

Defences:

- Was course of conduct pursued for purpose of preventing or detecting crime? (statutory agencies)? Or

- Was it pursued under statutory authority or obligation? Or

- In the particular circumstances of the case, was conduct reasonable?

2. PROCEDURAL CHECKLIST: PROTECTION FROM HARASSMENT: INTERIM INJUNCTIONS

- Part 8 CPR procedure applies for claims;

- High Court claims start in QBD;

- County Court : for district in which defendant resides or carries on business or claimant resides/carries on business;

- Both circuit and district judges have jurisdiction in county court;

- Save in restricted cases, application backed by evidence required;

- Application must state order applied for an why being sought together with date, time and place of hearing (CPR 23.6, 25PD 2.1);

- Application notice should be verified by statement of truth if relied upon as evidence;

- If court serving application, provide sufficient copies of application and supporting evidence for each respondent;

- Generally 3 clear days' notice required (although court has power to abridge and see below);

- Let respondent know of application as early as possible and serve as soon as practicable;

- Application must be supported by evidence setting out facts upon which applicant relies unless court orders otherwise;

- Evidence can be application notice or statement of case if verified by statement of truth, together with witness statement(s) if practicable;

- Draft order (together with disc) should be supplied wherever possible;

- **Urgent cases**/where overriding objective best served – court may dispense with notice /issue of claim (CPR23.3, Pt 23 PD paragraph 3) but generally, application notice, evidence in support and draft order should be filed in court two hours in advance wherever possible;

- There is power to grant injunction without notice to respondent parties where there are good reasons for not doing so (CPR 25.3, CPR 25 PD 4.1, 4.3, 4.5). In such cases the duty of full and fair disclosure applies

- If an injunction is granted without notice, order should provide for a rapid return date (CPR 25 PD 5.1(3));

- Even in the most urgent cases, draft order should be supplied if possible (CPR 25 PD 4.3). If application prior to claim, order should be headed "Claimant and Defendant in an intended action...."

- If injunction granted/refused before claim issued, claimant has to undertake to issue claim immediately or court may give directions for commencement of claim (CPR 25.2(b), CPR 25 PD 4.4);

- Where application notice/evidence in support dispensed with, both should be filed with court (and fee paid) on same or next working day as ordered by the court after matter dealt with;

- The claimant must undertake to serve these documents as soon as practicable after the hearing;

- In such circumstances, notice and any supporting evidence must be served on parties and anyone else against whom the order was sought or made unless the court directs otherwise and the order must contain a statement that the person who is served with the order has the right to apply to set aside or vary it within 7 days of service (CPR 23.9, 23.10)

3. APPLICATION FOR AN INJUNCTION (HARASSMENT OF INDIVIDUAL)

Application for an Injunction	**Parkshire County Court**
(General Form)	**Claim No**
	Claimant's name and reference
	Defendant's name and reference

X By application in pending proceedings
X Under statutory provision (section 3 of the Protection from Harassment Act 1997)
X This application is made under Part 8 of the Civil Procedure Rules
This application raises issues under the Human Rights Act 1998 (no)
The Claimant Catherine Xena Jenkins
Applies to the court for an injunction order in the following terms:

The Defendant Michael Duncan

be forbidden (whether by himself or by instructing or encouraging or permitting any other person) from

(1) entering the premises at Valleys View, Shuffles Bay, DY27 3RW or within 100 metres of that location;

(2) entering the claimant's place of work at Wolf Studios, Pinewood HH5 3XY or within a radius of 100 metres of that location;

(3) harassing, pestering or otherwise alarming or distressing the claimant;

(4)for the avoidance of any doubt, from following the claimant whether or not in a vehicle;

(5) threatening or assaulting the claimant:

(6) communicating with the claimant whether by spoken or written word and whether by letter, telephone, electronic mail or otherwise howsoever;

And that

(1) the time for service of notice upon the Defendant is abridged;

(2) the Defendant shall pay the costs of this application.

The grounds of this application are set out in the written evidence of Catherine Xena Jenkins sworn on (date)

This written evidence is served with this application.

This application is to be served upon Michael Duncan

Of : [address]

This application is filed by: Sharp and Co.

The Solicitors for the Claimant

Whose address for service is :

Odeon Buildings,

High Street

Pinewood HH3 2SF

Signed   Dated

(Continue as in Form 16A)

4. CLAIM FORM (HARASSMENT OF INDIVIDUAL)

Claim Form   **In the Parkshire County Court**

(CPR Part 8)   **Claim No.**

Catherine Xena Jenkins

Claimant

Michael Duncan

Defendant

Does your claim include any issues   No
under the Human Rights Act 1998

Details of Claim:

The claimant claims damages and an injunction under the Protection From
Harassment Act 1997. The defendant has been harassing, threatening,
pestering and following the claimant and is intent on continuing to do so
unless restrained.

Defendant's name Michael Duncan   Court Fee

and address   Solicitor's costs
Shuffles Farm

Shuffles   Issue date

Parkshire DY6 4SF

Statement of Truth

The Claimant believes that the facts
stated in these particulars of claim
are true.

Full name Dorothy Rose Parker

Name of Claimant's solicitor's firm :
Sharp and Co.

Signed   position or office held: Associate

Claimant's solicitor   Claimant's solicitor's address to which
                                                          documents should be sent

                                                          Odeon Buildings

                                                          High Street

                                                          Pinewood HH3 2SF

                                                          Email: drp@sharpco.com

                                                          Fax: SDX 2517 pinewood

5. CLAIMANT'S WITNESS STATEMENT (HARASSMENT OF INDIVIDUAL)

IN THE PARKSHIRE COUNTY   Claimant:
COURT

                                 CLAIM NO.
                                 CX Jenkins
                                 CXJ1

                                 1st:
                                 Dated:

BETWEEN:

CATHERINE XENA JENKINS

Claimant

-and-

MICHAEL DUNCAN

Defendant

Claimant's witness statement in support of an application for an injunction

I, Catherine Xena Jenkins, of Valleys View, Shuffles Bay, Parkshire, DY27 3RW, television actress, claimant in this action, STATE AS FOLLOWS:

1. I am the claimant in these proceedings. I make this statement, save so far as indicated otherwise, from my own knowledge and belief.

2. I am an actress and appear in the well known television series "Nuts in May".

3. I met the defendant, Michael Duncan, at an awards ceremony three months ago. Although he is much older than me we got on well. He told me that he was a member of a well known theatrical family. He told me that he lived in a stately home in Wiltshire with his elderly and frail father. I am relatively new to acting and had no reason to disbelieve him. We soon began a relationship and were talking about becoming engaged. We have never lived together, however.

4. In fact, I have since become aware, through watching it on television, that he is employed as an "extra" to sit in the bar in the well known farming soap opera "Over Hill and Dale".

5. I contacted the director of "Over Hill and Dale" who told me that Michael is not a famous actor but the pig man at the farm close to where the series is filmed. I immediately ended my relationship with Michael and no longer wish to have any contact with him.

6. Since I told him that I no longer wished to see him, 3 weeks ago, Michael has taken to "stalking" me. He started by leaving me messages on my mobile telephone. When I did not answer his many calls for me to ring him back, he began to send me text messages. I have printed these messages off and I refer to the bundle of documents now shown to me and marked "CXJ1". It will be seen that he has sent me up to 25 messages a day, mainly pleading with me to see him again, but the tone of the messages has become increasingly frightening and it will be seen from page 45 that over the last week he has threatened to "put an end" to us both on three occasions, mainly in texts sent late at night.

7. In addition, although I have now changed my email address, he started sending me frightening emails. Last Wednesday he sent one at 10 pm which said that he would be "watching" me. When I went to shut the curtains in my kitchen half an hour later I could clearly see him standing in my garden. He waved and walked away but I felt very intimidated.

8. Since then, until yesterday, he has been waiting by my gate when I drive out every morning at 6.30 am. Yesterday he jumped in his car and followed me all the way to work along country lanes. He drove very close behind me. In the evening he was waiting at the studio gates and I had to brake as he jumped in front of my car. Luckily I was with my co-star, Brad, who got out of the car and chased him down the road.

9. This morning, however, he was outside my garage door when I opened it and he grabbed my arm and was shouting at me to take him back. I managed to get away and run to my neighbour's house. I was very afraid, especially as he was shouting about me and Brad and saying if he could not have me, no one else would.

10. I seek the protection of an injunction granted by the court as I am finding it very difficult to cope with the defendant's campaign of harassment against me, which seems to be escalating rapidly. I am very afraid of what might happen given the defendant's threats and the rather isolated location of my home .

11. In the circumstances I would ask that the court abridge time for service of this application on the defendant as I am worried about what might happen if I wait any longer before acting. I called the police this morning but they seemed not to take the situation very seriously and Michael had gone by the time they arrived. My solicitors are endeavouring to serve the notice on the defendant today but if that fails I would ask that in the urgent circumstances the court dispenses with service.

I believe that the facts stated in this witness statement are true,

Signed   Dated

6. DRAFT ORDER (HARASSMENT OF INDIVIDUAL)

**IN THE
PARKSHIRE
COUNTY COURT**
BETWEEN:

CATHERINE XENA JENKINS

<u>Claimant</u>

-and-

MICHAEL DUNCAN

<u>Defendant</u>

Draft order

<u>If you do not obey this order you will be guilty of contempt of court and you may be fined or sent to prison or you may be guilty of a criminal offence for which you may be fined or sent to prison or both</u>

On the 25th of June 2008 the court considered an application for an injunction

The court ordered that the defendant Michael Duncan

Be forbidden (whether by himself or by instructing or encouraging or permitting any other person) from :

1. entering the premises at Valleys View, Shuffles Bay, DY 27 3RW or from approaching within 100 metres of those premises;

2. entering Wolf Studios, Pinewood HH5 3XY or within 100 metres of that location;

3. harassing, pestering or otherwise alarming or distressing the claimant;

4. following the claimant, whether or not in a vehicle;

5. threatening or assaulting the claimant;

6. communicating with the claimant whether by spoken or written word and whether in person or by letter, telephone, electronic mail or otherwise howsoever;

This order shall remain in force until the of 2008 at o'clock unless before then it is revoked by a further order of the court;

And that

1. Time for service of the notice of application, claim form, claimant's witness statement and this order on the defendant is abridged to 2 hours before the hearing on 25th June 2008;

2. the Defendant shall pay the costs of this application

Notice of Further Hearing (continue as in Form 16A)

7. APPLICATION FOR INJUNCTION (HARASSMENT BY PROTEST)

Application for Injunction

(box as in Form N244)

In the High Court of Justice

Queen's Bench Division

Claim No

Claimant's Name and ref.

Defendant's name and ref

date

Part A

We, |name| solicitors for the claimant George Brown (representing the employees of Build Force UK PLC)

Intend to apply to the court for an order (a draft of which is attached) that

The Defendants "Campaign to Stop Friar Tuck Runway" , Robin Good and Marian Sheriff (and any "protestor" as defined below)

Must remove from their website StopFriarTuck.com

(1) any reference to "causing havoc" or otherwise harassing employees at Build Force UK plc's ("the company's) site at Friar Tuck Airport;

(2) any request for information about the home addresses of (or any other personal information about) the company's employees.

And that they

Be forbidden (whether by themselves or by instructing or encouraging or permitting any other person) from

(1) harassing, molesting or pestering or threatening the claimant or any employee of Build Force UK PLC;

(2) congregating at the site at Friar Tuck Runway ("the site") or within 250 metres of that site other than on Wednesdays at 1pm for no longer than one hour for the purposes of peaceful protest;

(3) blocking the access of the claimant or any other employee of the company to the site at any time;

(4) approaching or communicating by whatever means with the claimant or any other employee of the company;

(5) approaching within 100 metres of the claimant's home address or the home addresses of Sam Malone or Dusty Binfield, employees of the company;

(6) damaging any property of any employee of the company;
and that "protestor" be defined as any of the defendants acting by themselves, their servants or agents and any other person acting in consort with the defendants and who has notice of the terms of this order.

And That

The 2nd and Third Defendants pay the costs of this application

Because the Respondents and the protestors as defined are harassing the claimant and the other employees of the company with the intention of causing the company to terminate its contractual obligations to build the new runway at Friar Tuck Airport. They are threatening to continue with their unlawful action unless restrained by order of the Court. The injunction is sought under the Protection From Harassment Act 1997. Part 8 of the CPR applies. The application raises issues under the Human Rights Act 1998.

Part B

We wish to rely on

The attached witness statement of George Brown sworn and signed on 22nd February 2008.

This written evidence is served with this application.

Signed   Dated

Address to which documents about this claim should be sent [layout as per N244]

Signed   Dated

Respondents' address

Campaign to Stop Friar Tuck Runway, 55 River Alley, Nottwood, Nottshire

Robin Good, 55 River Alley, Nottwood, Nottshire

Marian Sheriff , 55 River Alley, Nottwood, Nottshire

[Continue as per N 244]

8. CLAIMANT'S WITNESS STATEMENT IN SUPPORT OF INTERIM INJUNCTION (HARASSMENT BY PROTEST)

In the High Court of Justice	**Claimant**
Queen's Bench Division	**GBrown 1st**
Claim No	**GB1, GB2, GB3, GB4, GB5**
	Dated:

BETWEEN:

GEORGE BROWN (representing the employees of BUILD FORCE UK PLC)

<u>Claimant</u>

-and-

CAMPAIGN TO STOP FRIAR TUCK RUNWAY(1)

ROBIN GOOD(2)

MARIAN SHERIFF (3)

<u>Defendants</u>

Claimant's witness statement in support of interim injunction

I, George Brown, of Build Tower, Forest Lane, Nottingshire, Managing Director and claimant in these proceedings, STATE AS FOLLOWS:

1. I am the claimant in this matter and Managing Director of Build Force UK PLC ("the company"). I make this statement in support of my application for an interim injunction to stop the Defendants harassing myself and the other employees of Build Force in their efforts to force the company to terminate its contract to construct a third runway at Friar Tuck Airport.

2. The matters set out in this statement are within my own knowledge save where otherwise indicated and are true to the best of my knowledge, information and belief.

3. In or about January of this year, the company started work on construction of the new runway. It was well known locally that the construction project was controversial as many local people had opposed it, but the plans were eventually approved in the face of this opposition.

4. From the first day of our operations, both myself and the other employees of the company have been faced with a large scale protest by local people and others, including the 2nd and 3rd Defendants, who appear to have come from outside the area but are orchestrating the activities of the protestors.

5. Initially the protests and consequent harassment of the other workers (and I) was confined to the site at Friar Tuck airport but some of us are now being targeted at home.

6. Each day as the workers start to arrive at site at 6.30 am, the protestors are already present. There are usually 30 to 40 of them massed around the gate to the site. They carry megaphones, banners and other devices for transmitting what I can only describe as ear splitting sound effects. They carry banners bearing various messages protesting against the construction of the runway or against the company's activities such as "Build Force out now". I refer to the exhibit marked "GB1" containing a bundle of photographs taken of the protestors on various dates, which is shown to and verified by me and attached to this statement.

7. The protestors impede the passage of our vehicles on to the site but the protestors eventually move to let us in (usually after we have called the police). They then hang around the gates making a very disturbing level of noise which makes for a very unpleasant working environment.

8. On a number of occasions missiles such as cans, bottles and lumps of turf have been thrown over the perimeter fence and on two occasions workers have been struck but, thankfully, so far there have been no serious injuries.

9. As mentioned previously, the protestors now appear to have obtained home addresses for some employees, including myself. I refer to a bundle of letters marked "GB2" which is now shown to me and attached to this statement. The court will see that they comprise letters addressed to myself and made from words cut out of newspapers, threatening to damage my car, my home and stating that they know where my children go to school. They are stated to be from the 1st Defendant.

10. I am very much concerned by these threats, especially since, yesterday, when I left home to drive to work I found that paint stripper had been poured all over the bonnet of my car. I refer to the photograph labelled "GB3" which is now shown to me and attached to this statement together with a letter from my local garage confirming that the substance used was indeed paint stripper.

11. I have reported this to the police under crime reference xx334L but they say that it is virtually impossible to identify a culprit. I have been very much alarmed by this development as it shows that those responsible will carry out their threats. I refer to the statements of my colleagues Sam Mallone and Dusty Binfield whose vehicles were similarly attacked on their driveways two nights ago. The attacks seem clearly linked to the protests.

12. **The Defendants:** Many of the protestors carry placards stating "Support Campaign to Stop Friar Tuck Runway". The letters I have received at home are all stated to be from "Campaign to Stop Friar Tuck Runway". Owing to my concerns I searched the internet using the words "Campaign to Stop Friar Tuck Runway" and came across a website called "StopFriarTuckRunway.com".

13. There is now shown to me marked "GB4" and exhibited hereto information printed off that website. It will be seen that it names the 2nd and 3rd defendants as "co-ordinators" and gives an address for them and the campaign at 55 River Alley, Nottwood. I consider the website to be inflammatory as it encourages others to attend at the site at Friar Tuck airport and to "cause as much havoc as possible". It encourages others to send the co-ordinators details of the home addresses of company employees "and any other information you think we might find useful" and suggests methods by which employees can be harassed. There are details of a bank account to which donations can be made.

14. According to the website the Campaign has weekly meetings at Nottwood Javelin Club and they appear to have a list of subscribers to whom they send a monthly newsletter – see exhibit GB4. From the information on the website and the banners I have seen at the site together with the letters I have received I believe that the campaign is an organised group with the potential to carry out its threats.

15. The company has received resignations from 25 of its workforce of 200 over the last two weeks and we are struggling to replace these workers.

13. There is now shown to me marked "GB5" a document bearing the

signatures of 160 of the company's workforce (i.e. 80%) agreeing that I should make this claim and application for an injunction on their behalf as they are finding their working conditions intolerable.

14. I therefore ask the court to grant me the interim relief sought. My concern is that unless the unlawful activities of the protestors are curbed, the company will not be able to continue with the contract to build the runway and that unlawful action will have prevailed.

I believe that the facts stated in this witness statement are true:

Signed:

Dated:

9. DRAFT ORDER (HARASSMENT BY PROTEST)

In the High Court of Justice

Queen's Bench Division

Claim No

BETWEEN:

GEORGE BROWN (representing the employees of BUILD FORCE UK PLC)

<u>Claimant</u>

-and-

CAMPAIGN TO STOP FRIAR TUCK RUNWAY(1)

ROBIN GOOD(2)

MARIAN SHERIFF (3)

<u>Defendants</u>

Draft order

Before Mr(s) Justice sitting at . . . . on the 27th day of February 2008

Upon hearing from counsel for the Claimant and

AND Upon reading the statements of the Claimant George Brown (representing the employees of Build Force UK PLC) and of Sam Malone and Dusty Binfield dated

AND Upon the Claimant by his solicitors undertaking to display this order at the entrance to Build Force UK's site at Friar Tuck Airport and at distances of 50 metres around the perimeter fence

It is ordered that

The Defendants "Campaign to Stop Friar Tuck Runway" , Robin Good and Marian Sheriff (and any "protestor" as defined below)

Must remove from their website StopFriarTuck.com

(1) any reference to "causing havoc" or otherwise harassing protected persons as defined below at Build Force UK plc's ("the company's) site at Friar Tuck Airport;

(2) any request for information about the home addresses of (or other personal information about) the protected persons.

And that the Defendants and any "protestors" as defined below

Be forbidden (whether by themselves or by instructing or encouraging or permitting any other person) from

(1) harassing, molesting or pestering or threatening the claimant or any protected person;

(2) congregating at the site at Friar Tuck Runway ("the site") or within 250 metres of that site other than on Wednesdays for 1pm for no longer than one hour for the purposes of peaceful protest;

(3) blocking the access of the claimant or any other protected person ("the company") to the site at any time;

(4) approaching or communicating by whatever means with the claimant or any other protected person;

(5) approaching within 100 metres of the claimant's home address or the home addresses of Sam Malone or Dusty Binfield, protected persons;

(6) damaging any property of any protected person;

And that in this order "protestor" be defined as any of the defendants acting by themselves, their servants or agents and any other person acting in consort with the defendants and who has notice of the terms of this order;

And that in this order "protected persons" be defined as the claimant, any employee of Build Force UK PLC and any lawful visitor to the site at Friar Tuck Airport delineated on the attached map;

And that this order shall last until trial of this claim or further order

And That

Costs are reserved

This order is to be served upon:

Campaign to Stop Friar Tuck Runway, 55 River Alley, Nottwood, Nottshire

Robin Good, 55 River Alley, Nottwood, Nottshire

Marian Sheriff , 55 River Alley, Nottwood, Nottshire

Claimant's address for Service

Guisborne and Co.,

The Solicitors for the Claimant

Whose address for service is

Castle View House

Castle Lane

Nottwood NT3 6ZF

Fax : DX:

Penal Notice

Chapter 6

FAMILY LAW ACT 1996 INJUNCTIONS

INTRODUCTION

6.1   Part IV of the Family Law Act 1996 is entitled 'Family Homes and Domestic Violence'. However, Part IV covers a far wider range of situations than might be envisaged from the heading alone. It deals with problems between current and former spouses, current and former civil partners, current and former cohabitants, *and* other 'associated persons'. The powers of the court vary according to the type of relationship the proposed parties to the proceedings have (or had). It is important to check ss 30–42 and 62 of the Family Law Act 1996 to see what powers the court has in relation to the particular problem being experienced. The former sections set out the provisions on 'occupation orders' and 'non-molestation orders' and s 62 defines 'associated persons'.

MEANING OF 'NON-MOLESTATION ORDER' AND 'OCCUPATION ORDER'

6.2   An occupation order regulates who may occupy a specified property. It may exclude one party totally from that property and thus require them to live elsewhere or it may exclude them from certain rooms within the property, e g forbidding a husband to enter the bedroom that the wife is now sleeping in. Such an order might be made where there is good reason not to exclude the husband altogether but there needs to be some sort of system set up to deal with a difficult situation and prevent further escalations of the problem. Occupation orders used to be known under previous legislation as 'ouster orders' and that term may still sometimes be heard. However, the name was changed because the order will not always oust someone from a property and the term 'occupation order' more accurately reflects what the court is doing, ie regulating occupation.

6.3   A non-molestation order states that one person should not 'molest' another. Such an order will deal with violence or threats of violence, as well as behaviour by which one person harasses, pesters or annoys another. 'Molesting' is not specifically defined by the Family Law Act 1996, which is generally considered sensible because some people are very good at devising new ways of being unpleasant to other people, and the lack of a formal definition allows the law to evolve to cover new situations. Ten years ago, harassing a former partner by text message was unheard of. Now, it is a commonly cited complaint and the wording of the current law allows the court to deal with it.

6.4   In *Horner v Horner*[1] the court confirmed that a non-molestation order could be obtained in respect of conduct which could properly be regarded as such a degree of harassment as to call for the intervention of the court. In *Vaughan v Vaughan*[2] the court advised that molestation was behaviour intended 'to cause trouble, to vex, to annoy, to put to inconvenience'. One unnecessary telephone call at 3 am will not count as behaviour calling for the intervention of the court. Making a number of such calls might well be regarded differently.

6.5   The civil courts are familiar with the term 'molest' and persons have been committed to prison for contempt of court if they 'molested' someone else in breach of an injunction. Since the change in procedure whereby breach of a non-molestation injunction is usually dealt with as a criminal matter, uncertainty appears to have arisen with regard to the use of the term 'molest'. Anecdotally, this may be because the criminal system, whilst familiar with the term 'harass' (due to the Protection from Harassment Act 1997, see further Chapter 5), is not familiar with the term 'molest'.

6.6   It might seem surprising that the civil courts have in the past committed someone to prison whilst using that term, but now the criminal courts are reluctant to do so. It has been said by some practitioners that there are concerns about prosecuting on the basis of the word 'molest' due to the potential wideness (and thus possible uncertainty) of its meaning and the need in criminal proceedings for it to be clear as to what action a person is prohibited from taking. Equally, the civil system has been progressing towards a greater clarity of wording. The Court of Appeal, in such cases as *Manchester City Council v Lee,*[3] has made it plain that respondents should know exactly what it is they are not supposed to do. Chadwick LJ said:

> 'It cannot be sensible or a proper exercise of the statutory power to grant an injunction in terms which are not readily understandable by those whose conduct they are intended to restrain. Further, an injunction which leaves doubt as to what can and cannot be done is not a proper basis for committal proceedings.'

6.7   Therefore the draft order may be amended in an attempt to ensure that appropriate enforcement action will be carried out, rather than it being decided not to risk a failed prosecution because of doubts about the wording and whether the respondent could properly be said to be clear on what it was he was not supposed to do. This will be discussed further at **6.67** et seq under the sections dealing with the wording of orders and their enforcement.

6.8   Generally in this chapter, applicants are likely to be referred to as 'she' and respondents as 'he'. It is naturally accepted that not all victims are female

---

[1]   [1982] Fam 90.
[2]   [1973] 1 WLR 1159.
[3]   [2004] HLR 177.

and not all aggressors are male, but the terminology reflects the reality of life, which is that most of the persons seeking the court's assistance are female, and most of the respondents are male.

NON–MOLESTATION ORDERS

6.9 Applications for a non-molestation order are governed by s 42 of the Family Law Act 1996. The order will prohibit the respondent to the application from behaving in a specified way towards the applicant and/or a 'relevant child'. The applicant and the respondent must be 'associated persons'. Section 62 of the Family Law Act 1996 defines 'associated persons' as:

(1) persons who are or have been married to each other;

(2) persons who are or have been civil partners of each other;

(3) cohabitants or former cohabitants (which are defined as two persons who are neither married to each other nor civil partners but who are or have been living together as husband and wife or as if they were civil partners);

(4) persons who live or have lived in the same household otherwise than merely by reason of one of them being the other's employee, lodger, tenant or boarder;

(5) relatives (as further defined by s 63 of the Family Law Act 1996);

(6) persons who had agreed to marry each other (whether or not that agreement has been terminated);

(7) persons who had entered into a civil partnership agreement (as defined by s 73 of the Civil Partnership Act 2004 and whether or not that agreement has been terminated);

(8) persons who have or have had an intimate personal relationship with each other which is or was of significant duration;

(9) in relation to a child, persons who are the parents of the child, or who have or have had parental responsibility for the child. Natural and adoptive (or proposed adoptive) parents of a child may also be associated;

(10) persons who are parties to the same family proceedings (other than proceedings under Part IV of the Family Law Act 1996).

Definition of 'relative'

6.10 Section 63 of the Family Law Act 1996 defines a relative as the father, mother, stepfather, stepmother, son, daughter, stepson, stepdaughter, grandfather, grandmother, grandson or granddaughter of a person, or that person's spouse, former spouse, civil partner or former civil partner; or the brother, sister, uncle, aunt, nephew, niece, first cousin (whether of full blood or half blood or by marriage or civil partnership) of a person or that person's spouse or former spouse. In relation to a person who is or was cohabiting with another person, the definition includes any person who would fall into the categories listed above if the parties were married to each other or were civil partners of each other.

Definition of 'relevant child'

6.11 A 'relevant child' is defined as any child who is living with, or might reasonably be expected to live with, either party to the proceedings. It also includes any child in relation to whom an order under the Adoption Act 1976, the Adoption and Children Act 2002, or the Children Act 1989 is in question in the proceedings. Finally, as the catch-all, it covers 'any other child whose interests the court considers relevant'. It is clearly important that children, who normally need adults to take the steps to protect them, should be entitled to the court's protection and are not excluded from that required protection when one of the adults in their life is behaving badly.

RELATIONSHIPS COVERED BY THE ACT

6.12 The Act therefore covers situations which are predictable (spouses who have fallen out, cohabitants who have split up, etc) but also wider family groups, eg disputes between brothers and sisters or grandparents and grandchildren. It may not, however, cover problems in relationships where people dated each other for a short time but who did not live together or did not have a sexual relationship, or where the relationship, though perhaps intense, was only short lived. Persons in such situations would have to seek the court's assistance under other legislation. Case-law on this area has yet to evolve.

MAKING THE APPLICATION

6.13 Applications for non-molestation orders can be made either as stand-alone applications (ie the applicant wants only an injunction), or as part of other family proceedings, which s 62(2) of the Family Law Act 1996 defines as proceedings under:

- Parts II and IV of the Family Law Act 1996;

- the Matrimonial Causes Act 1973;

- the Adoption Act 1976;

- the Domestic Proceedings and Magistrates' Court Act 1978;

- Part III of the Matrimonial and Family Proceedings Act 1984;

- Parts I, II and IV of the Children Act 1989 and s 44 of that Act (where the court has made an emergency protection order with an exclusion requirement);

- s 30 of the Human Fertilisation and Embryology Act 1990;

- the Adoption and Children Act 2002; and

- Schs 5–7 of the Civil Partnership Act 2004,

together with any proceedings in relation to children under the inherent jurisdiction of the High Court.

Own motion non-molestation orders

6.14 The court can also make a non-molestation order of its own volition (ie without a formal application being made) in existing family proceedings where the intended respondent to the injunction is a party to those proceedings, and the court considers that an order ought to be made for the benefit of another party to the proceedings or a relevant child. Although the court can make such an order, it is at the court's discretion, and it will be wary about exercising such power. Courts will prefer legal representatives to take the steps they consider appropriate to obtain protection for their client. The provision does mean that if, for example, during the course of a Children Act 1989 matter, the parties became agitated and threats were made, the court could take immediate steps to try to protect the threatened person and children. Similarly, if a litigant in person required urgent protection but genuinely did not know how to make an application, the court could step in to ensure that protection was provided. However, there is a great deal of scope for potential problems. The court list is such that the court has not got the time to deal with a matter as a solicitor would to ensure that full and accurate information is provided. There will be concerns as to seeming already to have decided a matter because it was the court that identified the problem and made an order accordingly. In short, this is to be considered as fall-back protection, not the first line of defence.

6.15 If the application for a non-molestation order under the Family Law Act 1996 is made on the basis that the applicant and respondent were once engaged to be married, or had agreed to register as civil partners, the engagement or agreement to register must not have terminated more than 3 years before the application is made (s 33(2)). The 3 years starts to run on the day the engagement/agreement is terminated. If more than 3 years has elapsed, unless one of the other criteria for 'associated persons' applies (such as having fathered/given birth to the other's child), the applicant would not be able to use the Family Law Act 1996 but would need to seek assistance under other legislation.

PROCEDURE FOR 'ON NOTICE' APPLICATIONS FOR NON-MOLESTATION ORDERS

6.16 The rules governing the procedure are to be found in r 3.8 of the Family Proceedings Rules 1991[4] onwards. Whether the application is a stand-alone one, or made within existing family proceedings, the application must be made on Form FL401 (which deals with both non-molestation orders and occupation orders). It is a lengthy form, with accompanying notes, which should achieve the purpose of ensuring that the applicant is clear in her own mind as to what she is seeking from the court and setting out clearly for the court the basis on which its jurisdiction to act is founded.

6.17 The form begins with normal requests for information, such as the applicant's address. There may be circumstances in which the applicant is seeking a non-molestation order but does not want the respondent to know where she lives (for example, if he is sending threatening texts, or swearing at her in the street). The notes to the form confirm that such information can be left out of the form but the applicant would have to complete Form C8 (confidential address). This is essentially an application to the court to withhold the address from the respondent. Reasons as for it being withheld must be given. The reason may seem obvious ('In view of the threatening texts he has sent, I am frightened that if he knows where I live, he will come round and assault me') but it still needs to be stated. The court can only act on the information it has before it. If there is information that the court needs to know which is not expressly set out, the legal representatives will be doing their clients a disservice.

6.18 The form also requires the respondent's name, address and date of birth (if known). There may be occasions where the respondent's address is not known. In those circumstances, the applicant will need to consider how the respondent is to be served with the application and any court orders. It may be known that the respondent, for example, visits his mother once a week on a Friday and the process server may be able to serve him there. If, however, there is no address and no knowledge of his whereabouts, there will be difficulties in both service and enforcement. Orders of this nature are not going to be effective until the respondent knows that such an order has been made and what it is he must not do; and to achieve that, he needs to be served. Service will be dealt with below (including when it might be dispensed with) but the basic proposition is that the respondent must be served personally; and thus, his address or location must be known. Before starting any court proceedings, practitioners should consider what they want to achieve, and how they are

---

[4] SI 1991/1247.

going to achieve it. If basic information such as the address of the respondent is not known, it is doubtful whether protection for the applicant can be achieved.

6.19 The form asks whether a non-molestation order and/or an occupation order is sought, and whether the application is to be dealt with initially without notice being given to the respondent. The Family Proceedings Rules 1991 refer to these applications as ex parte applications (although Latin tags are now frowned on in civil proceedings). If the matter is to be dealt with (at least to start with) without the respondent's knowledge, the reasons must be set out in the witness statement which accompanies the application form. The granting of an injunction against someone before he has had an opportunity to give his side of the story is a serious step, and as such the court must have written reasons why such an order should be made. Again, the reason may be obvious ('In view of the incidents set out above, I am frightened that if he knows I am going to make this application, he will get very angry and if I do not already have the protection of a court order, he may assault me before the hearing on whether an order should be granted'), but it still has to be given.

6.20 The form then asks the applicant (if she is applying for a non-molestation order) to state briefly the order that she wants. This may be an order such as forbidding the respondent from using or threatening violence towards the applicant and/or specified children (with their full names and dates of birth being given), and/or intimidating, harassing or pestering her. The desired order may include (as well as the general wording above) specific examples of what the respondent must not do, such as contacting the applicant except through solicitors or sending text messages. The respondent must be clear about what it is he must not do. If there are specific matters that the applicant wishes the court to proscribe, these must be set out. This becomes all the more important when dealing with enforcement, in view of the new regime effective from 1 July 2007.

6.21 The applicant will need to advise whether an interpreter is required. If the applicant does not speak English, it is for the applicant to arrange her own interpreter. If, due to a disability, an interpreter or other facilities (eg hearing loop) are needed, this should be stated in the form so that the court can make the appropriate arrangements. The applicant must give details of any children living with, or likely to live with, the applicant or respondent, together with details of any other person living in the same household as the applicant or respondent, together with reasons as to why that person lives there. The court needs to know about all people who are likely to be affected by any order made, hence the need to provide this information. The applicant must advise the court of any current family proceedings or orders which are in force involving the applicant and respondent. It is clearly sensible that the court is aware of these when deciding what order should now be made. The application has to be supported by a statement signed by the applicant and sworn to be true, ie there must be direct sworn evidence from the applicant of the matters on which she wishes to rely.

6.22 Although reference is made above to making ex parte applications, the basic procedure envisages that such applications are made on notice to the respondent. On issue the court will fix a date a sufficient time in the future to enable the applicant to arrange for service on the respondent, who will then have the opportunity of attending court on the date fixed to oppose or otherwise deal with the application made. Service of such applications should be made by personal service on the respondent and service must occur not less than 2 days before the application is due to be heard. The 2 days excludes Saturdays, Sundays, Christmas Day, Good Friday and Bank Holidays. The applicant will need to provide the court with a time estimate for the hearing on notice (known as the 'return day'). The practice at different courts varies. Some will give a return day and allow (for example) 30 minutes when the court will essentially give directions as to how the matter may proceed (and may grant an interim injunction pending a fully contested hearing). Others may allow (for example) a 2-hour time estimate when they would expect to deal with the issues in full. Whatever the court's practice, the applicant should prepare the case so as to be able to satisfy the court as to the granting of either an interim or a final injunction.

6.23 As well as the application notice and affidavit, a draft order should be prepared and provided to the judge. The previous County Court Rules (of 1981) still apply to this type of application (as opposed to the Civil Procedure Rules 1998 which now govern civil matters and certain aspects of family proceedings). CCR Ord 13, r 6(6) confirms the necessity of preparing a draft order except in cases of urgency. On a normal return date, there is no excuse for not providing a draft order. If a draft order is not prepared, the applicant will be open to criticism from the judge and may believe that her legal representative has not prepared her case as well as he should have done. Preparing the draft order is also ultimately in the lawyer's own interests. The legal adviser will have thought about the wording and why it is required and thus be able to explain and seek to justify the proposed wording to the judge. If these steps are not taken, the applicant may be caught out when asked for appropriate justification, and thus certain wording may not appear in the final order because of insufficient preparation.

6.24 Even in straightforward and clear cases where standard orders are sought, it is advisable for the legal representative to prepare the draft. If the judge does not subsequently amend the order, it can simply be sealed and provided to the applicant for service. If during the course of the hearing, it becomes clear that amendment is required, it is generally easier to amend something previously prepared than to start with an entirely blank sheet totally afresh.

PROCEDURE FOR WITHOUT NOTICE APPLICATIONS

6.25 As discussed above, in cases of urgency, an applicant may make an application on an ex parte basis. Section 45 of the Family Law Act 1996 recognises that in cases of 'significant harm' (which is a wider definition than violence or threats of violence) a person may need immediate protection. Section 45 states that the court may, in any case where it considers it just and convenient to do so, make an occupation order or non-molestation order even though the respondent has not been given such notice of the proceedings as would otherwise be required by the rules. When considering whether to make an application ex parte, the court must have regard to all the circumstances, including:

(1) any risk of significant harm to the applicant or a relevant child attributable to the conduct of the respondent if the order is not made immediately;

(2) whether it is likely that the applicant will be deterred or prevented from pursuing the application if an order is not made immediately; and

(3) whether there is reason to believe that the respondent is aware of the proceedings but is deliberately evading service and that the applicant or a relevant child will be seriously prejudiced by the delay involved:
     (a) where the court is a magistrates' court, in effecting service of proceedings; or
     (b) in any other case, effecting substituted service.

6.26 An ex parte application may also be justified where the normal return date for an 'on notice' application is too far away (often because the court lists are very busy) but the matter is not serious enough to justify an injunction being granted on a without notice basis. For these cases, an ex parte application can still be made but with the intention of obtaining a more urgent return date. This type of situation is more likely to occur with applications for occupation orders (for example, someone could stay with family or friends for a few days pending the granting of an order allowing them to return and occupy, but having to do that for some weeks would cause problems; however, the matter itself is not serious enough to justify a without notice order). Without a direction from a judge confirming to the court staff that the matter needs to be listed urgently, the court staff will list the case in the usual way, which could be some weeks ahead. Under such circumstances, the application should be prepared in the usual 'on notice' way (but including in the supporting affidavit all the reasons why the matter needs to be dealt with in early course) and when the application is issued for an injunction, if the date the court offers for the return date is too far ahead, a request should be made to go ex parte before the judge. The court will need justification as to why some earlier date needs to be given.

6.27 When considering the information to be put in the affidavit in support of the ex parte application, applicants (and thus their legal representatives) must disclose all relevant information. In *Re S (A child) (Ex Parte Orders)*[5] it was said:

> 'Those who seek relief ex parte are under a duty to make the fullest and most candid and frank disclosure of all the relevant circumstances known to them. This duty is not confined to the material facts: it extends to all relevant matters, whether of fact or of law.'

In the absence of relevant information, the request for an injunction may be refused, or, if granted, may be discharged at a subsequent hearing and adverse costs orders made. An application for a non-molestation injunction or an occupation order will not generally require an undertaking in damages to be given. *Practice Direction (Injunction: Undertaking as to Damages)*[6] states:

> 'While such undertakings may be required when an interlocutory injunction is granted in an action under the general jurisdiction of the county courts, they are unnecessary and inappropriate in High Court and county court matrimonial and children's matters concerning personal conduct.'

Undertakings as to damages may be required when dealing with property matters.

6.28 If time pressures or other factors meant that the relevant information on urgency was not included within the supporting affidavit, the applicant may have to give evidence briefly on the point before the judge, otherwise the applicant may have to return at a later date with a re-sworn affidavit containing the additional required information. If done by way of additional sworn oral evidence (eg because there is insufficient time to have the affidavit amended and re-sworn), the reasons would need to be stated on the order, perhaps as a recital, confirming that the applicant gave sworn evidence and setting out the additional facts. The respondent must have in writing exactly what the case against him is, and this includes the reasons why the matter is so urgent.

6.29 In other cases, the court staff may be able to give an urgent date (eg because some other hearing is no longer proceeding) but the applicant must still attend before the judge to seek an abridgement of time for service as 2 requisite days' notice cannot be given because of the proximity of the return date itself, possible difficulties in tracing for service or other similar reasons. Again the applicant must be in a position to justify the request for abridging time for service. The rules are there for a reason and the aim is to give a respondent an opportunity to organise his response, seek legal advice, make childcare arrangements, arrange for time off work, etc.

---

5   [2001] 1 FLR 308.
6   [1974] 1 WLR 576.

6.30 The 'true' ex parte cases are those where the order is needed as a matter of urgency and there are proper reasons for not giving any warning of the application before it is made. The most common reason for wishing to obtain an order without notice is where the applicant is afraid that telling the respondent beforehand is likely to provoke the very behaviour which needs to be controlled and at a time when the applicant has no court protection. It is worth repeating that if an ex parte order is sought, the reason for doing so must be included in the supporting affidavit. It may seem that the reason is obvious when considering the rest of the information given in the affidavit, but the reason must be set out plainly, not by implication. If the reason is not given, the judge may send the applicant out to add an appropriate sentence to the affidavit and get it re-sworn, or may occasionally be prepared to hear formal evidence from the applicant on the point and add that information as a recital to the order. The judge may be reluctant to do so with a represented party. This latter step is more likely to occur with an unrepresented party who is unlikely to know all the rules but who clearly needs the court's protection.

6.31 A draft order should be prepared as part of the court papers, even in cases of urgency, for the same reasons as were given for on notice applications. The procedure for ex parte applications is to prepare (i) the application, (ii) the affidavit in support and (iii) a draft order, and to attend court to issue the application and ask to go before a judge. Before attending court to issue, it is prudent to telephone to check that a judge is available. Not all courts have judges every day and, even if they do, they may not be able for proper reason to deal with the case. It may still be desirable to issue in the local court, even though the hearing will take place elsewhere, or it may be preferable to issue in that other court to begin with. Telephoning the court first gives the court an approximate indication when the legal representative will appear and allows it to warn the judge of the incoming urgent matter, thus helping to ensure that matters proceed more smoothly.

6.32 If at all possible, the client should attend the hearing. The judge may seek clarification of matters and may need to hear further evidence. The affidavit may need to be amended and re-sworn. Without the client, the options are limited. If she cannot attend and has a good reason for this, the court may still be prepared to grant the order in her absence based on the evidence in the affidavit. However, there are obvious risks in the client not attending.

6.33 Although the rules require a notice of application, affidavit in support, draft order, etc, in extremely urgent cases, it is possible to attend before a judge without any documentation at all, the client giving oral evidence and there being an undertaking to file all the necessary paperwork within a specified time. This type of case is extremely rare. There will be few applications for non-molestation injunctions or occupation orders where an injunction is required so urgently that there is literally no time to prepare the necessary papers. However, if this occurs, even if no formal undertaking regarding the filing of all necessary paperwork is given, *Re S (A Child) (Ex Parte Orders)*[7] confirms that an applicant (and her legal advisers) have a duty to issue the papers and to serve the respondent with the application, sworn supporting evidence, court order and return date as soon as practicable.

6.34   Where a court makes an ex parte order, the respondent must be given an opportunity to make representations regarding the order 'as soon as just and convenient at a full hearing'. This is why a second hearing ('a return date') will generally be given by the court staff when dealing with an ex parte application. Some courts do not give a second date immediately – they make it clear within the order that the respondent has the right to request the court to list the matter for a hearing if he so wishes, and then leave it to him to ask for a hearing to be listed. This practice was approved by the Court of Appeal in *Re F*.[8] Injunctions are serious matters and, as such, any return date after an ex parte hearing should be listed promptly in the initial instance.

WHICH COURT, UNDERAGE PARTIES AND MENTAL CAPACITY

6.35   The application can be issued in any county court which is a divorce county court, family hearing centre or a care centre. Lambeth, Shoreditch and Woolwich County Courts also have jurisdiction, as does the Principal Registry. Not all magistrates' courts have jurisdiction. The family proceedings court in the magistrates' court does have jurisdiction. Applicants under 18 years of age must make the application in the High Court and applicants under 16 must seek leave of the High Court under s 43 of the Family Law Act 1996. There is no specific form of application. The usual application is made and is treated as an application for leave.

6.36   It should be noted that if an applicant wishes to take proceedings against a respondent who is under the age of 18, that respondent will require a litigation friend (here called a guardian ad litem) (CCR Ord 10; Family Proceedings Rules 1991, r 9). The power in r 9.2A to dispense with a litigation friend does not apply in Family Law Act proceedings (as confirmed by r 9.1(3)). The obvious difficulties as to what steps a court might wish (or be able) to take in relation to a defaulting minor will also need to be considered. There are statutory limitations on sending persons under the age of 18 to prison and such persons are unlikely to have assets which can be subjected to sequestration, nor have the means to pay a fine.[9] The court will be reluctant to make an order which cannot properly be enforced.

---

[7]   [2001] 1 FLR 308.
[8]   [2005] EWCA Civ 499.
[9]   See *Wookey v Wookey (including Re S (A Minor))* [1991] Fam 121.

6.37 However, in *H v H*[10] the Court of Appeal confirmed that a power of arrest on an occupation order (and also on a non-molestation injunction) could be made against a person under 18. The Court held that a power of arrest was not solely a precursor to committing a person for contempt. It also served the function of removing that person from the place where he was not supposed to be. In *Manchester City Council v Lee*[11] albeit under the anti-social behaviour legislation of the Housing Act 1996, a challenge was mounted as to whether such an injunction could be granted against a minor. The Court of Appeal, being able to deal with the case on other grounds, declined to decide the issue.

6.38 A respondent who is a patient within the meaning of the Mental Health Act 1983 must also have a litigation friend. The court should not grant an injunction against someone who does not have the capacity to understand what it is he is not supposed to do and who lacks the ability to control his behaviour. The fact that the respondent has learning difficulties or would be regarded as a 'vulnerable adult' does not mean that imprisonment cannot be imposed if he breaches an order, even when he is represented in the court proceedings by a litigation friend.[12] In the case of mental incapacity, the question is whether the respondent understands the proceedings and the nature and requirements of the order sought. Depending on the circumstances, an injunction may not be the appropriate course of action for someone to obtain protection from respondents with such difficulties or those under the age of 18.

CONDITIONS TO BE SATISFIED BEFORE INJUNCTION GRANTED

6.39 The phraseology of s 42(5) of the Family Law Act 1996 makes it clear that the granting of an injunction is a matter of discretion for the court. The court does not have to grant an injunction if it does not consider it appropriate.

6.40 Section 42(5) states:

'In deciding whether to exercise its powers under this section and, if so, in what manner, the Court shall have regard to all the circumstances including the need to secure the health safety and well being –

(a) of the applicant or in a case falling within subsection (2) (b), the person for whose benefit the order would be made; and
(b) of any relevant child.'

6.41 The court will first need to be satisfied there has been behaviour which amounts to molestation.[13] In *C v C*,[14] the court held that the wife's behaviour in

---

[10]   [2001] 1 FLR 641.
[11]   [2004] 1 WLR 349.
[12]   *Pluck v Pluck* [2007] EWCA Civ 1250; *Gull v Gull* [2007] EWCA Civ 900.
[13]   See **6.2** et seq above.
[14]   [1998] 1 FLR 554.

supplying information to a newspaper about the husband's behaviour during their marriage was not molestation for the purposes of s 42 of the Family Law Act 1996, which did not cover an invasion of privacy per se but which required deliberate conduct that clearly harassed and affected the other party to such a degree that the intervention of the court was called for. The court did not consider that the wife's behaviour did so and declined to continue an interim injunction previously granted. The court was influenced by the fact that s 42 falls within provisions relating to (essentially) domestic violence and that molestation would need to be considered in that light.

6.42   As outlined in *Horner v Horner*,[15] the court needs to be satisfied that judicial intervention is required before it will grant the injunction. The standard of proof (for the evidence of actual molestation, the need for protection of the applicant and the need for judicial intervention) is the usual civil standard, ie that something is more likely than not.

OCCUPATION ORDERS

6.43   Occupation orders are governed by ss 30–42 of the Family Law Act 1996. Which section is applicable will depend on the nature of the relationship between the applicant and the respondent and how the applicant comes to be in occupation of the relevant property.

6.44   Section 30 applies where one spouse or civil partner (ie not cohabitant) is entitled to occupy a dwelling house by virtue of a beneficial estate, interest, contract or by some enactment (hereinafter referred to as 'usual occupation rights'), but the other spouse or civil partner has no such rights. Section 30 gives the latter 'home rights' which are rights, if in occupation, not to be evicted or excluded from the dwelling house or any part of it except by order of the court, and, if not in occupation, a right to return with the leave of the court. The most likely scenario for this type of situation is where one person within the couple is named as the sole tenant, or is the sole owner of the property where they both live. Without these 'home rights', the spouse or civil partner with usual occupation rights would be able to exclude the other.

6.45   In order to prevent other legal difficulties arising, s 30 expressly confirms that if the spouse or civil partner with home rights pays the rent or mortgage or other outgoings affecting the dwelling house, that counts as if it were payment by the spouse or civil partner with usual occupation rights. In addition, if a tenant has to occupy premises as his only or principal home, occupation as the only or principal home by the spouse/civil partner with home rights will be treated as if it were occupation by the tenant as his only or principal home. This means that neither party has to worry about possible breaches of the mortgage or tenancy agreement, and thus loss of the home.

---

[15]   [1982] Fam 90 and see **6.4**.

6.46 Section 30 applies only to a dwelling house which was, or was intended to be, a matrimonial or civil partnership home. If it were not so intended (eg a property bought after the parties had separated), s 30 will not apply. 'Dwelling house' includes for the purposes of this section a caravan or houseboat or other structure occupied as a dwelling. The home rights last only as long as the marriage or civil partnership subsists (except to the extent that the court may order otherwise under s 33(5)) and provided the spouse/civil partner with usual occupation rights has himself the right to occupy. If a landlord can properly regain possession from the spouse/civil partner with usual occupation rights, he can also regain it from the spouse/civil partner with home rights. When advising a client about an occupation order, it is important to remember that a tenancy can be ended by the sole tenant (or, if a joint tenancy, by one of the joint tenants) surrendering the tenancy or serving a notice to quit. An injunction to prevent such action may therefore be required.

6.47 If the applicant has home rights and the respondent is the other spouse or civil partner, the court may (whilst the marriage or civil partnership still subsists) order that the home rights do not end on the death of the other spouse or civil partner or on the termination of the marriage or civil partnership (otherwise than by death). To ensure complete protection (eg in case the respondent tries to sell the property), the applicant should register her home rights as a charge with the Land Registry or under the Land Charges Act (see s 31 of the Family Law Act 1996).

POTENTIAL APPLICANTS AND RESPONDENTS

6.48 Section 33 sets out what the court may do for persons with the usual occupation rights, or home rights, and where the dwelling house is or at any time has been the home of the person entitled and of any other person with whom he is associated, or was intended by both those persons to be their home. The phrasing of s 33 is wide. The requirements on who can apply can cover spouses, civil partners, cohabitants, parents and adult offspring. In short, it covers anyone who has a right to occupy, who wishes to make an application against someone who is associated with that person and the application is in respect of a property which was or was intended to be their home. In relation to engaged couples or couples who agree to become civil partners, the application has to be made within 3 years of the termination of the engagement or agreement, pursuant to s 33(2) and (2A).

6.49 Under s 33(1), a person with either home rights or rights to occupy by virtue of a beneficial estate, interest, contract or under an enactment can apply for an order under s 33(3) to:

(a) enforce the applicant's entitlement to remain in occupation against the respondent;

(b)   require the respondent to permit the applicant to enter and remain in the dwelling house or part of the dwelling house;

(c)   regulate the occupation of the dwelling house by either or both parties;

(d)   prohibit, suspend or restrict the exercise by a respondent with usual occupation rights of the right to occupy;

(e)   restrict or terminate the home rights of a respondent where the applicant is a spouse or civil partner with usual occupation rights;

(f)   require the respondent to leave the dwelling house or part of the dwelling house;

(g)   exclude the respondent from a defined area in which the dwelling house is included (provided that the dwelling house is or at any time was the home of the person with usual occupation rights and of another person with whom the first person was associated, or was at any time intended by the first and the associated person to be their home).

6.50   If a person does not come within s 33, consideration must be given to ss 35–38 if an occupation order is required. Section 35 deals with situations where there are former spouses or former civil partners with no right to occupy (eg who had home rights which terminated under s 30(8) when the marriage or civil partnership ended) and the other former spouse or civil partner is entitled to occupy the dwelling house because he has the usual occupation rights. The dwelling house must have been the matrimonial or civil partnership home or have been intended to be such a home. The former spouse or civil partner without occupation rights may make application to the court for an occupation order.

6.51   Similarly, s 36 applies where one cohabitant or former cohabitant has the usual occupation rights but the other cohabitant does not. Again, the dwelling house must be the home in which they cohabited or it should be a home in which they at any time intended to cohabit.

6.52   Section 37 applies where a spouse/former spouse/civil partner/former civil partner and the other spouse/former spouse/civil partner/former civil partner occupy a dwelling house which is or was their matrimonial/civil partnership home but neither has the usual occupation rights. Section 38 applies where a cohabitant or former cohabitant and the other cohabitant or former cohabitant occupy a dwelling house which is the home in which they are or were cohabiting but neither has the usual occupation rights. There will clearly only be limited circumstances in which either of these sections applies (eg where the parties occupy premises under a bare licence).

PROCEDURE FOR 'ON NOTICE' APPLICATIONS

6.53 The procedure for 'on notice' applications is the same as set out above under non-molestation injunctions, and should be followed. As before, the application can be made as a free-standing application or within existing family proceedings.

Requirements for occupation orders

6.54 Form FL401 should be completed. Information relating to occupation orders as required by the form is dealt with below.

Details of property

6.55 Form FL401 requires the address of the property to which the application relates to be provided. It also asks whether the property is occupied by the applicant or the respondent, now or in the past, or whether it was intended to be occupied by the applicant or the respondent. The applicant must then state whether she is entitled to occupy the dwelling house and, if so, why. The applicant must also state whether the respondent is entitled to occupy and, if so, why. There are a number of questions designed to establish within which section of the Family Law Act 1996 the applicant falls. If she has matrimonial home rights, the applicant must state whether the title is registered or unregistered. A draft of the order sought must also be set out.

Maintenance of property

6.56 Paragraph 7 of Form FL401 requires that the applicant advise the court as to whether an order is needed that the respondent should deal with the repair and maintenance of the dwelling house, pay the rent, mortgage or other charges on the house, make payments to the applicant in respect of accommodation, grant either party the use of furniture or other contents (eg if a person needs to use a computer for his work) or require the other party to take reasonable steps to keep the dwelling house and any of the furniture or other contents secure. These are rights granted under s 40 of the Family Law Act 1996, which are limited in that they make no provision for enforcing these payments if the respondent neglects to make them, despite being ordered to do so.

Ownership and legal interest in property

6.57 In paragraph 8 of Form FL401, the applicant must advise whether the home is subject to mortgage or is rented, and in either case specify the name and address of the mortgagee or landlord. The landlord or mortgagee must be served with the application (see Family Proceedings Rules, r 3.8(11) and Family Proceedings Courts (Matrimonial Proceedings etc) Rules 1991,[16] r 3A(11)), by

---

[16]   SI 1991/1991.

first-class post and with Form FL416 advising it of its rights to make representations in writing or at any hearing.

Choice of venue

6.58 It should be noted that, as with non-molestation injunctions, occupation orders can only be obtained in divorce county courts, family hearing centres and care centres, or the family proceedings courts (ie not all county courts or magistrates' courts have jurisdiction). This may be important where a person has made an application for both a non-molestation injunction and an occupation order to the county court, which then considers transferring the matter to the magistrates' court. This may occur because of the new enforcement procedure, as breach of a non-molestation injunction granted from 1 July 2007 will now usually be dealt with in the magistrates' court. If one element of an order has to go to the magistrates' court, it may be sensible to transfer the whole matter to the magistrates' court. If there is a dispute as to a party's entitlement to occupy under the usual occupation rights, the magistrates' court does not have jurisdiction, unless it is unnecessary to determine the question in order to deal with the application or make the order.[17]

6.59 Before the change in enforcement procedure, only a county court could enforce a county court order. If the matter had been transferred to the magistrates' court, it would not have been able to enforce any order made by the county court. However, as breach of an order made from 1 July 2007 is now a criminal offence under s 42A of the Family Law Act 1996, breaches of non-molestation injunctions will generally ultimately end up in the magistrates' court. Breach of an occupation order will still fall to be dealt with as a contempt of court and thus as a civil matter, and if the matter is transferred in its entirety to the family proceedings court, that court will not be able to enforce the county court occupation order. As a consequence of this, orders obtained in the county court may now be deliberately phrased to cease to be effective once an order made in the magistrates' court has been served. This allows the matter to be transferred, limits the life of the county court order (and thus reduces the time available for its breach which would then require county court enforcement), allows a magistrates' court order to be made, which that court can then enforce if necessary, but still provide uninterrupted cover to the applicant.

CONDITIONS TO BE SATISFIED BEFORE INJUNCTION GRANTED

6.60 When considering what order to make under s 33, the court must look at *all* the circumstances (including but not limited to):

---

[17] See s 59 of the Family Law Act 1996.

(1)　the housing needs and housing resources of each of the parties and any relevant child;

(2)　the financial resources of each of the parties;

(3)　the likely effect of any order, or of any decision by the court not to exercise its powers under s 33(3) on the health, safety or well-being of the parties and of any relevant child; and

(4)　the conduct of each of the parties in relation to each other and otherwise.

6.61　This enables the court to consider all relevant factors and make the most appropriate decision on the facts. If it appears to the court that the applicant or any relevant child is likely to suffer significant harm which is attributable to the conduct of the respondent if an occupation order is not made, the court *must* make an order unless it appears that the respondent or any relevant child is likely to suffer significant harm if the order is made and the harm likely to be suffered by either the respondent or the relevant child is as great as or greater than the harm likely to be suffered by the applicant or their relevant child (attributable to the conduct of the respondent) if the order is not made. Basically, the court must balance the interests of both parties and any relevant children carefully. If the balance of harm is equal, the housing needs, resources, conduct, etc may well be the decisive factor. The court will consider s 33(7) factors first, and if that does not determine the issue, it will consider s 33(6). Other factors are considered in addition for applications under the other relevant sections, including how much time has elapsed since the parties lived together or dissolved their marriage/civil partnership, whether they are seeking property adjustment orders, how long their cohabitation lasted, the nature of their relationship and the level of commitment involved. The relevant sections should be studied to ensure that all relevant information is provided to the court.

6.62　Occupation orders cannot be made after the death of either of the parties and any order made will cease to have effect on the death of one of the parties, unless a specific order to extend the time has been made pursuant to s 33(5). This subsection relates to a situation where the applicant has home rights and the respondent is the other spouse or civil partner. Under such circumstances, the court can order that the rights do not terminate on the death of the other spouse or civil partner, or the termination of the marriage or civil partnership. The court can exercise its powers in any case where it considers that, in all the circumstances, it is just and reasonable to do so.

PROCEDURE FOR WITHOUT NOTICE APPLICATIONS

6.63　The procedure for non-molestation injunctions set out above should be followed in relation to without notice applications for occupation orders. Non-molestation injunctions and occupation orders are often issued together (for obvious reasons). Ex parte occupation orders, by themselves, are unlikely to be granted, but there may be situations where a hearing is required at short notice, in which case an ex parte application should be made to request an early hearing date and abridge time for service. To grant an occupation order on an ex parte basis is a very draconian measure. The respondent would have had no opportunity to put his side of the case, and no opportunity to find alternative accommodation. Granting a non-molestation injunction on an ex parte basis is different because it essentially only tells a respondent not to do something which he should not be doing in any event and thus is not an infringement of his legal rights, whereas an occupation order is likely to be a severe restriction of his normal rights. As stated above, an applicant may wish to make an ex parte application where the situation is not urgent enough to justify making an order immediately but the usual 'on notice' application would be too far away. The applicant may be able to stay with friends for a few days but not for a few weeks. The application is thus made ex parte so that the court can be requested to list the matter more urgently. The court may be prepared to grant an ex parte order where the applicant has said on oath that the respondent has already vacated the property and, for example, confirms that he is already living elsewhere (so that the court is not, essentially, being asked to make someone homeless). Such an order will generally specifically state within it that 'the respondent having already vacated the property will be forbidden from returning'. Whether the court will be prepared to make such an order will depend on the apparent cogency of the evidence put before it and the harm the court is trying to prevent.

UNDERTAKINGS

6.64 Section 46 of the Family Law Act 1996 is the statutory recognition of the fact that the court may accept an undertaking by a party in place of the court making a formal order. This can apply to both occupation orders and non-molestation orders. Powers of arrest can now only be attached to occupation orders and not to non-molestation orders. A power of arrest cannot be attached to an undertaking, and s 46 specifically states that no undertaking can be accepted where the court would otherwise have attached a power of arrest. The reason for the specific reference to a power of arrest is due to the terms of s 47, under which the court 'shall' attach a power of arrest when it makes an occupation order if it appears to the court that the respondent has used or threatened violence against the applicant or a relevant child. The court can only decide not to attach a power of arrest if it is satisfied that in all the circumstances of the case, the applicant or child will be adequately protected without such a power of arrest.

6.65 The position with regard to undertakings and powers of arrest used to be the same for both occupation orders and non-molestation injunctions. However, the Domestic Violence, Crime and Victims Act 2004 brought in new enforcement provisions for both undertakings and non-molestation orders. As will be seen below, breaches of non-molestation injunctions are now generally enforced through the criminal law and no power of arrest can be attached to a non-molestation injunction. Section 46(3A) states that a court shall not accept an undertaking in proceedings for a non-molestation order in cases where it appears that the respondent has used or threatened violence against the applicant or a relevant child and, for the protection of the applicant or child, it is necessary to make a non-molestation order so that any breach may be punishable under s 42A.

6.66 An undertaking is now enforceable as if it were an order of the court (made in the same terms as the undertaking), with the ultimate penalty for a breach being committal to prison. This means that for injunction orders made from 1 July 2007, an applicant may now apply for a warrant for arrest for breach of an undertaking. Before the recent amendment brought in by the Domestic Violence, Crime and Victims Act 2004 to s 46(4), an applicant could only issue an application to commit for breach of an undertaking, and there was no power to arrest the respondent or have him held in custody pending the determination of the final hearing.

TERMS OF THE ORDER

Non-molestation orders

6.67 Section 42(6) provides that a non-molestation order may be expressed so as to refer to molestation in general, to particular acts of molestation, or to both.

6.68 However, as briefly discussed above at **6.6**, it appears that there may be some difficulties in the criminal system with the meaning of 'molest'. An order may prohibit the respondent from 'molesting' the applicant. It may also prohibit specific acts, such as contacting the applicant except through solicitors, or prohibiting the sending of text messages, etc. Although the new enforcement system has only been effective since 1 July 2007, stories have emerged of the police being reluctant to take action and, rather than taking the matter through the criminal courts, they have instead issued cautions. It has also been said that the Criminal Prosecution Service (CPS) has been uncertain as to the actual meaning of 'molest' and how to prove it, and thus has not wished to prosecute. Whilst these tales may be apocryphal, it may be best to ensure that there are paragraphs within the non-molestation order which prohibit specific known activities that have occurred, so that if the respondent repeats those activities, such as texting the applicant or contacting her except through solicitors, the police and CPS have a direct and clear order on which they can take action. Equally, as stated in *Manchester City Council v Lee* (see **6.6**), it must be clearly set out for the respondent what it is he is forbidden from doing.

6.69 It may seem like trite law, but any order which is made must be proportionate to the acts complained of. Mummery LJ in *Manchester City Council v Lee* reminded us that:

'Careful consideration needs to be given by the court in each case to the scope of the injunction which is justified by the evidence. In the exercise of its discretion the court must ensure that the injunction granted is framed in terms appropriate and proportionate to the facts of the case.'

Whilst this was an anti-social behaviour injunction case, the principle still applies.

6.70 Occupation orders made under s 33 'may declare' that the applicant has usual occupation rights, or that she has home rights. If the application is made under s 35 (one former spouse or former civil partner with no existing right to occupy) or s 36 (one cohabitant or former cohabitant with no existing right to occupy), the order must contain a provision that if the applicant is in occupation, she has the right not to be excluded from the property or any part of it by the respondent for the period specified by the order, and a provision prohibiting the respondent from evicting or excluding the applicant during that period. If the applicant is not in occupation, the order must contain a provision giving the applicant the right to enter and occupy the property for the period specified in the order and requiring the respondent to permit the exercise of that right.

DURATION OF ORDERS

6.71 A non-molestation order may be made for a specific period of time (eg until 12 noon on 31 December 2008) or until further order. As many non-molestation orders are made on an ex parte basis, a further hearing will usually be ordered to give the respondent the opportunity to make representations about the order. Some courts have taken the view that provided the order states clearly that the respondent may apply on, for example, 2 days' notice for a hearing at which he can make representations, that is sufficient. Other courts list the matter for a further hearing regardless. As the enforcement will now generally be by criminal proceedings, and a further order will be required, many county courts may proceed to transfer the matter to the magistrates' court for the 'on notice' hearing. Historically, an order made in the county court could not be enforced in the magistrates' court and vice versa. Equally, the magistrates' court would not be able to vary an order made by the county court. To avoid possible problems, many county courts are adopting a version of an order whereby the county court order (made ex parte) will only remain effective until such time as the magistrates' court order is served, but is thereafter discharged. As the order remains in force until service of the new order, there is no gap in the protection given to the applicant, but the way is clear for the magistrates' court to make such order as it considers fit at the full hearing. Such an order may therefore state that it is effective for, for example, 6 weeks or until service of any order made by the family proceedings court which varies, discharges or otherwise replaces the order made by the county court.

6.72 The length of time for which an occupation order may be made varies according to which section of the Family Law Act 1996 governed the grant of the order. If it is made under s 33 (where the applicant has usual occupation rights or home rights – see **6.44**), s 33(10) provides that the order may be made for a specified period, until the occurrence of a specified event or until further order. If the order is made under s 35 (where the applicant is a former spouse/civil partner who has no existing rights to occupy the property), it can only be made for up to 6 months in the initial instance, but may be extended on one or more occasions for a further maximum of 6 months on each occasion (s 35(10)). If the order is made under s 36 (a co-habitant or former co-habitant with no existing right to occupy), it can only be made for a period of up to 6 months, with a power to extend for a further specified period of up to 6 months, but only one such extension is permitted. If the order is made under s 37 (where neither spouse/civil partner has rights to occupy, the rule is the same as for s 35). If the order is made under s 38 (neither cohabitant or former cohabitant is entitled to occupy the property), the rule is the same as for s 36.

6.73 When calculating time-limits, time starts to run from the making of the initial order, even if made ex parte (s 45(4)), and for the purposes of ss 36 and 38, the initial ex parte order and the 'on notice' order count as one order (so that it is clear that the making of those two orders does not count as the first order and then the one permitted extension).

ENFORCEMENT OF THE ORDER

6.74 Section 42A introduced a new section regarding enforcement of non-molestation injunctions. Under the new section 'a person who without reasonable excuse does anything that he is prohibited from doing by a non-molestation order is guilty of an offence'. The section makes it clear that a person cannot be guilty of an offence in respect of his conduct until such time as he becomes aware of the existence of an order, and then does something which is prohibited. The phrasing of the section means that the respondent does not actually need to know the exact wording of the order, nor does he necessarily need to have been personally served with the order; it may be sufficient for him to have been told, for example by telephone, of the order and approximately what the order said.

6.75 Although breach of a non-molestation order is a criminal offence, there may still be circumstances where civil enforcement can occur, but these are limited. If the matter is dealt with in the criminal courts, the respondent's breach of the order cannot be dealt with as a contempt of court. If the matter is dealt with as a contempt of court, no action can then be brought in the criminal courts. The level of punishment in the criminal courts is higher than in the civil courts – a respondent could be imprisoned for up to 5 years in the Crown Court but only a maximum of 2 years in the civil courts. As from 1 July 2007, there is no longer a power of arrest attached to non-molestation injunctions. A matter will no longer be brought before a civil court following an arrest when the respondent is alleged to have breached the order, and thus the civil enforcement procedure will not commence automatically. It is far more likely that the police and CPS will first consider the matter and decide what action, if any, to take through the criminal system. If no criminal proceedings are brought, it is still open to the applicant to apply to commit the respondent to prison. If, however, the police decide to administer a caution to the respondent in respect of the breach and he accepts this, no civil proceedings can then be brought.

6.76 It appears that some applicants may be dissuaded from bringing injunction proceedings because they do not wish to criminalise the respondent's behaviour. A person imprisoned as a result of a criminal conviction may be seen differently from one imprisoned as a result of civil proceedings. In addition, whilst the respondent would not have obtained a criminal record if he had not behaved wrongly (save for miscarriages of justice), a number of respondents (and some applicants) might still view the applicant as being the cause of their conviction, to no one's benefit. Some applicants also do not wish to lose the 'control' they have over what steps should be taken in the proceedings. A number of practitioners regard the change in the law as a retrograde step.

POWER OF ARREST

6.77 Under s 47 of the Family Law Act 1996, whilst a power of arrest can no longer be attached to a non-molestation injunction, it can still be attached to an occupation order if the court considers that the respondent has used or threatened violence against the applicant or a relevant child. The court is at liberty not to attach a power of arrest *only* if satisfied in all the circumstances of the case that the applicant or child would be adequately protected without such a power being attached. The court is not under the same compulsion to attach a power of arrest to an ex parte order, the making of an order ex parte being a draconian measure in any event. For ex parte orders, the court 'may' attach a power of arrest if it appears that the respondent has used or threatened violence against the applicant or a relevant child and there is a risk of significant harm to the applicant or child, attributable to the conduct of the respondent, if the power of arrest is not attached to the order immediately. As stated above, ex parte occupation orders are rarely granted in any event. The power of arrest can be for a shorter period than the actual order. It may also be extended on one or more occasions. It is more usual for the power of arrest to be granted for the same length of time as the main order.

6.78 Powers of arrest on occupation orders are generally most likely to be attached to an order excluding a respondent from a defined area in which the dwelling house is located. The order must be served before it takes effect. Once it has been served, Form FL406 must be delivered to the police to alert them to the relevant provisions of the order so that they can take appropriate action in the event of, for example, a telephone call from the applicant telling them that the respondent is outside her home. Form FL406 should be delivered to the officer in charge of the police station for the applicant's address. The court may specify another police station where, for example, the police station for the applicant's address does not have a domestic violence unit. Rule 3.9A of the Family Proceedings Rules deals with service on the police. A statement regarding service on the respondent must also be delivered to the police with Form FL406. The rule makes it clear that the statement can cover personal service, or that the respondent has been made aware of the terms of the order, for example by oral advice as to what the order said, or the fact that the respondent was present in court when the order was made. It is important that the respondent is served before the police are notified to ensure that they do not arrest him for potential breaches when he is not aware that any order has been made. Form FL406 should not refer to any provisions of the order to which no power of arrest has been attached. This is presumably to ensure that the police do not arrest someone for breach of a specific term of an injunction where no power of arrest was actually granted in relation to that term.

6.79 Where an order is granted with a power of arrest and, subsequently, the provision regarding the power of arrest is varied or discharged, the 'proper officer', ie the appropriate member of the court staff (rather than the applicant's solicitor) must immediately inform the police of the new order and deliver a copy to the officer. Section 47(6) makes it clear that the police do not need to obtain a warrant before arresting the respondent. A constable may arrest without warrant a person whom he has reasonable cause for suspecting is in breach of an order where a power of arrest is attached to the relevant provision.

6.80 Once a respondent has been arrested under a power of arrest, he must be brought before the appropriate court (ie a circuit judge or district judge in the county court if the county court made the order, or the family proceedings court if that court made the order) within 24 hours. The 24 hours starts to run from the time of the arrest. When calculating the 24-hour period, no account is taken of Christmas Day, Good Friday or any Sunday. As set out in the President's Direction of 17 December 1997, if the respondent cannot conveniently be brought before the relevant judicial authority sitting in a place normally used as a courtroom within the 24-hour period, he may be brought before the court at 'any convenient place'. This may mean a judge attending at the local police station to deal with the arrested person. If for any reason the respondent is not brought before the court within the 24-hour period, he must be released immediately.

6.81 The respondent must be given notice in writing of the alleged breach of the order which has led to his arrest.[18] In the absence of the applicant, this may mean the court being obliged to set out the breaches. Although the court has power to deal with the matter in full on the first hearing, it is unlikely, generally, that this will occur. There are a number of issues to be considered. The judge

---

[18] See *Newman v Modern Bookbinders* [2000] 2 All ER 814.

must first consider whether the arrest was lawful. If the arrest was made under a power of arrest, and the arresting officer had reasonable grounds to believe that the injunction had actually been served and that the arrested person had broken a provision of the order to which a power of arrest had been attached, the arrest will be considered lawful. If the respondent accepts that the arrest was lawful, the matter can proceed to the next stage. If he disputes the lawfulness of the arrest, there will need to be a hearing regarding the lawfulness of the arrest. The arresting officer is unlikely to be present at the time the matter first comes before the relevant judicial authority. If he is present, the court can proceed to deal with the question of lawfulness, although it may still need to adjourn for other reasons. If the question of the lawfulness of the arrest can be dealt with, the attendance of the officer at the next hearing may be dispensed with.

6.82 The matter may be adjourned if it has not been possible to arrange for the attendance of the applicant or her solicitor at the first hearing. Equally, the respondent may not have had the opportunity to seek legal advice. When there is a possibility that a person may be sent to prison for contempt of court, the court will give that person at least one opportunity to obtain legal advice.[19] Therefore, although the court may at the first hearing 'determine whether the facts, and the circumstances which led to the arrest, amounted to disobedience of the order', it is actually more likely to adjourn the matter to another occasion because it cannot yet determine the facts, or the respondent may need to seek representation.

6.83 The matter should be dealt with within 14 days of the day on which the respondent was arrested and the respondent should be given not less than 2 days' notice of the adjourned hearing (Family Proceedings Rules 1991, r 3.9A). However, this provision is not mandatory and it is not clear whether the court loses its power to deal summarily with the matter after the expiration of the 14 days. The applicant may still apply to commit the respondent even if the 14 days has expired. It may therefore not be unusual for a matter to be adjourned beyond the 14 days but with an order that the applicant proceed by way of an application to commit. The court will regard the matter as one of seriousness and urgency and will therefore try to hear the matter within the 14 days, but there may be good and proper reasons for the next hearing to be slightly beyond the 14 days.

6.84 If the matter is not dealt with on the first occasion, the court may remand the respondent on bail or in custody, rather than just release him. The respondent may not be remanded for a period exceeding 8 clear days unless he is remanded on bail and he and the other party consent, when the court can remand him for a longer period. The court can commit the respondent to the custody of a constable for a period not exceeding 3 clear days. If the matter were, for example, adjourned to a date 10 days subsequently but the respondent was remanded in custody for the maximum 8-day period, the respondent would

---

[19] See *King v Read and Slack* [1999] 1 FLR 425.

have to be brought back to court at the expiry of the 8-day period for a further remand. The court may remand for a longer period where it is satisfied that any person who has been remanded under para 2 of Sch 5 to the Family Law Act 1996 is unable to attend or be brought before the court at the expiration of the period for which he was remanded due to illness or accident.

6.85 The respondent may also be remanded for up to 4 weeks where the court considers that a medical report may be required. The respondent may be remanded in custody for up to 3 weeks for a report to be obtained or up to 4 weeks on bail. If there is reason to suspect that the respondent is suffering from a mental illness or severe mental impairment, the court can remand for a report on the respondent's mental condition. The court has the same power as the Crown Court under s 35 of the Mental Health Act 1983 (Family Law Act 1996, s 48).

WARRANTS FOR ARREST

6.86 Where a power of arrest was not attached to the order, or not attached to certain provisions of the order, and the applicant considers that the respondent is in breach of those provisions, the applicant may apply for a warrant for arrest. The application should be made in Form FL408 and is generally made without notice being given to the respondent. Again, the application should be made to the court which made the order alleged to have been breached since magistrates' courts cannot enforce county court orders and vice versa (this relates to civil enforcement of, for example, occupation orders, not criminal enforcement of non-molestation orders). The court must not issue a warrant unless the application has been substantiated on oath and the court has reasonable grounds for believing that the respondent has failed to comply with the order. In the High Court, the warrant would be executed by the Tipstaff; in the county court, the bailiffs (or by the police at the request of the county court); and in the magistrates' court, by the police alone. In the magistrates' court, the justices' clerk takes the responsibility for delivering the warrant to the police (Family Proceedings Courts (Matrimonial Proceedings etc) Rules 1991, r 20(3)).

6.87 An application for a warrant for arrest cannot be made where there *was* a power of arrest attached to the relevant provision but no arrest was actually made, for whatever reason. The applicant would have to proceed instead by way of an application to commit. If the respondent is brought before the court under a warrant for arrest and the court does not deal with the matter immediately, it may remand him. The provisions on remand are the same as for persons arrested under a power of arrest.

COMMITTAL FOR CONTEMPT OF COURT

6.88 Applications to commit a respondent to prison in relation to occupation orders may occur, for example, where no power of arrest was attached to an order, or where one was attached but has not been acted on by the police, or where it was acted upon by the police but due to the possible time constraints mentioned in **6.83**, the court has directed the applicant proceed by way of an application to commit. In relation to non-molestation injunctions, such applications may occur where no criminal enforcement has been undertaken in respect of any alleged breach.

6.89 Applications in the High Court in respect of occupation orders or non-molestation injunctions are the least likely to be made since occupation orders or non-molestation injunctions are generally granted by the county courts or magistrates' courts. However, if such an application is necessary, it is made by a summons supported by an affidavit in the Family Division, or an application supported by affidavit in the Queen's Bench Division. In the county court, the usual method is by way of issuing an application requesting the issue of a notice in Form N78 (supported by affidavit) and, in the magistrates' court, the filing of a request (supported by a statement declaring the facts given to be true) for the issue of a notice in Form FL418. In both cases, the filing of a draft, completed form will generally be taken as the application notice itself.

6.90 It is clear from practice directions and the appropriate rules that the draft form should identify and list the provisions of the order or undertaking which it is alleged have been disobeyed or broken. The draft form must set out every alleged breach. It is insufficient to say, for example, 'see attached affidavit'. It is a fundamental requirement of any type of situation where the respondent might be sent to prison that he has clear written notice of the case he has to meet.

6.91 The procedure on committal is set out in CPR Sch 2 (the relevant rule is CCR Ord 29) in the county court, and r 20(8) and (9) of the Family Proceeding Courts (Matrimonial Proceedings etc) Rules 1991 in the magistrates' court. In the county court, the applicant files the draft form and affidavit in support and the application is duly issued by the court staff. Form N78 is entitled 'Notice to show good reason why you should not be committed to prison'. The respondent is thus under no illusion as to what might occur. As before, the form and the affidavit in support must be served personally upon the respondent if the hearing of the application to commit is to be effective. There is a power in the court to dispense with service if the court thinks that it just to do so, or to order substituted service. As might be appreciated, it would be very unusual to dispense with service, but it might occur if the court were satisfied on evidence that, for example, the respondent was deliberately evading service. This was the case in *Wright v Jess*.[20]

---

[20]   [1987] 2 FLR 373.

6.92 Where a person has been served but fails to attend the hearing, the court may proceed in his absence. However, as is generally the case when an order for committal is made in someone's absence, the court should provide for the respondent to be brought back before it as soon as possible once he has actually been arrested. This applies both to cases where the respondent was served but did not attend and where service was dispensed with.

6.93 The respondent will then be given the opportunity to deal with the allegations made. This is likely to be by way of a complete rehearing as the respondent is entitled to the same.[21] *Lamb v Lamb*[22] is authority for the proposition that the court cannot sentence the respondent to a longer period of imprisonment, having heard him, than it imposed when dealing with the matter in his absence. As with powers of arrest or warrants for arrest, if it appears that the respondent might be sent to prison, he should be given an opportunity to obtain legal representation, which might therefore entail an adjournment. The court does not have power to grant legal aid (public funding).

BURDEN OF PROOF

6.94 In relation to obtaining an injunction, the applicant must show on the balance of probabilities that the facts she alleges are true (and sufficient to justify the order being made). When alleging a breach of an order, the onus will be on the applicant to demonstrate that the respondent has breached the order and, as the ultimate penalty is imprisonment, the breach must be proven beyond reasonable doubt, ie the criminal level of proof, rather than the civil level of something being more likely than not. If the respondent disputes the allegations, the applicant's evidence will be heard first as the burden of proof is on the applicant.

COSTS

6.95 The usual rules on costs apply. Costs are within the discretion of the court. Under normal circumstances where a party has been successful in either obtaining an injunction or defending the grant of an injunction, that party might reasonably expect to be awarded his or her costs. However, if a party has been successful on only one part, she might only receive part of her costs and the other party might be awarded part of his costs against her. If both parties have the benefit of public funding certificates (legal aid), they may both be content with no order for costs save public funding assessment as any other order for costs may be meaningless if the paying party does not have the means to pay. If matters are settled on the basis of an undertaking, it would be

---

[21] See *Aslam v Singh* [1987] 1 FLR 278.
[22] [1984] FLR 278.

unusual for there to be an order for costs in favour of one party as there would have been no determination by the court of any wrongdoing so as to justify a costs award.

FORMS

6.96 Reproduced below are draft orders for a non-molestation order; an occupation order where the applicant has an estate, interest or matrimonial home rights; and an occupation order where the applicant has no existing rights of occupation (including former spouses and cohabitants) to which a power of arrest has been attached. Like all precedents, they will require careful tailoring to suit the circumstances of any particular case but will hopefully provide a useful starting point. The authors are very grateful to HHJ John Platt, who kindly agreed for the forms which follow to be included in this book.

FORMS AND PRECEDENTS

6.97 Forms and precedents relating to Family Law Act 1996 injunctions are reproduced below.

1. NON-MOLESTATION ORDER UNDER SECTION 42 OF THE FAMILY LAW ACT 1996

ORDER	**In the NAME County Court**	
Non-molestation Order under section 42 of the Family Law Act 1996	Case No.	
	Applicant Ref	
	Respondent Ref	

To: [*Respondent's name*]

of: [*Respondent's address*]

IMPORTANT NOTICE TO THE RESPONDENT [*insert name*]

You must obey this Order. You should read it carefully. If you do not understand anything in this Order you should go to a solicitor, Legal Advice Centre or Citizens Advice Bureau. You have a right to apply to the court to change or cancel this Order.

If, without reasonable excuse, you do anything which you are forbidden from doing by this Order, you will be committing a criminal offence and liable on conviction to a term of imprisonment not exceeding five years or to a fine or to both.

Alternatively, if you do not obey this Order, you will be guilty of contempt of court and may be sent to prison.

In this Order the Applicant is [*name of Applicant*] and the Respondent is [name of Respondent]

On [*date*] District Judge NAME sitting at NAME County Court, ADDRESS considered an application for an Order OR heard the solicitor for the Applicant and [*record other attendances*]

THE COURT ORDERED THAT:

From and after personal service of this Order upon him the Respondent [*whether by himself or acting jointly with any other person*] is forbidden to: [*delete as appropriate*] OR

From and after the time when the Respondent is made aware of the terms of this Order whether by personal service or telephone or otherwise the Respondent [*whether by himself or acting jointly with any other person*] is forbidden to: [*delete as appropriate*]

[*delete the following numbered paragraphs as appropriate*]

1   Use or threaten any unlawful violence towards the Applicant

2   Use or threaten any violence towards [*name of child or children*]

3   Come within [ ] metres of the Applicant's home at [*address*]

4   Come within [ ] metres of the Applicant's place of work at [*address*]

5   Come within [ ] metres of any property at which he/she is aware that the Applicant is living

6   Come within [ ] metres of [*address of school*] between the hours of 8am and 9am and 3 pm and 4 pm except by prior written invitation from the school authorities [*adjust to collection and delivery times for child*]

7   Send any threatening or abusive letters, text messages or other communication to the Applicant

8   Communicate with the Applicant whether by letter, telephone, text message or other means of communication except [through her solicitors] **OR** [for the purpose of making arrangements for contact between the Respondent and [*name(s) of child or children*]]

9   Threaten the Applicant

10   Damage or attempt to damage or threaten to damage any property belonging to the Applicant or jointly owned by the parties

11   Damage or attempt to damage or threaten to damage any of the contents of [*address occupied by the Applicant*]

The Respondent is also forbidden to instruct or encourage any other person to do anything which he is forbidden to do by the terms of this Order [*delete as appropriate*]

This Order will remain in force until [*specify event or date*] OR a further Order of the Court.

AND THE COURT ORDERED that:

A   This Order will be re-considered at a further hearing on [a date specified in this Order] *or* [to be fixed by the proper officer on request by the Respondent].

B   Respondent to file and serve any affidavit in evidence in support of his/her case not less than 48 hours before the review hearing.

C   There be no order as to costs save that there be a detailed assessment of the Applicant's publicly funded costs **OR** Costs reserved to the listed hearing.

This Order has been made under section 42 of the Family Act 1996 following a hearing on notice to the Respondent at which the Respondent **did / did not** attend. [*complete as appropriate*] **OR**

This Order is made without notice to the Respondent under sections 42 and 45 of the Family Act 1996.

NOTICE TO THE RESPONDENT [*delete if Order made on notice*]

This Order has been made without any notice of the proceedings being given to you and on the basis of the affidavit evidence of the Applicant a copy of which has been served with this Order.

If you think the Order should be set aside or varied you may apply for this at a full hearing which will take place as soon as just and convenient. At the hearing the court will hear evidence from both parties and decide whether to confirm, or vary, or set aside the Order.

Unless a hearing has been fixed by this Order **the court will fix a hearing as soon as you come to the office, or telephone or write to the court to ask for the date to be fixed. The hearing will normally take place within seven days of your request and both you and the Applicant will receive at least 48 hours notice of the hearing date. You must file any affidavit evidence on which you rely at the court office and serve copies on the Applicant if possible not less than 48 hours before the hearing.**

Notice of Further Hearing [*if applicable*]

The court will re-consider the application and whether the Order should continue at a further hearing at **NAME County Court, ADDRESS**

on the . . . . . . day of . . . . . . 20 . . . . . ., at . . . . . . o'clock

If you do not attend at the time shown the court may make an Order in your absence

NOTE TO ARRESTING OFFICER

Under section 42A of the Family Law Act 1996 breach of a non-molestation Order is a criminal offence punishable by up to five years imprisonment. It is an arrestable offence and it is not necessary to obtain a warrant.

'A person who without reasonable excuse does anything that he is prohibited from doing by a non-molestation Order is guilty of an offence'.

FAMILY LAW ACT 1996, Section 42A(1)

2. OCCUPATION ORDER UNDER FAMILY LAW ACT 1996 SECTION 33 ONLY

ORDER	In the NAME County Court	
	Case No.	
Occupation Order under Family Law Act 1996 section 33 only	Applicant Ref	
Applicant has estate or interest or matrimonial home rights	Respond-ent Ref	

IMPORTANT NOTICE TO THE RESPONDENT [INSERT NAME]

You must obey this Order. You should read it carefully. If you do not understand anything in this Order you should go to a solicitor, Legal Advice Centre or Citizens advice Bureau. You have a right to apply to the court to change or cancel the Order.

You must obey the instructions contained in this Order. If you do not, you will be guilty of contempt of court and may be sent to prison.

In this Order the Applicant is [*name of Applicant*] and the Respondent is [*name of Respondent*]

On [*date*] District Judge NAME sitting at NAME County Court, ADDRESS considered an application for an Order OR heard the solicitor for the Applicant and [the solicitor for the Respondent in the presence of both parties – *or as appropriate*]

THE COURT DECLARED that:

1   The Applicant is entitled to occupy [*address of home or intended home*] as his / her home. **OR**

2   The Applicant has matrimonial home rights in [*address of home or intended home*]. **AND**

3   The Applicant's matrimonial home rights shall not end when the Respondent dies or their marriage is dissolved and shall continue until [*date*] or further order.

AND THE COURT ORDERED that the Respondent:

1   shall allow the Applicant to occupy [*address of home or intended home*]

2   shall allow the Applicant to occupy part of [*address of home or intended home*] namely: [*specify part*]

3   shall not come within [ ] metres of [*address of Applicant's home*]

4   shall not obstruct, harass or interfere with the Applicant's peaceful occupation of [*address of home or intended home*]

5   shall not occupy [*address of home or intended home*] **OR**

6   shall not occupy [*address of home or intended home*] between [*specify dates or times*] **OR**

7   shall not occupy [*part of address of home or intended home*] [between [*specify dates or times*]]

8   shall leave [*address or part of address*] [forthwith] [within hours / days] of service on him/her of this Order.] **AND / OR**

9   having left [*address or part of address*] shall not return to, enter or attempt to enter [or go within [*specify distance*] of] it.

The Respondent is also forbidden to instruct or encourage any other person to do anything which he is forbidden to do by the terms of this Order

AND THE COURT ALSO ORDERED that:

1   The [Applicant/Respondent] shall maintain and repair [*address of home or intended home*]. **AND/OR**

2   The [Applicant/Respondent] shall pay the rent for [*address of home or intended home*]. **OR**

3   The [Applicant/Respondent] shall pay the mortgage payments on [*address of home or intended home*]. **OR**

4   The [Applicant/Respondent] shall pay the following for [*address of home or intended home*]: [*specify outgoings as bullet points*].

5   The [*party in occupation*] shall pay to the [*other party*] £XX each [*week, month, etc*] for [*address of home etc*].

6   The [*party in occupation*] shall keep and use the [*furniture*] [*contents*] [*specify if necessary*] of [*address of home or intended home*] and the [Applicant / Respondent] shall return to the [*party in occupation*] the [*furniture*] [*contents* [*specify if necessary*]] [no later than [*date/time*]].

7   The [*party in occupation*] shall take reasonable care of the [*furniture*] [*contents*] [*specify if necessary*] of [*address of home or intended home*].

8   The [*party in occupation*] shall take all reasonable steps to keep secure [*address of home or intended home*] and the furniture or other contents [*specify if necessary*].

This Order will remain in force until [*specify event or date*] **OR** a further Order of the Court.

This Order is made with/without [***delete as appropriate***] notice to the Respondent under section 33 of the Family Act 1996.

AND THE COURT ORDERED that:

A   This Order will be re-considered at a further hearing on a date [specified in this Order] **OR** [to be fixed by the proper officer on request by the Respondent].

B   Respondent to file and serve any affidavit in evidence in support of his/her case not less than 48 hours before the review hearing.

C   There be no order as to costs save that there be a detailed assessment of the Applicant's publicly funded costs **OR** Costs reserved to the listed hearing.

NOTICE TO THE RESPONDENT [*delete if Order made on notice*]

This Order has been made without any notice of the proceedings being given to you and on the basis of the affidavit evidence of the Applicant a copy of which has been served with this Order.

If you think the Order should be set aside or varied you may apply for this at a full hearing which will take place as soon as just and convenient. At the hearing the court will hear evidence from both parties and decide whether to confirm, or vary, or set aside the Order.

Unless a hearing has been fixed by this Order the court will fix a hearing as soon as you come to the office, or telephone or write to the court to ask for the date to be fixed. The hearing will normally take place within seven days of your request and both you and the Applicant will receive at least 48 hours notice of the hearing date. You must file any affidavit evidence on which you rely at the court office and serve copies on the Applicant if possible not less than 48 hours before the hearing.

Notice of Further Hearing [if applicable]

The court will re-consider the application and whether the Order should continue at a further hearing at NAME County Court, ADDRESS

on the . . . . . . day of . . . . . . 20 . . . . . ., at . . . . . . o'clock

If you do not attend at the time shown the court may make an Order in your absence

3. OCCUPATION ORDER UNDER FAMILY LAW ACT 1996 SECTIONS 35, 36, 37 & 38 ONLY

ORDER	In the NAME County Court	
	Case No.	
Occupation Order under Family Law Act 1996 sections 35, 36, 37 & 38 only	Applicant Ref	
Applicant has no existing rights of occupation (including former spouse and cohabitant)	Respond-ent Ref	

IMPORTANT NOTICE TO THE RESPONDENT [INSERT NAME]

You must obey this Order. You should read it carefully. If you do not understand anything in this Order you should go to a solicitor, Legal Advice Centre or Citizens advice Bureau. You have a right to apply to the court to change or cancel the Order.

You must obey the instructions contained in this Order. If you do not, you will be guilty of contempt of court and may be sent to prison.

In this Order the Applicant is [*name of Applicant*] and the Respondent is [*name of Respondent*]

On [*date*] District Judge NAME sitting at NAME County Court, ADDRESS considered an application for an Order OR heard the solicitor for the Applicant and [the solicitor for the Respondent in the presence of both parties – *or as appropriate*]

THE COURT DECLARED that:

1 The Applicant has the right to occupy [*address of home or intended home*] and the Respondent shall allow the Applicant to do so

AND THE COURT ORDERED that the Respondent:

2 shall not evict or exclude the Applicant from [*address of home or intended home*] or any part of it

3 shall not occupy [*address of home or intended home*] **OR**

4   shall not occupy [*address of home or intended home*] between [*specify dates or times*] **OR**

5   shall not occupy [*part of address of home or intended home*] [between [*specify dates or times*]]

6   shall leave [*address or part of address*] [forthwith] [within hours / days] of service on him/her of this Order.] **AND / OR**

7   having left [*address or part of address*] shall not return to, enter or attempt to enter [or go within [*specify distance*] of] it.

[for Orders made under sections 37 & 38 check statutory provisions before including above paras]

The Respondent is also forbidden to instruct or encourage any other person to do anything which he is forbidden to do by the terms of this Order

AND THE COURT ALSO ORDERED that: [for Orders made under sections 35 & 36 only]

8   The [Applicant/Respondent] shall maintain and repair [*address of home or intended home*]. **AND/OR**

9   The [Applicant/Respondent] shall pay the rent for [*address of home or intended home*]. **OR**

10   The [Applicant/Respondent] shall pay the mortgage payments on [*address of home or intended home*]. **OR**

11   The [Applicant/Respondent] shall pay the following for [*address of home or intended home*]: [*specify outgoings as bullet points*].

12   The [*party in occupation*] shall pay to the [*other party*] £XX each [*week, month, etc*] for [*address of home etc*].

13   The [*party in occupation*] shall keep and use the [*furniture*] [*contents*] [*specify if necessary*] of [*address of home or intended home*] and the [Applicant / Respondent] shall return to the [*party in occupation*] the [*furniture*] [*contents* [*specify if necessary*]] [no later than [*date/time*]].

14   The [*party in occupation*] shall take reasonable care of the [*furniture*] [*contents*] [*specify if necessary*] of [*address of home or intended home*].

15   The [*party in occupation*] shall take all reasonable steps to keep secure [*address of home or intended home*] and the furniture or other contents [*specify if necessary*].

This Order will remain in force until [*specify event or date*] **OR** a further Order of the Court.

This Order is made with/without [*delete as appropriate*] notice to the Respondent under Family Act 1996 section 35 36 37 38 [*delete as appropriate*]

AND THE COURT ORDERED that:

A   This Order will be re-considered at a further hearing on a date [specified in this Order] **OR** [to be fixed by the proper officer on request by the Respondent].

B   Respondent to file and serve any affidavit in evidence in support of his/her case not less than 48 hours before the review hearing.

C   There be no order as to costs save that there be a detailed assessment of the Applicant's publicly funded costs **OR** Costs reserved to the listed hearing.

NOTICE TO THE RESPONDENT [delete if Order made on notice]

This Order has been made without any notice of the proceedings being given to you and on the basis of the affidavit evidence of the Applicant a copy of which has been served with this Order.

If you think the Order should be set aside or varied you may apply for this at a full hearing which will take place as soon as just and convenient. At the hearing the court will hear evidence from both parties and decide whether to confirm, or vary, or set aside the Order.

Unless a hearing has been fixed by this Order the court will fix a hearing as soon as you come to the office, or telephone or write to the court to ask for the date to be fixed. The hearing will normally take place within seven days of your request and both you and the Applicant will receive at least 48 hours notice of the hearing date. You must file any affidavit evidence on which you rely at the court office and serve copies on the Applicant if possible not less than 48 hours before the hearing.

Notice of Further Hearing [if applicable]

The court will re-consider the application and whether the Order should continue at a further hearing at NAME County Court, ADDRESS

on the . . . . . . day of . . . . . . 20 . . . . . ., at . . . . . . o'clock

If you do not attend at the time shown the court may make an Order in your absence

4. RECORD OF OCCUPATION ORDER TO WHICH THE POWER OF ARREST HAS BEEN ATTACHED

Record of Occupation Order to which the Power of Arrest has been attached	In the NAME County Court	
	Case No.	
Family Law Act 1996 sections 33-38	Applicant *Ref*	
	Respond-ent *Ref*	

On [*date*] District Judge NAME sitting at NAME County Court, ADDRESS considered an application for an Order **OR** heard the solicitor for the Applicant and [the solicitor for the Respondent in the presence of both parties – *or as appropriate*]

THE COURT ORDERED THAT the Respondent [*name of Respondent*]:

from and after a time when the Respondent is made aware of the terms of this Order, whether by personal service or by telephone or otherwise:

[SET OUT HERE THE NUMBERED PARAGRAPHS INCLUDED IN THE ORDER THAT ARE CAPABLE OF BEING ENFORCED BY THE POWER OF ARREST]

The Respondent is also forbidden to instruct or encourage any other person to do anything which he is forbidden to do by the terms of this Order

This order lasts until [*specify event or date*] **OR** a further order is made.

POWER OF ARREST

The Court is satisfied that the Respondent has used or threatened violence against the Applicant and the following child [*name of child or children*] and that there is risk of significant harm to the Applicant and the above child attributable to the conduct of the Respondent if the power of arrest is not attached immediately.

A Power of Arrest is attached to the Order whereby any constable may (under the power of given by sections 33-38 of the Family Law Act 1996) arrest without warrant the Respondent if the constable has any reasonable cause for suspecting that the Respondent may be in breach of any provision to which the power of arrest is attached.

APPENDIX

CONTENTS

LOCAL GOVERNMENT ACT 1972

1972 Chapter 70

PART XI
GENERAL PROVISIONS AS TO LOCAL AUTHORITIES

LEGAL PROCEEDINGS

222 Power of local authorities to prosecute or defend legal proceedings

(1) Where a local authority consider it expedient for the promotion or protection of the interests of the inhabitants of their area –

(a) they may prosecute or defend or appear in any legal proceedings and, in the case of civil proceedings, may institute them in their own name, and

(b) they may, in their own name, make representations in the interests of the inhabitants at any public inquiry held by or on behalf of any Minister or public body under any enactment.

(2) In this section 'local authority' includes the Common Council and the London Fire and Emergency Planning Authority.

Amendments—Greater London Authority Act 1999, s 328, Sch 29, Pt I, para 20.

265A Application in relation to the Broads Authority

(1) Subject to subsections (2) and (3) below, the following provisions of this Act shall have effect as if the Broads Authority were a local authority and the Broads were its local government area—

(a)   section 70;

(b)   sections 80(1)(a) and (2), 85, 92, *94 to 98*, 99 and 100;

(c)   sections 101 to 106;

(d)   sections 111 to 119;

(e)   sections 120 to 123 and 128 to 131;

(f)   sections 135, 136, 139, 140, 140A, 140C, 143 and 144;

(g)   sections 153 and 173 to 177; and

(h)   sections 222, 223, 225, 228 to 234 and 239.

(2) The Navigation Committee of the Broads Authority shall be treated, for the purposes of this Act and of any other enactment relating to the committees of local authorities (but subject to section 9 of the Norfolk and Suffolk Broads Act 1988), as a committee of the Authority appointed under section 102 of this Act.

(3) Sections 120 to 123, 128 and 224 shall have effect as if the Authority were a principal council.

Amendments—Inserted by Norfolk and Suffolk Broads Act 1988, s 21, Sch 6, Para 10 (1).

Prospective amendments—Words in italics prospectively repealed by the Local Government and Housing Act 1989, s 194, Sch 12, Part 11; Words in italics prospectively repealed by the Local Government Act 2000, s 107, Sch 6.

270 General provisions as to interpretation

(1) In this Act, except where the context otherwise requires, the following expressions have the following meanings respectively, that is to say –

'alternative arrangements' has the same meaning as in Part II of the Local Government Act 2000;

'appropriate Minister', in relation to the making of an order or regulation or the giving of a direction with respect to any matter, means the Minister in charge of any Government department concerned with that matter; but the validity of any order, regulation or direction purporting to be made or given by any Minister by virtue of a power conferred on the appropriate Minister by this Act shall not be affected by any question as to whether or not that Minister was the appropriate Minister for the purpose;

'bank holiday break' means any bank holiday not included in the Christmas break or the Easter break and the period beginning with the last week day before that bank holiday and ending with the next week day which is not a bank holiday;

'the Broads' has the same meaning as in the Norfolk and Suffolk Broads Act 1988;

'Christmas break' means the period beginning with the last week day before Christmas Day and ending with the first week day after Christmas Day which is not a bank holiday;

'the City' means the City of London;

'Common Council' means the Common Council of the City;

'county' without more, means, in relation to England, a metropolitan county or a non-metropolitan county, but in the expressions 'county council', 'council of a county', 'county councillor' and 'councillor of a county' means, in relation to England, a non-metropolitan county only;

'district', without more, means, in relation to England, a metropolitan district or a non-metropolitan district;

'Easter break' means the period beginning with the Thursday before and ending with the Tuesday after Easter Day;

'elected mayor' has the same meaning as in Part II of the Local Government Act 2000;

'electoral area' means any area for which councillors are elected to any local authority;

'executive', 'executive arrangements' and 'executive leader' have the same meaning as in Part II of the Local Government Act 2000;

'existing', in relation to a local government or other area or a local authority or other body, except in sections 1 and 20 above, means that area or body as it existed immediately before the passing of this Act;

'financial year' means the period of twelve months ending with 31st March in any year;

'grouped', in relation to a parish or community, means grouped by or by virtue of any provision of this Act or any previous corresponding enactment under a common parish or community council, and 'grouping order' shall be construed accordingly;

'joint authority' means an authority established by Part IV of the Local Government Act 1985;

'joint waste authority' means an authority established for an area in England by an order under section 207 of the Local Government and Public Involvement in Health Act 2007;

'land' includes any interest in land and any easement or right in, to or over land;

'leader and cabinet executive' means—
  (a) in relation to England: a leader and cabinet executive (England);
  (b) in relation to Wales: a leader and cabinet executive (Wales);

'leader and cabinet executive (England)' has the same meaning as in Part 2 of the Local Government Act 2000;

'leader and cabinet executive (Wales)' has the same meaning as in Part 2 of the Local Government Act 2000;

'local authority' means a county council, a district council, a London borough council or a parish council but, in relation to Wales, means a county council, county borough council or community council;

'local government area' means—
  (a) in relation to England, a county, Greater London, a district, a London borough or a parish;
  (b) in relation to Wales, a county, county borough or community;

'local government elector' means a person registered as a local government elector in the register of electors in accordance with the provisions of the Representation of the People Acts;

'local statutory provision' means a provision of a local Act (including an Act confirming a provisional order) or a provision of a public general Act passed with respect only to the whole or part of an existing local government area or a provision of an instrument made under any such local or public general Act or of an instrument in the nature of a local enactment made under any other Act;

'mayor and cabinet executive' and 'mayor and council manager executive' have the same meaning as in Part II of the Local Government Act 2000;

'new', in relation to any area or authority, means an area or authority established by or under this Act including one established by virtue of any provision of the Local Government (Wales) Act 1994;

'1933 Act' means the Local Government Act 1933;

'1963 Act' means the London Government Act 1963;

'open space' has the meaning assigned to it by section 336(1) of the Town and Country Planning Act 1990;

'prescribed' means prescribed by regulations made by the Secretary of State;

'preserved county' means any county created by this Act as a county in Wales, as it stood immediately before the passing of the Local Government (Wales) Act 1994 but subject to any provision of the Act of 1994, or any provision made under this Act, redrawing its boundaries;

'principal area' means a non-metropolitan county, a district or a London borough but, in relation to Wales, means a county or county borough;

'principal council' means a council elected for a principal area;

'public body' includes—

    (a)   a local authority and a joint board on which, and a joint committee on which, a local authority or parish meeting are represented;

    (b)   any trustees, commissioners or other persons who, for public purposes and not for their own profit, act under any enactment or instrument for the improvement of any place, for the supply of water to any place, or for providing or maintaining a cemetery or market in any place; and

    (c)   any other authority having powers of levying or issuing a precept for any rate for public purposes;

and 'district' means, in relation to a public body other than a local authority, the area for which the public body acts;

'specified papers', in relation to a parish or community, means the public books, writings and papers of the parish or community (including any photographic copies thereof) and all documents directed by law to be kept therewith;

'the Temples' means the Inner Temple and the Middle Temple;

'Welsh Commission' has the meaning assigned to it by section 53 above.

(2) In this Act and in any other enactment, whether passed before, at the same time as, or after this Act, the expression 'non-metropolitan county' means any county other than a metropolitan county, and the expression 'non-metropolitan district' means any district other than a metropolitan district.

(3) Any reference in this Act to a proper officer and any reference which by virtue of this Act is to be construed as such a reference shall, in relation to any purpose and any local authority or other body or any area, be construed as a reference to an officer appointed for that purpose by that body or for that area, as the case may be.

(4) In any provision of this Act which applies to a London borough, except Schedule 2 to this Act, –

  (a)   any reference to the chairman of the council or of any class of councils comprising the council or to a member of a local authority shall be construed as or, as the case may be, as including a reference to the mayor of the borough;

  (b)   any reference to the vice-chairman of the council or any such class of councils shall be construed as a reference to the deputy mayor of the borough; and

  (c)   any reference to the proper officer of the council or any such class of councils shall be construed as a reference to the proper officer of the borough.

(4A) Where a London borough council are operating executive arrangements which involve a mayor and cabinet executive , subsection (4) above shall have effect with the omission of paragraphs (a) and (b).

(5) In this Act, except where the context otherwise requires, references to any enactment shall be construed as references to that enactment as amended, extended or applied by or under any other enactment, including any enactment contained in this Act.

Amendment—SI 2001/2237,arts 1(2), 2(a), 9; Definition inserted by Norfolk and Suffolk Broads Act 1988, s 21, Sch 6, para 10 (9); Local Government Act 1992, s 29, Sch 4, Part II; Local Government Act 1985, s 102, Sch 16, para 8; Local Government (Wales) Act 1994, s 1 (7), (8); Local Government Act 2000, s 46, Sch 3, para 12(1), (2), s 108 (4), (6) (b); Local Government and Public Involvement in Health Act 2007, s 74 (1), s 209 (2), Sch 13, Pt 1, paras 1, 24, s 245(2); Local Government, Planning and Land Act 1980, s 118, Sch 23; Planning (Consequential Provisions) Act 1990, s 4, Sch 2, para 28(3); Statute Law (Repeals) Act 2004.

MAGISTRATES COURTS' ACT 1980

1980 Chapter 43

Limitation of time

127 Limitation of time

(1) Except as otherwise expressly provided by any enactment and subject to subsection (2) below, a magistrates' court shall not try an information or hear a complaint unless the information was laid, or the complaint made, within 6 months from the time when the offence was committed, or the matter of complaint arose.

(2) Nothing in–

(a)   subsection (1) above; or
(b)   subject to subsection (4) below, any other enactment (however framed or worded) which, as regards any offence to which it applies, would but for this section impose a time-limit on the power of a magistrates' court to try an information summarily or impose a limitation on the time for taking summary proceedings,

shall apply in relation to any indictable offence.

(3) Without prejudice to the generality of paragraph (b) of subsection (2) above, that paragraph includes enactments which impose a time-limit that applies only in certain circumstances (for example, where the proceedings are not instituted by or with the consent of the Director of Public Prosecutions or some other specified authority).

(4) Where, as regards any indictable offence, there is imposed by any enactment (however framed or worded, and whether falling within subsection (2)(b) above or not) a limitation on the time for taking proceedings on indictment for that offence no summary proceedings for that offence shall be taken after the latest time for taking proceedings on indictment.

HOUSING ACT 1985

1985 Chapter 68

82 Security of tenure

(1) A secure tenancy which is either –

(a)   a weekly or other periodic tenancy, or
(b)   a tenancy for a term certain but subject to termination by the landlord,

cannot be brought to an end by the landlord except by obtaining an order mentioned in subsection (1A).

(1A) These are the orders –

(a)   an order of the court for the possession of the dwelling-house;
(b)   an order under subsection (3);
(c)   a demotion order under section 82A.

(2) Where the landlord obtains an order for the possession of the dwelling-house, the tenancy ends on the date on which the tenant is to give up possession in pursuance of the order.

(3) Where a secure tenancy is a tenancy for a term certain but with a provision for re-entry or forfeiture, the court shall not order possession of the dwelling-house in pursuance of that provision, but in a case where the court would have made such an order it shall instead make an order terminating the tenancy on a date specified in the order and section 86 (periodic tenancy arising on termination of fixed term) shall apply.

(4) Section 146 of the Law of Property Act 1925 (restriction on and relief against forfeiture), except subsection (4) (vesting in under-lessee), and any other

enactment or rule of law relating to forfeiture, shall apply in relation to proceedings for an order under subsection (3) of this section as if they were proceedings to enforce a right of re-entry or forfeiture.

Amendments—Anti-Social Behaviour Act 2003, s 14(1)(a), (b).

82A Demotion because of anti-social behaviour

(1) This section applies to a secure tenancy if the landlord is –

    (a)   a local housing authority;
    (b)   a housing action trust;
    (c)   a registered social landlord.

(2) The landlord may apply to a county court for a demotion order.

(3) A demotion order has the following effect –

    (a)   the secure tenancy is terminated with effect from the date specified in the order;
    (b)   if the tenant remains in occupation of the dwelling-house after that date a demoted tenancy is created with effect from that date;
    (c)   it is a term of the demoted tenancy that any arrears of rent payable at the termination of the secure tenancy become payable under the demoted tenancy;
    (d)   it is also a term of the demoted tenancy that any rent paid in advance or overpaid at the termination of the secure tenancy is credited to the tenant's liability to pay rent under the demoted tenancy.

(4) The court must not make a demotion order unless it is satisfied –

    (a)   that the tenant or a person residing in or visiting the dwelling-house has engaged or has threatened to engage in –
        (i)   housing-related anti-social conduct, or
        (ii)   conduct to which section 153B of the Housing Act 1996 (use of premises for unlawful purposes) applies, and
    (b)   that it is reasonable to make the order.

(5) Each of the following has effect in respect of a demoted tenancy at the time it is created by virtue of an order under this section as it has effect in relation to the secure tenancy at the time it is terminated by virtue of the order-

    (a)   the parties to the tenancy;
    (b)   the period of the tenancy;
    (c)   the amount of the rent;
    (d)   the dates on which the rent is payable.

(6) Subsection (5)(b) does not apply if the secure tenancy was for a fixed term and in such a case the demoted tenancy is a weekly periodic tenancy.

(7) If the landlord of the demoted tenancy serves on the tenant a statement of any other express terms of the secure tenancy which are to apply to the demoted tenancy such terms are also terms of the demoted tenancy.

(7A) In subsection (4)(a) 'housing-related anti-social conduct' has the same meaning as in section 153A of the Housing Act 1996.

(8) For the purposes of this section a demoted tenancy is –

- (a) a tenancy to which section 143A of the Housing Act 1996 applies if the landlord of the secure tenancy is a local housing authority or a housing action trust;
- (b) a tenancy to which section 20B of the Housing Act 1988 applies if the landlord of the secure tenancy is a registered social landlord.

Amendment—Inserted by the Anti-social Behaviour Act 2003, s 14(2); Police and Justice Act 2006, s 52, Sch 14, para 12(1), (2), (3).

85A Proceedings for possession: anti-social behaviour

(1) This section applies if the court is considering under section 84(2)(a) whether it is reasonable to make an order for possession on ground 2 set out in Part 1 of Schedule 2 (conduct of tenant or other person).

(2) The court must consider, in particular –

- (a) the effect that the nuisance or annoyance has had on persons other than the person against whom the order is sought;
- (b) any continuing effect the nuisance or annoyance is likely to have on such persons;
- (c) the effect that the nuisance or annoyance would be likely to have on such persons if the conduct is repeated.

Amendments—Inserted by Anti-Social Behaviour Act 2003, s 16(1).

HOUSING ACT 1988

1988 Chapter 50

6A Demotion because of anti-social behaviour

(1) This section applies to an assured tenancy if the landlord is a registered social landlord.

(2) The landlord may apply to a county court for a demotion order.

(3) A demotion order has the following effect –

- (a) the assured tenancy is terminated with effect from the date specified in the order;
- (b) if the tenant remains in occupation of the dwelling-house after that date a demoted tenancy is created with effect from that date;
- (c) it is a term of the demoted tenancy that any arrears of rent payable at the termination of the assured tenancy become payable under the demoted tenancy;
- (d) it is also a term of the demoted tenancy that any rent paid in advance or overpaid at the termination of the assured tenancy is credited to the tenant's liability to pay rent under the demoted tenancy.

(4) The court must not make a demotion order unless it is satisfied –

    (a)   that the tenant or a person residing in or visiting the dwelling-house has engaged or has threatened to *engage in conduct to which section 153A or 153B of the Housing Act 1996 (anti-social behaviour or use of premises for unlawful purposes) applies, and* [engage in

    (i)   housing-related anti-social conduct, or

    (ii)   conduct to which section 153B of the housing Act 1996 (use of premises for unlawful purposes) applies, and]

    (b)   that it is reasonable to make the order.

(5) The court must not entertain proceedings for a demotion order unless –

    (a)   the landlord has served on the tenant a notice under subsection (6), or

    (b)   the court thinks it is just and equitable to dispense with the requirement of the notice.

(6) The notice must –

    (a)   give particulars of the conduct in respect of which the order is sought;

    (b)   state that the proceedings will not begin before the date specified in the notice;

    (c)   state that the proceedings will not begin after the end of the period of twelve months beginning with the date of service of the notice.

(7) The date specified for the purposes of subsection (6)(b) must not be before the end of the period of two weeks beginning with the date of service of the notice.

(8) Each of the following has effect in respect of a demoted tenancy at the time it is created by virtue of an order under this section as it has effect in relation to the assured tenancy at the time it is terminated by virtue of the order –

    (a)   the parties to the tenancy;

    (b)   the period of the tenancy;

    (c)   the amount of the rent;

    (d)   the dates on which the rent is payable.

(9) Subsection (8)(b) does not apply if the assured tenancy was for a fixed term and in such a case the demoted tenancy is a weekly periodic tenancy.

(10) If the landlord of the demoted tenancy serves on the tenant a statement of any other express terms of the assured tenancy which are to apply to the demoted tenancy such terms are also terms of the demoted tenancy.

(10A) In subsection (4) (a) ' housing-related anti-social conduct' has the same meaning as in section 153A of the Housing Act 1996.

(11) For the purposes of this section a demoted tenancy is a tenancy to which section 20B of the Housing Act 1988 applies.

Amendments—Anti-Social Behaviour Act 2003, s 14(4).

Prospective Amendments—Words in italics prospectively repealed and subsequent words substituted; subsection (10A) prospectively inserted by Police and Justice Act 2006,ss 52, Sch 14, para 15(1), (2), (3).

9A Proceedings for possession: anti-social behaviour

(1) This section applies if the court is considering under section 7(4) whether it is reasonable to make an order for possession on ground 14 set out in Part 2 of Schedule 2 (conduct of tenant or other person).

(2) The court must consider, in particular –

    (a)   the effect that the nuisance or annoyance has had on persons other than the person against whom the order is sought;

    (b)   any continuing effect the nuisance or annoyance is likely to have on such persons;

    (c)   the effect that the nuisance or annoyance would be likely to have on such persons if the conduct is repeated.

Amendments—Inserted by Anti-Social Behaviour Act 2003, s 16(2).

20B Demoted assured shorthold tenancies

(1) An assured tenancy is an assured shorthold tenancy to which this section applies (a demoted assured shorthold tenancy) if –

    (a)   the tenancy is created by virtue of an order of the court under section 82A of the Housing Act 1985 or section 6A of this Act (a demotion order), and

    (b)   the landlord is a registered social landlord.

(2) At the end of the period of one year starting with the day when the demotion order takes effect a demoted assured shorthold tenancy ceases to be an assured shorthold tenancy unless subsection (3) applies.

(3) This subsection applies if before the end of the period mentioned in subsection (2) the landlord gives notice of proceedings for possession of the dwelling house.

(4) If subsection (3) applies the tenancy continues to be a demoted assured shorthold tenancy until the end of the period mentioned in subsection (2) or (if later) until one of the following occurs –

    (a)   the notice of proceedings for possession is withdrawn;

    (b)   the proceedings are determined in favour of the tenant;

    (c)   the period of six months beginning with the date on which the notice is given ends and no proceedings for possession have been brought.

(5) Registered social landlord has the same meaning as in Part 1 of the Housing Act 1996.

Amendments—Inserted by Anti-Social Behaviour Act 2003, s 15(1).

FAMILY LAW ACT 1996

1996 Chapter 27

PART IV
FAMILY HOMES AND DOMESTIC VIOLENCE

Rights to occupy matrimonial or civil partnership home

30 Rights concerning home where one spouse or civil partner has no estate, etc

(1) This section applies if –

(a) one spouse or civil partner ('A') is entitled to occupy a dwelling-house by virtue of–
(i) a beneficial estate or interest or contract; or
(ii) any enactment giving A the right to remain in occupation; and
(b) the other spouse or civil partner ('B')is not so entitled.

(2) Subject to the provisions of this Part, B the spouse not so entitled has the following rights ('home rights') –

(a) if in occupation, a right not to be evicted or excluded from the dwelling-house or any part of it by A except with the leave of the court given by an order under section 33;
(b) if not in occupation, a right with the leave of the court so given to enter into and occupy the dwelling-house.

(3) If B is entitled under this section to occupy a dwelling-house or any part of a dwelling-house, any payment or tender made or other thing done by B in or towards satisfaction of any liability of A in respect of rent, mortgage payments or other outgoings affecting the dwelling-house shall, whether or not it is made or done in pursuance of an order under section 40, be as good as if made or done by A.

(4) B's occupation by virtue of this section –

(a) is to be treated, for the purposes of the Rent (Agriculture) Act 1976 and the Rent Act 1977 (other than Part V and sections 103 to 106 of that Act), as occupation by A as A's residence, and
(b) if B occupies the dwelling-house as B's only or principal home, is to be treated, for the purposes of the Housing Act 1985, Part I of the Housing Act 1988 and Chapter I of Part V of the Housing Act 1996, as occupation by A as A's only or principal home.

(5) If B–

(a) is entitled under this section to occupy a dwelling-house or any part of a dwelling-house, and
(b) makes any payment in or towards satisfaction of any liability of A in respect of mortgage payments affecting the dwelling-house,

the person to whom the payment is made may treat it as having been made by A, but the fact that that person has treated any such payment as having been so made does not affect any claim of B against A to an interest in the dwelling-house by virtue of the payment.

(6) If B is entitled under this section to occupy a dwelling-house or part of a dwelling-house by reason of an interest of A under a trust, all the provisions of subsections (3) to (5) apply in relation to the trustees as they apply in relation to A.

(7) This section does not apply to a dwelling-house which –

    (a)   in the case of spouses, has at no time been, and was at no time intended by them to be, a matrimonial home of theirs; and

    (b)   in the case of civil partners, has at no time been, and was at no time intended by them to be, a civil partnership home of theirs.

(8) B's home rights continue –

    (a)   only so long as the marriage or civil partnership subsists, except to the extent that an order under section 33(5) otherwise provides; and

    (b)   only so long as A is entitled as mentioned in subsection (1) to occupy the dwelling-house, except where provision is made by section 31 for those rights to be a charge on an estate or interest in the dwelling-house.

(9) It is hereby declared that a person –

    (a)   who has an equitable interest in a dwelling-house or in its proceeds of sale, but

    (b)   is not a person in whom there is vested (whether solely or as joint tenant) a legal estate in fee simple or a legal term of years absolute in the dwelling-house,

is to be treated, only for the purpose of determining whether he has home rights, as not being entitled to occupy the dwelling-house by virtue of that interest.

Amendments—Civil Partnership Act 2004, s 82, Sch 9, Part 1, para 1(1), (2), (a), (i),(ii),(2)(b), (3), (a), (b), (c), (4), (a), (b),(5) (b), (5), (c), (ii),(6), (b), (c), (d), (7), (a) (b), (8), (9), (a), (b), (c), (10), (a), (b).

31 Effect of home rights as charge on dwelling-house

(1) Subsections (2) and (3) apply if, at any time during a marriage or civil parntership, A is entitled to occupy a dwelling-house by virtue of a beneficial estate or interest.

(2) B's home rights are a charge on the estate or interest.

(3) The charge created by subsection (2) has the same priority as if it were an equitable interest created at whichever is the latest of the following dates–

    (a)   the date on which A acquires the estate or interest;

(b)   the date of the marriage or of the formation of the civil partnership; and

(c)   1st January 1968 (the commencement date of the Matrimonial Homes Act 1967).

(4) Subsections (5) and (6) apply if, at any time when B's home rights are a charge on an interest of A under a trust, there are, apart from A or B, no persons, living or unborn, who are or could become beneficiaries under the trust.

(5) The rights are a charge also on the estate or interest of the trustees for A.

(6) The charge created by subsection (5) has the same priority as if it were an equitable interest created (under powers overriding the trusts) on the date when it arises.

(7) In determining for the purposes of subsection (4) whether there are any persons who are not, but could become, beneficiaries under the trust, there is to be disregarded any potential exercise of a general power of appointment exercisable by either or both of A and B alone (whether or not the exercise of it requires the consent of another person).

(8) Even though B's home rights are a charge on an estate or interest in the dwelling-house, those rights are brought to an end by–

(a)   the death of A, or

(b)   the termination (otherwise than by death) of the marriage or civil partnership,

unless the court directs otherwise by an order made under section 33(5).

(9) If–

(a)   B's home rights are a charge on an estate or interest in the dwelling-house, and

(b)   that estate or interest is surrendered to merge in some other estate or interest expectant on it in such circumstances that, but for the merger, the person taking the estate or interest would be bound by the charge,

the surrender has effect subject to the charge and the persons thereafter entitled to the other estate or interest are, for so long as the estate or interest surrendered would have endured if not so surrendered, to be treated for all purposes of this Part as deriving title to the other estate or interest under A or, as the case may be, under the trustees for A, by virtue of the surrender.

(10) If the title to the legal estate by virtue of which A is entitled to occupy a dwelling-house (including any legal estate held by trustees for that spouse) is registered under the Land Registration Act 2002 or any enactment replaced by that Act–

(a)   registration of a land charge affecting the dwelling-house by virtue of this Part is to be effected by registering a notice under that Act; and

(b)   B's home rights are not to be capable of falling within paragraph 2 of Schedule 1 or 3 to that Act

(11) (*repealed*)

(12) If–

   (a)   B's home rights are a charge on the estate of A or of trustees of A, and

   (b)   that estate is the subject of a mortgage,

then if, after the date of the creation of the mortgage ('the first mortgage'), the charge is registered under section 2 of the Land Charges Act 1972, the charge is, for the purposes of section 94 of the Law of Property Act 1925 (which regulates the rights of mortgagees to make further advances ranking in priority to subsequent mortgages), to be deemed to be a mortgage subsequent in date to the first mortgage.

(13) It is hereby declared that a charge under subsection (2) or (5) is not registrable under subsection (10) or under section 2 of the Land Charges Act 1972 unless it is a charge on a legal estate.

Amendments—Land Registration Act 2002, ss 133, 135, Sch 11, para 34, Sch 13; Civil Partnership Act 2004, s 82, Sch 9, Part 1, para 2.

32 Further provisions relating to home rights

Schedule 4 (provisions supplementary to sections 30 and 31) has effect.

Amendments—Civil Partnership Act 2004, s 82, Sch 9, Part 1, para 3.

Occupation orders

33 Occupation orders where applicant has estate or interest etc or has home rights

(1) If–

   (a)   a person ('the person entitled')–

      (i)   is entitled to occupy a dwelling-house by virtue of a beneficial estate or interest or contract or by virtue of any enactment giving him the right to remain in occupation, or

      (ii)   has home rights in relation to a dwelling-house, and

   (b)   the dwelling-house–

      (i)   is or at any time has been the home of the person entitled and of another person with whom he is associated, or

      (ii)   was at any time intended by the person entitled and any such other person to be their home,

the person entitled may apply to the court for an order containing any of the provisions specified in subsections (3), (4) and (5).

(2) If an agreement to marry is terminated, no application under this section may be made by virtue of section 62(3)(e) by reference to that agreement after the end of the period of three years beginning with the date on which it is terminated.

(2A) If a civil partnership agreement (as defined by section 73 of the Civil Partnership Act 2004) is terminated, no application under this section may be made by virtue of section 62(3)(eza) by reference to that agreement after the end of the period of three years beginning with the day on which it is terminated.

(3) An order under this section may–

(a)   enforce the applicant's entitlement to remain in occupation as against the other person ('the respondent');

(b)   require the respondent to permit the applicant to enter and remain in the dwelling-house or part of the dwelling-house;

(c)   regulate the occupation of the dwelling-house by either or both parties;

(d)   if the respondent is entitled as mentioned in subsection (1)(a)(i), prohibit, suspend or restrict the exercise by him of his right to occupy the dwelling-house;

(e)   if the respondent has home rights in relation to the dwelling-house and the applicant is the other spouse or civil partner, restrict or terminate those rights;

(f)   require the respondent to leave the dwelling-house or part of the dwelling-house; or

(g)   exclude the respondent from a defined area in which the dwelling-house is included.

(4) An order under this section may declare that the applicant is entitled as mentioned in subsection (1)(a)(i) or has home rights.

(5) If the applicant has home rights and the respondent is the other spouse or civil partner, an order under this section made during the marriage or civil partnership may provide that those rights are not brought to an end by–

(a)   the death of the other spouse or civil partner; or

(b)   the termination (otherwise than by death) of the marriage or civil partnership.

(6) In deciding whether to exercise its powers under subsection (3) and (if so) in what manner, the court shall have regard to all the circumstances including–

(a)   the housing needs and housing resources of each of the parties and of any relevant child;

(b)   the financial resources of the parties;

(c)   the likely effect of any order, or of any decision by the court not to exercise its powers under subsection (3), on the health, safety or well-being of the parties and of any relevant child; and

(d)   the conduct of the parties in relation to each other and otherwise.

(7) If it appears to the court that the applicant or any relevant child is likely to suffer significant harm attributable to conduct of the respondent if an order under this section containing one or more of the provisions mentioned in subsection (3) is not made, the court shall make the order unless it appears to the court that–

(a)   the respondent or any relevant child is likely to suffer significant harm if the order is made; and

(b)   the harm likely to be suffered by the respondent or child in that event is as great as, or greater than, the harm attributable to conduct of the respondent which is likely to be suffered by the applicant or child if the order is not made.

(8) The court may exercise its powers under subsection (5) in any case where it considers that in all the circumstances it is just and reasonable to do so.

(9) An order under this section–

(a)   may not be made after the death of either of the parties mentioned in subsection (1); and

(b)   except in the case of an order made by virtue of subsection (5)(a), ceases to have effect on the death of either party.

(10) An order under this section may, in so far as it has continuing effect, be made for a specified period, until the occurrence of a specified event or until further order.

Amendments—Civil Partnership Act 2004, s 82, Sch 9, Part 1, para 4, (1), (4), (b), Part 3.

34 Effect of order under s 33 where rights are charge on dwelling-house

(1) If B's home rights are a charge on the estate or interest of A or of trustees for the A–

(a)   an order under section 33 against A has, except so far as a contrary intention appears, the same effect against persons deriving title under A or under the trustees and affected by the charge, and

(b)   sections 33(1), (3), (4) and (10) and 30(3) to (6) apply in relation to any person deriving title under A or under the trustees and affected by the charge as they apply in relation to A.

(2) The court may make an order under section 33 by virtue of subsection (1)(b) if it considers that in all the circumstances it is just and reasonable to do so.

Amendments—Civil Partnership Act 2004, s 82, Sch 9, Part 1, para 5.

35 One former spouse or former civil partner with no existing right to occupy

(1) This section applies if–

(a)   one former spouse or former civil partner is entitled to occupy a dwelling-house by virtue of a beneficial estate or interest or contract, or by virtue of any enactment giving him the right to remain in occupation;

(b)   the other former spouse or former civil partner is not so entitled; and

(c)   the dwelling-house–

   (i)   in the case of former spouses, was at any time their matrimonial home or was at any time intended by them to be their matrimonial home, or

(ii) in the case of former civil partners, was at any time their civil partnership home or was at any time intended by them to be their civil partnership home.

(2) The former spouse or former civil partner not so entitled may apply to the court for an order under this section against the other former spouse or former civil partner ('the respondent').

(3) If the applicant is in occupation, an order under this section must contain provision–

(a) giving the applicant the right not to be evicted or excluded from the dwelling-house or any part of it by the respondent for the period specified in the order; and

(b) prohibiting the respondent from evicting or excluding the applicant during that period.

(4) If the applicant is not in occupation, an order under this section must contain provision–

(a) giving the applicant the right to enter into and occupy the dwelling-house for the period specified in the order; and

(b) requiring the respondent to permit the exercise of that right.

(5) An order under this section may also–

(a) regulate the occupation of the dwelling-house by either or both of the parties;

(b) prohibit, suspend or restrict the exercise by the respondent of his right to occupy the dwelling-house;

(c) require the respondent to leave the dwelling-house or part of the dwelling-house; or

(d) exclude the respondent from a defined area in which the dwelling-house is included.

(6) In deciding whether to make an order under this section containing provision of the kind mentioned in subsection (3) or (4) and (if so) in what manner, the court shall have regard to all the circumstances including–

(a) the housing needs and housing resources of each of the parties and of any relevant child;

(b) the financial resources of each of the parties;

(c) the likely effect of any order, or of any decision by the court not to exercise its powers under subsection (3) or (4), on the health, safety or well-being of the parties and of any relevant child;

(d) the conduct of the parties in relation to each other and otherwise;

(e) the length of time that has elapsed since the parties ceased to live together;

(f) the length of time that has elapsed since the marriage or civil partnership was dissolved or annulled; and

(g) the existence of any pending proceedings between the parties–

(i)   for an order under section 23A or 24 of the Matrimonial Causes Act 1973 (property adjustment orders in connection with divorce proceedings etc);

(ia)   for a property adjustment order under Part 2 of Schedule 5 to the Civil Partnership Act 2004;

(ii)   for an order under paragraph 1(2)(d) or (e) of Schedule 1 to the Children Act 1989 (orders for financial relief against parents); or

(iii) relating to the legal or beneficial ownership of the dwelling-house.

(7) In deciding whether to exercise its power to include one or more of the provisions referred to in subsection (5) ('a subsection (5) provision') and (if so) in what manner, the court shall have regard to all the circumstances including the matters mentioned in subsection (6)(a) to (e).

(8) If the court decides to make an order under this section and it appears to it that, if the order does not include a subsection (5) provision, the applicant or any relevant child is likely to suffer significant harm attributable to conduct of the respondent, the court shall include the subsection (5) provision in the order unless it appears to the court that–

(a)   the respondent or any relevant child is likely to suffer significant harm if the provision is included in the order; and

(b)   the harm likely to be suffered by the respondent or child in that event is as great as or greater than the harm attributable to conduct of the respondent which is likely to be suffered by the applicant or child if the provision is not included.

(9) An order under this section–

(a)   may not be made after the death of either of the former spouses or former civil partners; and

(b)   ceases to have effect on the death of either of them.

(10) An order under this section must be limited so as to have effect for a specified period not exceeding six months, but may be extended on one or more occasions for a further specified period not exceeding six months.

(11) A former spouse or former civil partner who has an equitable interest in the dwelling-house or in the proceeds of sale of the dwelling-house but in whom there is not vested (whether solely or as joint tenant) a legal estate in fee simple or a legal term of years absolute in the dwelling-house is to be treated (but only for the purpose of determining whether he is eligible to apply under this section) as not being entitled to occupy the dwelling-house by virtue of that interest.

(12) Subsection (11) does not prejudice any right of such a former spouse or former civil partner to apply for an order under section 33.

(13) So long as an order under this section remains in force, subsections (3) to (6) of section 30 apply in relation to the applicant–

(a)   as if he were B (the person entitled to occupy the dwelling-house by virtue of that section); and

(b)   as if the respondent were A (the person entitled as mentioned in subsection (1)(a) of that section).

Amendments—Civil Partnership Act 2004, s 82, Sch 9, Part 1, para 6.

36 One cohabitant or former cohabitant with no existing right to occupy

(1) This section applies if–

(a)   one cohabitant or former cohabitant is entitled to occupy a dwelling-house by virtue of a beneficial estate or interest or contract or by virtue of any enactment giving him the right to remain in occupation;

(b)   the other cohabitant or former cohabitant is not so entitled; and

(c)   that dwelling-house is the home in which they cohabit or a home in which they at any time cohabited or intended to cohabit.

(2) The cohabitant or former cohabitant not so entitled may apply to the court for an order under this section against the other cohabitant or former cohabitant ('the respondent').

(3) If the applicant is in occupation, an order under this section must contain provision–

(a)   giving the applicant the right not to be evicted or excluded from the dwelling-house or any part of it by the respondent for the period specified in the order, and

(b)   prohibiting the respondent from evicting or excluding the applicant during that period.

(4) If the applicant is not in occupation, an order under this section must contain provision–

(a)   giving the applicant the right to enter into and occupy the dwelling-house for the period specified in the order; and

(b)   requiring the respondent to permit the exercise of that right.

(5) An order under this section may also–

(a)   regulate the occupation of the dwelling-house by either or both of the parties;

(b)   prohibit, suspend or restrict the exercise by the respondent of his right to occupy the dwelling-house;

(c)   require the respondent to leave the dwelling-house or part of the dwelling-house; or

(d)   exclude the respondent from a defined area in which the dwelling-house is included.

(6) In deciding whether to make an order under this section containing provision of the kind mentioned in subsection (3) or (4) and (if so) in what manner, the court shall have regard to all the circumstances including–

   (a)   the housing needs and housing resources of each of the parties and of any relevant child;

   (b)   the financial resources of each of the parties;

   (c)   the likely effect of any order, or of any decision by the court not to exercise its powers under subsection (3) or (4), on the health, safety or well-being of the parties and of any relevant child;

   (d)   the conduct of the parties in relation to each other and otherwise;

   (e)   the nature of the parties' relationship and in particular the level of commitment involved in it;

   (f)   the length of time during which they have cohabited;

   (g)   whether there are or have been any children who are children of both parties or for whom both parties have or have had parental responsibility;

   (h)   the length of time that has elapsed since the parties ceased to live together; and

   (i)   the existence of any pending proceedings between the parties–

       (i)   for an order under paragraph 1(2)(d) or (e) of Schedule 1 to the Children Act 1989 (orders for financial relief against parents), or

       (ii)   relating to the legal or beneficial ownership of the dwelling-house.

(7) In deciding whether to exercise its powers to include one or more of the provisions referred to in subsection (5) ('a subsection (5) provision') and (if so) in what manner, the court shall have regard to all the circumstances including–

   (a)   the matters mentioned in subsection (6)(a) to (d); and

   (b)   the questions mentioned in subsection (8).

(8) The questions are–

   (a)   whether the applicant or any relevant child is likely to suffer significant harm attributable to conduct of the respondent if the subsection (5) provision is not included in the order; and

   (b)   whether the harm likely to be suffered by the respondent or child if the provision is included is as great as or greater than the harm attributable to conduct of the respondent which is likely to be suffered by the applicant or child if the provision is not included.

(9) An order under this section–

   (a)   may not be made after the death of either of the parties; and

   (b)   ceases to have effect on the death of either of them.

(10) An order under this section must be limited so as to have effect for a specified period not exceeding six months, but may be extended on one occasion for a further specified period not exceeding six months.

(11) A person who has an equitable interest in the dwelling-house or in the proceeds of sale of the dwelling-house but in whom there is not vested (whether solely or as joint tenant) a legal estate in fee simple or a legal term of years absolute in the dwelling-house is to be treated (but only for the purpose of

determining whether he is eligible to apply under this section) as not being entitled to occupy the dwelling-house by virtue of that interest.

(12) Subsection (11) does not prejudice any right of such a person to apply for an order under section 33.

(13) So long as the order remains in force, subsections (3) to (6) of section 30 apply in relation to the applicant–

(a)   as if he were B (the person entitled to occupy the dwelling-house by virtue of that section); and

(b)   as if the respondent were A (the person entitled as mentioned in subsection (1)(a) of that section).

Amendments—Civil Partnership Act 2004, s 82, Sch 9, Part 1, para 7; Domestic Violence, Crime and Victims Act 2004, ss 2(2), 58(1), Sch 10, para 34(1), (3).

37 Neither spouse or civil partner entitled to occupy

(1) This section applies if–

(a)   one spouse or former spouse and the other spouse or former spouse occupy a dwelling-house which is or was the matrimonial home; but

(b)   neither of them is entitled to remain in occupation–

(i)   by virtue of a beneficial estate or interest or contract; or

(ii)   by virtue of any enactment giving him the right to remain in occupation.

(1A) This section also applies if–

(a)   one civil partner or former civil partner and the other civil partner or former civil partner occupy a dwelling-house which is or was the civil partnership home; but

(b)   neither of them is entitled to remain in occupation–

(i)   by virtue of a beneficial estate or interest or contract; or

(ii)   by virtue of any enactment giving him the right to remain in occupation.

(2) Either of the parties may apply to the court for an order against the other under this section.

(3) An order under this section may–

(a)   require the respondent to permit the applicant to enter and remain in the dwelling-house or part of the dwelling-house;

(b)   regulate the occupation of the dwelling-house by either or both of the parties;

(c)   require the respondent to leave the dwelling-house or part of the dwelling-house; or

(d)   exclude the respondent from a defined area in which the dwelling-house is included.

(4) Subsections (6) and (7) of section 33 apply to the exercise by the court of its powers under this section as they apply to the exercise by the court of its powers under subsection (3) of that section.

(5) An order under this section must be limited so as to have effect for a specified period not exceeding six months, but may be extended on one or more occasions for a further specified period not exceeding six months.

Amendments—Civil Partnership Act 2004, s 82, Sch 9, Part 1, para 8.

38 Neither cohabitant or former cohabitant entitled to occupy

(1) This section applies if–

- (a) one cohabitant or former cohabitant and the other cohabitant or former cohabitant occupy a dwelling-house which is the home in which they cohabit or cohabited; but
- (b) neither of them is entitled to remain in occupation–
  - (i) by virtue of a beneficial estate or interest or contract; or
  - (ii) by virtue of any enactment giving him the right to remain in occupation.

(2) Either of the parties may apply to the court for an order against the other under this section.

(3) An order under this section may–

- (a) require the respondent to permit the applicant to enter and remain in the dwelling-house or part of the dwelling-house;
- (b) regulate the occupation of the dwelling-house by either or both of the parties;
- (c) require the respondent to leave the dwelling-house or part of the dwelling-house; or
- (d) exclude the respondent from a defined area in which the dwelling-house is included.

(4) In deciding whether to exercise its powers to include one or more of the provisions referred to in subsection (3) ('a subsection (3) provision') and (if so) in what manner, the court shall have regard to all the circumstances including–

- (a) the housing needs and housing resources of each of the parties and of any relevant child;
- (b) the financial resources of each of the parties;
- (c) the likely effect of any order, or of any decision by the court not to exercise its powers under subsection (3), on the health, safety or well-being of the parties and of any relevant child;
- (d) the conduct of the parties in relation to each other and otherwise; and
- (e) the questions mentioned in subsection (5).

(5) The questions are–

- (a) whether the applicant or any relevant child is likely to suffer significant harm attributable to conduct of the respondent if the subsection (3) provision is not included in the order; and

(b)   whether the harm likely to be suffered by the respondent or child if the provision is included is as great as or greater than the harm attributable to conduct of the respondent which is likely to be suffered by the applicant or child if the provision is not included.

(6) An order under this section shall be limited so as to have effect for a specified period not exceeding six months, but may be extended on one occasion for a further specified period not exceeding six months.

Amendments—Domestic Violence, Crime and Victims Act 2004, s 58(1), Sch 10, para 35.

39 Supplementary provisions

(1) In this Part an 'occupation order' means an order under section 33, 35, 36, 37 or 38.

(2) An application for an occupation order may be made in other family proceedings or without any other family proceedings being instituted.

(3) If–

(a)   an application for an occupation order is made under section 33, 35, 36, 37 or 38, and

(b)   the court considers that it has no power to make the order under the section concerned, but that it has power to make an order under one of the other sections,

the court may make an order under that other section.

(4) The fact that a person has applied for an occupation order under sections 35 to 38, or that an occupation order has been made, does not affect the right of any person to claim a legal or equitable interest in any property in any subsequent proceedings (including subsequent proceedings under this Part).

40 Additional provisions that may be included in certain occupation orders

(1) The court may on, or at any time after, making an occupation order under section 33, 35 or 36–

(a)   impose on either party obligations as to–
    (i)   the repair and maintenance of the dwelling-house; or
    (ii)   the discharge of rent, mortgage payments or other outgoings affecting the dwelling-house;
(b)   order a party occupying the dwelling-house or any part of it (including a party who is entitled to do so by virtue of a beneficial estate or interest or contract or by virtue of any enactment giving him the right to remain in occupation) to make periodical payments to the other party in respect of the accommodation, if the other party would (but for the order) be entitled to occupy the dwelling-house by virtue of a beneficial estate or interest or contract or by virtue of any such enactment;
(c)   grant either party possession or use of furniture or other contents of the dwelling-house;

(d)   order either party to take reasonable care of any furniture or other contents of the dwelling-house;

(e)   order either party to take reasonable steps to keep the dwelling-house and any furniture or other contents secure.

(2) In deciding whether and, if so, how to exercise its powers under this section, the court shall have regard to all the circumstances of the case including–

(a)   the financial needs and financial resources of the parties; and

(b)   the financial obligations which they have, or are likely to have in the foreseeable future, including financial obligations to each other and to any relevant child.

(3) An order under this section ceases to have effect when the occupation order to which it relates ceases to have effect.

41

....

Amendments—Repealed by Domestic Violence, Crime and Victims Act 2004, ss 2(1), 58(1), Sch 11.

Non-molestation orders

42 Non-molestation orders

(1) In this Part a 'non-molestation order' means an order containing either or both of the following provisions–

(a)   provision prohibiting a person ('the respondent') from molesting another person who is associated with the respondent;

(b)   provision prohibiting the respondent from molesting a relevant child.

(2) The court may make a non-molestation order–

(a)   if an application for the order has been made (whether in other family proceedings or without any other family proceedings being instituted) by a person who is associated with the respondent; or

(b)   if in any family proceedings to which the respondent is a party the court considers that the order should be made for the benefit of any other party to the proceedings or any relevant child even though no such application has been made.

(3) In subsection (2) 'family proceedings' includes proceedings in which the court has made an emergency protection order under section 44 of the Children Act 1989 which includes an exclusion requirement (as defined in section 44A(3) of that Act).

(4) Where an agreement to marry is terminated, no application under subsection (2)(a) may be made by virtue of section 62(3)(e) by reference to that agreement after the end of the period of three years beginning with the day on which it is terminated.

(4ZA) If a civil partnership agreement (as defined by section 73 of the Civil Partnership Act 2004) is terminated, no application under this section may be made by virtue of section 62(3)(eza) by reference to that agreement after the end of the period of three years beginning with the day on which it is terminated.

(4A) A court considering whether to make an occupation order shall also consider whether to exercise the power conferred by subsection (2)(b).

(4B) In this Part 'the applicant', in relation to a non-molestation order, includes (where the context per-mits) the person for whose benefit such an order would be or is made in exercise of the power conferred by subsection (2)(b).

(5) In deciding whether to exercise its powers under this section and, if so, in what manner, the court shall have regard to all the circumstances including the need to secure the health, safety and well-being–

   (a)   of the applicant; and
   (b)   of any relevant child.

(6) A non-molestation order may be expressed so as to refer to molestation in general, to particular acts of molestation, or to both.

(7) A non-molestation order may be made for a specified period or until further order.

(8) A non-molestation order which is made in other family proceedings ceases to have effect if those proceedings are withdrawn or dismissed.

Amendments—Civil Partnership Act 2004, s 82, Sch 9, Part 1, para 9; Domestic Violence, Crime and Victims Act 2004, s 58(1), (2), Sch 10, para 36(1), (2), (3).

42A Offence of breaching non-molestation order

(1) A person who without reasonable excuse does anything that he is prohibited from doing by a non-molestation order is guilty of an offence.

(2) In the case of a non-molestation order made by virtue of section 45(1), a person can be guilty of an offence under this section only in respect of conduct engaged in at a time when he was aware of the existence of the order.

(3) Where a person is convicted of an offence under this section in respect of any conduct, that conduct is not punishable as a contempt of court.

(4) A person cannot be convicted of an offence under this section in respect of any conduct which has been punished as a contempt of court.

(5) A person guilty of an offence under this section is liable –

   (a)   on conviction on indictment, to imprisonment for a term not exceeding five years, or a fine, or both;
   (b)   on summary conviction, to imprisonment for a term not exceeding 12 months, or a fine not exceeding the statutory maximum, or both.

(6) A reference in any enactment to proceedings under this Part, or to an order under this Part, does not include a reference to proceedings for an offence under this section or to an order made in such proceedings.

'Enactment' includes an enactment contained in subordinate legislation within the meaning of the Interpretation Act 1978 (c 30).

Amendment—Domestic Violence, Crime and Victims Act 2004, s 1.

Further provisions relating to occupation and non-molestation orders

43 Leave of court required for applications by children under sixteen

(1) A child under the age of sixteen may not apply for an occupation order or a non-molestation order except with the leave of the court.

(2) The court may grant leave for the purposes of subsection (1) only if it is satisfied that the child has sufficient understanding to make the proposed application for the occupation order or non-molestation order.

44 Evidence of agreement to marry or form a civil partnership

(1) Subject to subsection (2), the court shall not make an order under section 33 or 42 by virtue of section 62(3)(e) unless there is produced to it evidence in writing of the existence of the agreement to marry.

(2) Subsection (1) does not apply if the court is satisfied that the agreement to marry was evidenced by–

(a)   the gift of an engagement ring by one party to the agreement to the other in contemplation of their marriage, or

(b)   a ceremony entered into by the parties in the presence of one or more other persons assembled for the purpose of witnessing the ceremony.

(3) Subject to subsection (4), the court shall not make an order under section 33 or 42 by virtue of section 62(3)(eza) unless there is produced to it evidence in writing of the existence of the civil partnership agreement (as defined by section 73 of the Civil Partnership Act 2004).

(4) Subsection (3) does not apply if the court is satisfied that the civil partnership agreement was evidenced by–

(a)   a gift by one party to the agreement to the other as a token of the agreement, or

(b)   a ceremony entered into by the parties in the presence of one or more other persons assembled for the purpose of witnessing the ceremony.

Amendments—Civil Partnership Act 2004, s 82, Sch 9, Part 1, para 10.

45 Ex parte orders

(1) The court may, in any case where it considers that it is just and convenient to do so, make an occupation order or a non-molestation order even though

the respondent has not been given such notice of the proceedings as would otherwise be required by rules of court.

(2) In determining whether to exercise its powers under subsection (1), the court shall have regard to all the circumstances including–

(a) any risk of significant harm to the applicant or a relevant child, attributable to conduct of the respondent, if the order is not made immediately;

(b) whether it is likely that the applicant will be deterred or prevented from pursuing the application if an order is not made immediately; and

(c) whether there is reason to believe that the respondent is aware of the proceedings but is deliberately evading service and that the applicant or a relevant child will be seriously prejudiced by the delay involved–

(i) where the court is a magistrates' court, in effecting service of proceedings; or

(ii) in any other case, in effecting substituted service.

(3) If the court makes an order by virtue of subsection (1) it must afford the respondent an opportunity to make representations relating to the order as soon as just and convenient at a full hearing.

(4) If, at a full hearing, the court makes an occupation order ('the full order'), then–

(a) for the purposes of calculating the maximum period for which the full order may be made to have effect, the relevant section is to apply as if the period for which the full order will have effect began on the date on which the initial order first had effect; and

(b) the provisions of section 36(10) or 38(6) as to the extension of orders are to apply as if the full order and the initial order were a single order.

(5) In this section–

'full hearing' means a hearing of which notice has been given to all the parties in accordance with rules of court;

'initial order' means an occupation order made by virtue of subsection (1); and

'relevant section' means section 33(10), 35(10), 36(10), 37(5) or 38(6).

46 Undertakings

(1) In any case where the court has power to make an occupation order or non-molestation order, the court may accept an undertaking from any party to the proceedings.

(2) No power of arrest may be attached to any undertaking given under subsection (1).

(3) The court shall not accept an undertaking under subsection (1) instead of making an occupation order in any case where apart from this section a power of arrest would be attached to the order.

(3A) The court shall not accept an undertaking under subsection (1) instead of making a non-molestation order in any case where it appears to the court that –

    (a)   the respondent has used or threatened violence against the applicant or a relevant child; and

    (b)   for the protection of the applicant or child it is necessary to make a non-molestation order so that any breach may be punishable under section 42A.

(4) An undertaking given to a court under subsection (1) is enforceable as if the court had made an occupation order or a non-molestation order in terms corresponding to those of the undertaking.

(5) This section has effect without prejudice to the powers of the High Court and the county court apart from this section.

Amendments—Domestic Violence, Crime and Victims Act 2004, s 58(1), Sch 10, para 37.

47 Arrest for breach of order

(1) ...

(2) If–

    (a)   the court makes an occupation order; and

    (b)   it appears to the court that the respondent has used or threatened violence against the applicant or a relevant child,

it shall attach a power of arrest to one or more provisions of the order unless the court is satisfied that in all the circumstances of the case the applicant or child will be adequately protected without such a power of arrest.

(3) Subsection (2) does not apply in any case where the occupation order is made by virtue of section 45(1), but in such a case the court may attach a power of arrest to one or more provisions of the order if it appears to it–

    (a)   that the respondent has used or threatened violence against the applicant or a relevant child; and

    (b)   that there is a risk of significant harm to the applicant or child, attributable to conduct of the respondent, if the power of arrest is not attached to those provisions immediately.

(4) If, by virtue of subsection (3), the court attaches a power of arrest to any provisions of an occupation order, it may provide that the power of arrest is to have effect for a shorter period than the other provisions of the order.

(5) Any period specified for the purposes of subsection (4) may be extended by the court (on one or more occasions) on an application to vary or discharge the occupation order.

(6) If, by virtue of subsection (2) or (3), a power of arrest is attached to certain provisions of an order, a constable may arrest without warrant a person whom he has reasonable cause for suspecting to be in breach of any such provision.

(7) If a power of arrest is attached under subsection (2) or (3) to certain provisions of the order and the respondent is arrested under subsection (6)–

(a) he must be brought before the relevant judicial authority within the period of 24 hours beginning at the time of his arrest; and

(b) if the matter is not then disposed of forthwith, the relevant judicial authority before whom he is brought may remand him.

In reckoning for the purposes of this subsection any period of 24 hours, no account is to be taken of Christmas Day, Good Friday or any Sunday.

(8) If the court –

(a) has made a non-molestation order, or

(b) has made an occupation order but has not attached a power of arrest under subsection (2) or (3) to any provision of the order, or has attached that power only to certain provisions of the order,

then, if at any time the applicant considers that the respondent has failed to comply with the order, he may apply to the relevant judicial authority for the issue of a warrant for the arrest of the respondent.

(9) The relevant judicial authority shall not issue a warrant on an application under subsection (8) unless–

(a) the application is substantiated on oath; and

(b) the relevant judicial authority has reasonable grounds for believing that the respondent has failed to comply with the order.

(10) If a person is brought before a court by virtue of a warrant issued under subsection (9) and the court does not dispose of the matter forthwith, the court may remand him.

(11) Schedule 5 (which makes provision corresponding to that applying in magistrates' courts in civil cases under sections 128 and 129 of the Magistrates' Courts Act 1980) has effect in relation to the powers of the High Court and a county court to remand a person by virtue of this section.

(12) If a person remanded under this section is granted bail (whether in the High Court or a county court under Schedule 5 or in a magistrates' court under section 128 or 129 of the Magistrates' Courts Act 1980), he may be required by the relevant judicial authority to comply, before release on bail or later, with such requirements as appear to that authority to be necessary to secure that he does not interfere with witnesses or otherwise obstruct the course of justice.

Amendments—Domestic Violence, Crime and Victims Act 2004, s 58(1), Sch 10, para 38.

48 Remand for medical examination and report

(1) If the relevant judicial authority has reason to consider that a medical report will be required, any power to remand a person under section 47(7)(b) or (10) may be exercised for the purpose of enabling a medical examination and report to be made.

(2) If such a power is so exercised, the adjournment must not be for more than 4 weeks at a time unless the relevant judicial authority remands the accused in custody.

(3) If the relevant judicial authority so remands the accused, the adjournment must not be for more than 3 weeks at a time.

(4) If there is reason to suspect that a person who has been arrested–

(a)   under section 47(6), or
(b)   under a warrant issued on an application made under section 47(8),

is suffering from *mental illness or severe mental impairment*[mental disorder within the meaning of the Mental Health Act 1983], the relevant judicial authority has the same power to make an order under section 35 of the *Mental Health Act 1983* [that Act] (remand for report on accused's mental condition) as the Crown Court has *under section 35 of the Act of 1983* [that section] in the case of an accused person within the meaning of that section.

Prospective Amendments—Words in italics repealed and subsequent words in square brackets substituted by the Mental Health Act 2007, s 1(4), Sch 1, Pt2,para 20(1), (2), (a) from a date to be appointed.

49 Variation and discharge of orders

(1) An occupation order or non-molestation order may be varied or discharged by the court on an application by–

(a)   the respondent, or
(b)   the person on whose application the order was made.

(2) In the case of a non-molestation order made by virtue of section 42(2)(b), the order may be varied or discharged by the court even though no such application has been made.

(3) If B's home rights are, under section 31, are a charge on the estate or interest of the other spouse or of trustees for A, an order under section 33 against A may also be varied or discharged by the court on an application by any person deriving title under A or under the trustees and affected by the charge.

(4) If, by virtue of section 47(3), a power of arrest has been attached to certain provisions of an occupation order, the court may vary or discharge the order under subsection (1) in so far as it confers a power of arrest (whether or not any application has been made to vary or discharge any other provision of the order).

Amendments—Civil Partnership Act 2004, s 82, Sch 9, Part 1, para 11; Domestic Violence, Crime and Victims Act 2004, s 58(1), Sch 10, para 39, Sch 11.

Enforcement powers of magistrates' courts

50 Power of magistrates' court to suspend execution of committal order

(1) If, under section 63(3) of the Magistrates' Courts Act 1980, a magistrates' court has power to commit a person to custody for breach of a relevant requirement, the court may by order direct that the execution of the order of committal is to be suspended for such period or on such terms and conditions as it may specify.

(2) In subsection (1) 'a relevant requirement' means–

    (a)   an occupation order or non-molestation order;

    (b)   an exclusion requirement included by virtue of section 38A of the Children Act 1989 in an interim care order made under section 38 of that Act; or

    (c)   an exclusion requirement included by virtue of section 44A of the Children Act 1989 in an emergency protection order under section 44 of that Act.

51 Power of magistrates' court to order hospital admission or guardianship

(1) A magistrates' court shall have the same power to make a hospital order or guardianship order under section 37 of the Mental Health Act 1983 or an interim hospital order under section 38 of that Act in the case of a person suffering from *mental illness or severe mental impairment* [mental disorder within the meaning of that Act] who could otherwise be committed to custody for breach of a relevant requirement as a magistrates' court has under those sections in the case of a person convicted of an offence punishable on summary conviction with imprisonment.

(2) In subsection (1) 'a relevant requirement' has the meaning given by section 50(2).

Prospective Amendments—Words in italics repealed and subsequent words in square brackets substituted by the Mental Health Act 2007, s 1(4), Sch 1, Pt2,para 20(1), (2), (a).

Interim care orders and emergency protection orders

52 Amendments of Children Act 1989

Schedule 6 makes amendments of the provisions of the Children Act 1989 relating to interim care orders and emergency protection orders.

Transfer of tenancies

53 Transfer of certain tenancies

Schedule 7 makes provision in relation to the transfer of certain tenancies on divorce etc or on separation of cohabitants.

Dwelling-house subject to mortgage

54 Dwelling-house subject to mortgage

(1) In determining for the purposes of this Part whether a person is entitled to occupy a dwelling-house by virtue of an estate or interest, any right to possession of the dwelling-house conferred on a mortgagee of the dwelling-house under or by virtue of his mortgage is to be disregarded.

(2) Subsection (1) applies whether or not the mortgagee is in possession.

(3) Where a person ('A') is entitled to occupy a dwelling-house by virtue of an estate or interest, a connected person does not by virtue of–

    (a)   any home rightsconferred by section 30, or
    (b)   any rights conferred by an order under section 35 or 36,

have any larger right against the mortgagee to occupy the dwelling-house than A has by virtue of his estate or interest and of any contract with the mortgagee.

(4) Subsection (3) does not apply, in the case of home rights, if under section 31 those rights are a charge, affecting the mortgagee, on the estate or interest mortgaged.

(5) In this section 'connected person', in relation to any person, means that person's spouse, former spouse,civil partner, former civil partner, cohabitant or former cohabitant.

Amendments—Civil Partnership Act 2004, s 82, Sch 9, Part 1, para 12.

55 Actions by mortgagees: joining connected persons as parties

(1) This section applies if a mortgagee of land which consists of or includes a dwelling-house brings an action in any court for the enforcement of his security.

(2) A connected person who is not already a party to the action is entitled to be made a party in the circumstances mentioned in subsection (3).

(3) The circumstances are that–

    (a)   the connected person is enabled by section 30(3) or (6) (or by section 30(3) or (6) as applied by section 35(13) or 36(13)), to meet the mortgagor's liabilities under the mortgage;
    (b)   he has applied to the court before the action is finally disposed of in that court; and
    (c)   the court sees no special reason against his being made a party to the action and is satisfied–
        (i)   that he may be expected to make such payments or do such other things in or towards satisfaction of the mortgagor's liabilities or obligations as might affect the outcome of the proceedings; or
        (ii)   that the expectation of it should be considered under section 36 of the Administration of Justice Act 1970.

(4) In this section 'connected person' has the same meaning as in section 54.

56 Actions by mortgagees: service of notice on certain persons

(1) This section applies if a mortgagee of land which consists, or substantially consists, of a dwelling-house brings an action for the enforcement of his security, and at the relevant time there is–

(a)   in the case of unregistered land, a land charge of Class F registered against the person who is the estate owner at the relevant time or any person who, where the estate owner is a trustee, preceded him as trustee during the subsistence of the mortgage; or

(b)   in the case of registered land, a subsisting registration of–

(i)   a notice under section 31(10);

(ii)   a notice under section 2(8) of the Matrimonial Homes Act 1983; or

(iii)   a notice or caution under section 2(7) of the Matrimonial Homes Act 1967.

(2) If the person on whose behalf–

(a)   the land charge is registered, or

(b)   the notice or caution is entered,

is not a party to the action, the mortgagee must serve notice of the action on him.

(3) If–

(a)   an official search has been made on behalf of the mortgagee which would disclose any land charge of Class F, notice or caution within subsection (1)(a) or (b),

(b)   a certificate of the result of the search has been issued, and

(c)   the action is commenced within the priority period,

the relevant time is the date of the certificate.

(4) In any other case the relevant time is the time when the action is commenced.

(5) The priority period is, for both registered and unregistered land, the period for which, in accordance with section 11(5) and (6) of the Land Charges Act 1972, a certificate on an official search operates in favour of a purchaser.

Jurisdiction and procedure etc

57 Jurisdiction of courts

(1) For the purposes of this Part 'the court' means the High Court, a county court or a magistrates' court.

(2) Subsection (1) is subject to the provision made by or under the following provisions of this section, to section 59 and to any express provision as to the jurisdiction of any court made by any other provision of this Part.

(3) The Lord Chancellor may, after consulting the Lord Chief Justice, by order specify proceedings under this Act which may only be commenced in–

   (a)   a specified level of court;

   (b)   a court which falls within a specified class of court; or

   (c)   a particular court determined in accordance with, or specified in, the order.

(4) The Lord Chancellor may, after consulting the Lord Chief Justice by order specify circumstances in which specified proceedings under this Part may only be commenced in–

   (a)   a specified level of court;

   (b)   a court which falls within a specified class of court; or

   (c)   a particular court determined in accordance with, or specified in, the order.

(5) The Lord Chancellor may, after consulting the Lords Chief Justice, by order provide that in specified circumstances the whole, or any specified part of any specified proceedings under this Part shall be transferred to–

   (a)   a specified level of court;

   (b)   a court which falls within a specified class of court; or

   (c)   a particular court determined in accordance with, or specified in, the order.

(6) An order under subsection (5) may provide for the transfer to be made at any stage, or specified stage, of the proceedings and whether or not the proceedings, or any part of them, have already been transferred.

(7) An order under subsection (5) may make provision as the Lord Chancellor thinks appropriate, after consulting the Lord Chief Justice for excluding specified proceedings from the operation of section 38 or 39 of the Matrimonial and Family Proceedings Act 1984 (transfer of family proceedings) or any other enactment which would otherwise govern the transfer of those proceedings, or any part of them.

(8) For the purposes of subsections (3), (4) and (5), there are three levels of court–

   (a)   the High Court;

   (b)   any county court; and

   (c)   any magistrates' court.

(9) The Lord Chancellor may, after consulting the Lord Chief Justice, by order make provision for the principal registry of the Family Division of the High Court to be treated as if it were a county court for specified purposes of this Part, or of any provision made under this Part.

(10) Any order under subsection (9) may make such provision as the Lord Chancellor thinks expedient, after consulting the Lord Chief Justice, for the purpose of applying (with or without modifications) provisions which apply in relation to the procedure in county courts to the principal registry when it acts as if it were a county court.

(11) In this section 'specified' means specified by an order under this section.

(12) The Lord Chief Justice may nominate a judicial office holder (as defined in section 109(4) of the Constitutional Reform Act 2005) to exercise his functions under this section.

Amendments—Constitutional Reform Act 2005, s 15(1), Sch 4, Pt 1, paras 252, 253(1), (6).

58 Contempt proceedings

The powers of the court in relation to contempt of court arising out of a person's failure to comply with an order under this Part may be exercised by the relevant judicial authority.

59 Magistrates' courts

(1) A magistrates' court shall not be competent to entertain any application, or make any order, involving any disputed question as to a party's entitlement to occupy any property by virtue of a beneficial estate or interest or contract or by virtue of any enactment giving him the right to remain in occupation, unless it is unnecessary to determine the question in order to deal with the application or make the order.

(2) A magistrates' court may decline jurisdiction in any proceedings under this Part if it considers that the case can more conveniently be dealt with by another court.

(3) The powers of a magistrates' court under section 63(2) of the Magistrates' Courts Act 1980 to suspend or rescind orders shall not apply in relation to any order made under this Part.

60 Provision for third parties to act on behalf of victims of domestic violence

(1) Rules of court may provide for a prescribed person, or any person in a prescribed category, ('a representative') to act on behalf of another in relation to proceedings to which this Part applies.

(2) Rules made under this section may, in particular, authorise a representative to apply for an occupation order or for a non-molestation order for which the person on whose behalf the representative is acting could have applied.

(3) Rules made under this section may prescribe–

  (a) conditions to be satisfied before a representative may make an application to the court on behalf of another; and
  (b) considerations to be taken into account by the court in determining whether, and if so how, to exercise any of its powers under this Part when a representative is acting on behalf of another.

(4) Any rules made under this section may be made so as to have effect for a specified period and may make consequential or transitional provision with respect to the expiry of the specified period.

(5) Any such rules may be replaced by further rules made under this section.

61 Appeals

(1) An appeal shall lie to the High Court against–

  (a)   the making by a magistrates' court of any order under this Part, or
  (b)   any refusal by a magistrates' court to make such an order,

but no appeal shall lie against any exercise by a magistrates' court of the power conferred by section 59(2).

(2) On an appeal under this section, the High Court may make such orders as may be necessary to give effect to its determination of the appeal.

(3) Where an order is made under subsection (2), the High Court may also make such incidental or consequential orders as appear to it to be just.

(4) Any order of the High Court made on an appeal under this section (other than one directing that an application be re-heard by a magistrates' court) shall, for the purposes–

  (a)   of the enforcement of the order, and
  (b)   of any power to vary, revive or discharge orders,

be treated as if it were an order of the magistrates' court from which the appeal was brought and not an order of the High Court.

(5) The Lord Chancellor may, after consulting the Lord Chief Justice, by order make provision as to the circumstances in which appeals may be made against decisions taken by courts on questions arising in connection with the transfer, or proposed transfer, of proceedings by virtue of any order under section 57(5).

(6) Except to the extent provided for in any order made under subsection (5), no appeal may be made against any decision of a kind mentioned in that subsection.

(7) The Lord Chief Justice may nominate a judicial office holder (as defined in section 109(4) of the Constitutional Reform Act 2005) to exercise his functions under this section.

Amendments—Constitutional Reform Act 2005, s 15(1), Sch 4, Pt 1, paras 252, 254(1), (2).

General

62 Meaning of 'cohabitants', 'relevant child' and 'associated persons'

(1) For the purposes of this Part–

  (a)   'cohabitants' are two persons who are neither married to each other nor civil partners of each other but are living together as husband and wife or as if they were civil partners; and
  (b)   'cohabit' and 'former cohabitants' are to be read accordingly, but the latter expression does not include cohabitants who have subsequently married each other or become civil partners of each other.

(2) In this Part, 'relevant child', in relation to any proceedings under this Part, means–

(a) any child who is living with or might reasonably be expected to live with either party to the proceedings;

(b) any child in relation to whom an order under the Adoption Act 1976, the Adoption and Children Act 2002 or the Children Act 1989 is in question in the proceedings; and

(c) any other child whose interests the court considers relevant.

(3) For the purposes of this Part, a person is associated with another person if–

(a) they are or have been married to each other;

(aa) they are or have been civil partners of each other;

(b) they are cohabitants or former cohabitants;

(c) they live or have lived in the same household, otherwise than merely by reason of one of them being the other's employee, tenant, lodger or boarder;

(d) they are relatives;

(e) they have agreed to marry one another (whether or not that agreement has been terminated);

(eza) they have entered into a civil partnership agreement (as defined by section 73 of the Civil Partnership Act 2004) (whether or not that agreement has been terminated;

(ea) they have or have had an intimate personal relationship with each other which is or was of significant duration;

(f) in relation to any child, they are both persons falling within subsection (4); or

(g) they are parties to the same family proceedings (other than proceedings under this Part).

(4) A person falls within this subsection in relation to a child if–

(a) he is a parent of the child; or

(b) he has or has had parental responsibility for the child.

(5) If a child has been adopted or falls within subsection (7), two persons are also associated with each other for the purpose of this Part if–

(a) one is a natural parent of the child or a parent of such a natural parent; and

(b) the other is the child or any person–

   (i) who had become a parent of the child by virtue of an adoption order or has applied for an adoption order, or

   (ii) with whom the child has at any time been placed for adoption.

(6) A body corporate and another person are not, by virtue of subsection (3)(f) or (g), to be regarded for the purposes of this Part as associated with each other.

(7) A child falls within this subsection if–

(a) an adoption agency, within the meaning of section 2 of the Adoption and Children Act 2002, has power to place him for adoption under section 19 of that Act (placing children with parental consent) or he has become the subject of an order under section 21 of that Act (placement orders), or

(b) he is freed for adoption by virtue of an order made–
    (i) in England and Wales, under section 18 of the Adoption Act 1976,
    (ii) in Scotland, under section 18 of the Adoption (Scotland) Act 1978, or
    (iii) in Northern Ireland, under Article 17(1) or 18(1) of the Adoption (Northern Ireland) Order 1987.

Amendments—Adoption and Children Act 2002, s 139(1), Sch 3, paras 85, 86, 87; Civil Partnership Act 2004, s 82, Sch 9, Pt 1, para 13; Domestic Violence, Crime and Victims Act 2004, ss 3, 58(1), Sch 10, para 40.

Prospective amendments—Domestic Violence, Crime and Victims Act 2004, s 4

63 Interpretation of Part IV

(1) In this Part–

'adoption order' means an adoption order within the meaning of section 72(1) of the Adoption Act 1976 or section 46(1) of the Adoption and Children Act 2002;

'associated', in relation to a person, is to be read with section 62(3) to (6);

'child' means a person under the age of eighteen years;

'cohabit', 'cohabitant' and 'former cohabitant' have the meaning given by section 62(1);

'the court' is to be read with section 57;

'development' means physical, intellectual, emotional, social or behavioural development;

'dwelling-house' includes (subject to subsection (4))–
    (a) any building or part of a building which is occupied as a dwelling,
    (b) any caravan, house-boat or structure which is occupied as a dwelling,

and any yard, garden, garage or outhouse belonging to it and occupied with it;

'family proceedings' means any proceedings–
    (a) under the inherent jurisdiction of the High Court in relation to children; or
    (b) under the enactments mentioned in subsection (2);

'harm'–
    (a) in relation to a person who has reached the age of eighteen years, means ill-treatment or the impairment of health; and
    (b) in relation to a child, means ill-treatment or the impairment of health or development;

'health' includes physical or mental health;

'home rights' has the meaning given by section 30;

'ill-treatment' includes forms of ill-treatment which are not physical and, in relation to a child, includes sexual abuse;

'mortgage', 'mortgagor' and 'mortgagee' have the same meaning as in the Law of Property Act 1925;

'mortgage payments' includes any payments which, under the terms of the mortgage, the mortgagor is required to make to any person;

'non-molestation order' has the meaning given by section 42(1);

'occupation order' has the meaning given by section 39;

'parental responsibility' has the same meaning as in the Children Act 1989;

'relative', in relation to a person, means–

    (a)   the father, mother, stepfather, stepmother, son, daughter, stepson, stepdaughter, grandmother, grandfather, grandson or grand-daughter of that person or of that person's spouse, former spouse, civil partner or former civil partner, or

    (b)   the brother, sister, uncle, aunt, niece, nephew or first cousin (whether of the full blood or of the half blood or by marriage or civil partnership) of that person or of that person's spouse, former spouse, civil partner or former civil partner,

and includes, in relation to a person who is cohabiting or has cohabited with another person, any person who would fall within paragraph (a) or (b) if the parties were married to each other or were civil partners of each other;

'relevant child', in relation to any proceedings under this Part, has the meaning given by section 62(2);

'the relevant judicial authority', in relation to any order under this Part, means–

    (a)   where the order was made by the High Court, a judge of that court;

    (b)   where the order was made by a county court, a judge or district judge of that or any other county court; or

    (c)   where the order was made by a magistrates' court, any magistrates' court.

(2) The enactments referred to in the definition of 'family proceedings' are–

    (a)   Part II;

    (b)   this Part;

    (ba) Part 4A;

    (c)   the Matrimonial Causes Act 1973;

    (d)   the Adoption Act 1976;

    (e)   the Domestic Proceedings and Magistrates' Court Act 1978;

    (f)   Part III of the Matrimonial and Family Proceedings Act 1984;

    (g)   Parts I, II and IV of the Children Act 1989;

    (h)   section 30 of the Human Fertilisation and Embryology Act 1990.

    (i)   the Adoption and Children Act 2002;

    (j)   Schedules 5 to 7 to the Civil Partnership Act 2004.

(3) Where the question of whether harm suffered by a child is significant turns on the child's health or development, his health or development shall be compared with that which could reasonably be expected of a similar child.

(4) For the purposes of sections 31, 32, 53 and 54 and such other provisions of this Part (if any) as may be prescribed, this Part is to have effect as if paragraph (b) of the definition of 'dwelling-house' were omitted.

(5) It is hereby declared that this Part applies as between the parties to a marriage even though either of them is, or has at any time during the marriage been, married to more than one person.

Amendments—Adoption and Children Act 2002, s 139(1), Sch 3, paras 85, 88; Civil Partnership Act 2004, s 82, Sch 9, Pt 1, para 14; Domestic Violence, Crime and Victims Act 2004, s 58(1), Sch 10, para 41.

Prospective Amendments—para (ba) prospectively inserted by the Forced Marriage (Civil Protection) Act 2007, s 3(1), (2).

HOUSING ACT 1996

(1996 Chapter 52)

153A Anti-social behaviour injunction

(1) In this section –

'anti-social behaviour injunction' means an injunction that prohibits the person in respect of whom it is granted from engaging in housing-related anti-social conduct of a kind specified in the injunction;

'anti-social conduct' means conduct capable of causing nuisance or annoyance to some person (who need not be a particular identified person);

'conduct' means conduct anywhere;

'housing-related' means directly or indirectly relating to or affecting the housing management functions of a relevant landlord.

(2) The court on the application of a relevant landlord may grant an anti-social behaviour injunction if the condition in subsection (3) is satisfied.

(3) The condition is that the person against whom the injunction is sought is engaging, has engaged or threatens to engage in housing-related conduct capable of causing a nuisance or annoyance to –

(a) a person with a right (of whatever description) to reside in or occupy housing accommodation owned or managed by a relevant landlord,

(b) a person with a right (of whatever description) to reside in or occupy other housing accommodation in the neighbourhood of housing accommodation mentioned in paragraph (a),

(c) a person engaged in lawful activity in, or in the neighbourhood of, housing accommodation mentioned in paragraph (a), or

(d) a person employed (whether or not by a relevant landlord) in connection with the exercise of a relevant landlord's housing management functions.

(4) Without prejudice to the generality of the court's power under subsection (2), a kind of conduct may be described in an anti-social behaviour injunction by reference to a person or persons and, if it is, may (in particular) be described by reference –

(a)   to persons generally,
(b)   to persons of a description specified in the injunction, or
(c)   to persons, or a person, specified in the injunction.

Amendments—Section substituted by Police and Justice Act 2006, s 26.

153B Injunction against unlawful use of premises

(1) This section applies to conduct which consists of or involves using or threatening to use housing accommodation owned or managed by a relevant landlord for an unlawful purpose.

(2) The court on the application of the relevant landlord may grant an injunction prohibiting the person in respect of whom the injunction is granted from engaging in conduct to which this section applies.

Amendments—Anti-Social Behaviour Act 2003, s 13(3).

153C Injunctions: exclusion order and power of arrest

(1) This section applies if the court grants an injunction under subsection (2) of section 153A or 153B and it thinks that either of the following paragraphs applies –

(a)   the conduct consists of or includes the use or threatened use of violence;
(b)   there is a significant risk of harm to a person mentioned in any of paragraphs (a) to (d) of section 153A(3).

(2) The court may include in the injunction a provision prohibiting the person in respect of whom it is granted from entering or being in –

(a)   any premises specified in the injunction;
(b)   any area specified in the injunction.

(3) The court may attach a power of arrest to any provision of the injunction.

Amendments—Anti-Social Behaviour Act 2003, s 13(3); Police and Justice Act 2006, s 52, Sch 14, para 32(a).

153D Injunction against breach of tenancy agreement

(1) This section applies if a relevant landlord applies for an injunction against a tenant in respect of the breach or anticipated breach of a tenancy agreement on the grounds that the tenant –

(a)   is engaging or threatening to engage in conduct that is capable of causing nuisance or annoyance to any person, or
(b)   is allowing, inciting or encouraging any other person to engage or threaten to engage in such conduct.

(2) The court may proceed under subsection (3) or (4) if it is satisfied –

    (a)   that the conduct includes the use or threatened use of violence, or

    (b)   that there is a significant risk of harm to any person.

(3) The court may include in the injunction a provision prohibiting the person in respect of whom it is granted from entering or being in –

    (a)   any premises specified in the injunction;

    (b)   any area specified in the injunction.

(4) The court may attach a power of arrest to any provision of the injunction.

(5) Tenancy agreement includes any agreement for the occupation of residential accommodation owned or managed by a relevant landlord.

Amendments—Anti-Social Behaviour Act 2003, s 13(3).

153E Injunctions: supplementary

(1) This section applies for the purposes of sections 153A to 153D.

(2) An injunction may –

    (a)   be made for a specified period or until varied or discharged;

    (b)   have the effect of excluding a person from his normal place of residence.

(3) An injunction may be varied or discharged by the court on an application by –

    (a)   the person in respect of whom it is made;

    (b)   the relevant landlord.

(4) If the court thinks it just and convenient it may grant or vary an injunction without the respondent having been given such notice as is otherwise required by rules of court.

(5) If the court acts under subsection (4) it must give the person against whom the injunction is made an opportunity to make representations in relation to the injunction as soon as it is practicable for him to do so.

(6) The court is the High Court or a county court.

(7) Each of the following is a relevant landlord –

    (a)   a housing action trust;

    (b)   a local authority (within the meaning of the Housing Act 1985);

    (c)   a registered social landlord.

(8) A charitable housing trust which is not a registered social landlord is also a relevant landlord for the purposes of section 153D.

(9) Housing accommodation includes –

    (a)   flats, lodging-houses and hostels;

    (b)   any yard, garden, outhouses and appurtenances belonging to the accommodation or usually enjoyed with it;

(c) in relation to a neighbourhood, the whole of the housing accommodation owned or managed by a relevant landlord in the neighbourhood and any common areas used in connection with the accommodation.

(10) A landlord owns housing accommodation if either of the following paragraphs applies to him –

(a) he is a person (other than a mortgagee not in possession) who is for the time being entitled to dispose of the fee simple in the premises, whether in possession or in reversion;

(b) he is a person who holds or is entitled to the rents and profits of the premises under a lease which (when granted) was for a term of not less than three years.

(11) The housing management functions of a relevant landlord include –

(a) functions conferred by or under any enactment;

(b) the powers and duties of the landlord as the holder of an estate or interest in housing accommodation.

(12) Harm includes serious ill-treatment or abuse (whether physical or not).

Amendments—Anti-Social Behaviour Act 2003, s 13(3).

154 Powers of arrest: ex-parte applications for injunctions

(1) In determining whether to exercise its power under section 153C(3) or 153D(4) to attach a power of arrest to an injunction which it intends to grant on an ex-parte application, the High Court or a county court shall have regard to all the circumstances including –

(a) whether it is likely that the applicant will be deterred or prevented from seeking the exercise of the power if the power is not exercised immediately, and

(b) whether there is reason to believe that the respondent is aware of the proceedings for the injunction but is deliberately evading service and that the applicant or any person of a description mentioned in any of paragraphs (a) to (d) of section 153A(3) (as the case may be) will be seriously prejudiced if the decision as to whether to exercise the power were delayed until substituted service is effected.

(2) Where the court exercises its power as mentioned in subsection (1), it shall afford the respondent an opportunity to make representations relating to the exercise of the power as soon as just and convenient at a hearing of which notice has been given to all the parties in accordance with rules of court.

Amendments—Anti-Social Behaviour Act 2003, s 13(4)(a), (b); Police and Justice Act 2006, s 52, Sch 14, para 32(b).

155 Arrest and remand

(1) If a power of arrest is attached to certain provisions of an injunction by virtue of section 153C(3) or 153D(4), a constable may arrest without warrant a

person whom he has reasonable cause for suspecting to be in breach of any such provision or otherwise in contempt of court in relation to a breach of any such provision. A constable shall after making any such arrest forthwith inform the person on whose application the injunction was granted.

(2) Where a person is arrested under subsection (1) –

   (a) he shall be brought before the relevant judge within the period of 24 hours beginning at the time of his arrest, and
   (b) if the matter is not then disposed of forthwith, the judge may remand him.

In reckoning for the purposes of this subsection any period of 24 hours no account shall be taken of Christmas Day, Good Friday or any Sunday.

(3) If the court has granted an injunction in circumstances such that a power of arrest could have been attached under section 153C(3) or 153D(4) but –

   (a) has not attached a power of arrest under the section in question to any provisions of the injunction, or
   (b) has attached that power only to certain provisions of the injunction,

then, if at any time the applicant considers that the respondent has failed to comply with the injunction, he may apply to the relevant judge for the issue of a warrant for the arrest of the respondent.

(4) The relevant judge shall not issue a warrant on an application under subsection (3) unless –

   (a) the application is substantiated on oath, and
   (b) he has reasonable grounds for believing that the respondent has failed to comply with the injunction.

(5) If a person is brought before a court by virtue of a warrant issued under subsection (4) and the court does not dispose of the matter forthwith, the court may remand him.

(6) Schedule 15 (which makes provision corresponding to that applying in magistrates' courts in civil cases under sections 128 and 129 of the Magistrates' Courts Act 1980) applies in relation to the powers of the High Court and a county court to remand a person under this section.

(7) If a person remanded under this section is granted bail by virtue of subsection (6), he may be required by the relevant judge to comply, before release on bail or later, with such requirements as appear to the judge to be necessary to secure that he does not interfere with witnesses or otherwise obstruct the course of justice.

Amendments—Anti-Social Behaviour Act 2003, s 13(5) (a), (b).

156 Remand for medical examination and report

(1) If the relevant judge has reason to consider that a medical report will be required, any power to remand a person under section 155 may be exercised for the purpose of enabling a medical examination and report to be made.

(2) If such a power is so exercised the adjournment shall not be for more than 4 weeks at a time unless the judge remands the accused in custody.

(3) If the judge so remands the accused, the adjournment shall not be for more than 3 weeks at a time.

(4) If there is reason to suspect that a person who has been arrested –

(a)   under section 155(1), or
(b)   under a warrant issued under section 155(4),

is suffering from *mental illness or severe mental impairment*, [mental disorder within the meaning of the Mental Health Act 1983], the relevant judge shall have the same power to make an order under section 35 of the *Mental Health Act 1983* [that Act] (remand for report on accused's mental condition) as the Crown Court has under *section 35 of that Act* [that section] in the case of an accused person within the meaning of that section.

Prospective Amendments—Words in italics prospectively repealed and subsequent words in square brackets substituted by the Mental Health Act 2007, s 1(4), Sch 1, Pt 2, para 21(a) (b) (c)

157   Powers of arrest: supplementary provisions

(1) If in exercise of its power under section 153C(3) or 153D(4) the High Court or a county court attaches a power of arrest to any provisions of an injunction, it may provide that the power of arrest is to have effect for a shorter period than the other provisions of the injunction.

(2) Any period specified for the purposes of subsection (1) may be extended by the court (on one or more occasions) on an application to vary or discharge the injunction.

(3) If a power of arrest has been attached to certain provisions of an injunction by virtue of section 153C(3) or 153D(4), the court may vary or discharge the injunction in so far as it confers a power of arrest (whether or not any application has been made to vary or discharge any other provision of the injunction).

(4) An injunction may be varied or discharged under subsection (3) on an application by the respondent or the person on whose application the injunction was made.

Amendments—Anti-Social Behaviour Act 2003, s 13 (1), (6)(a), (b), Sch 3; SI 2004/1502.

158   Interpretation: Chapter III

(1) For the purposes of this Chapter –

'charitable housing trust' means a housing trust, within the meaning of the Housing Associations Act 1985, which is a charity within the meaning of the Charities Act 1993;
'relevant judge', in relation to an injunction, means –
(a)   where the injunction was granted by the High Court, a judge of that court,

(b)   where the injunction was granted by a county court, a judge or district judge of that or any other county court;

'tenancy' includes a licence, and 'tenant' and 'landlord' shall be construed accordingly.

(2) (*repealed*)

Amendments—Anti-Social Behaviour Act 2003, ss 13(7)(a), (b), 92, Sch 3.

****

PROTECTION FROM HARASSMENT ACT 1997

1997 Chapter 40

1 Prohibition of harassment

(1) A person must not pursue a course of conduct–

(a)   which amounts to harassment of another, and
(b)   which he knows or ought to know amounts to harassment of the other.

(1A) A person must not pursue a course of conduct –

(a)   which involves harassment of two or more persons, and
(b)   which he knows or ought to know involves harassment of those persons, and
(c)   by which he intends to persuade any person (whether or not one of those mentioned above) –
    (i)   not to do something that he is entitled or required to do, or
    (ii)   to do something that he is not under any obligation to do.

(2) For the purposes of this section, the person whose course of conduct is in question ought to know that it amounts to or involves harassment of another if a reasonable person in possession of the same information would think the course of conduct amounted to or involved harassment of the other.

(3) Subsection (1) or (1A) does not apply to a course of conduct if the person who pursued it shows–

(a)   that it was pursued for the purpose of preventing or detecting crime,
(b)   that it was pursued under any enactment or rule of law or to comply with any condition or requirement imposed by any person under any enactment, or
(c)   that in the particular circumstances the pursuit of the course of conduct was reasonable.

Amendments—Subsection inserted: Organized Crime and Police Act 2005, s 125(1), (2)(a), (b), (c), (SI 2005/1521, art 3(1)(m)).

2 Offence of harassment

(1) A person who pursues a course of conduct in breach of section 1(1) or (1A) is guilty of an offence.

(2) A person guilty of an offence under this section is liable on summary conviction to imprisonment for a term not exceeding six months, or a fine not exceeding level 5 on the standard scale, or both.

(3) ....

Amendments—Words substituted: Organized Crime and Police Act 2005, s 125(1), (3), (SI 2005/1521, art 3(1)(m)); Subsection repealed: Police Reform Act 2002, s 107(2), Sch 8, (Police Reform Act 2002 (Commencement No 1) Order 2002, SI 2002/2306).

3 Civil remedy

(1) An actual or apprehended breach of section 1(1) may be the subject of a claim in civil proceedings by the person who is or may be the victim of the course of conduct in question.

(2) On such a claim, damages may be awarded for (among other things) any anxiety caused by the harassment and any financial loss resulting from the harassment.

(3) Where–

    (a)   in such proceedings the High Court or a county court grants an injunction for the purpose of restraining the defendant from pursuing any conduct which amounts to harassment, and

    (b)   the plaintiff considers that the defendant has done anything which he is prohibited from doing by the injunction,

the plaintiff may apply for the issue of a warrant for the arrest of the defendant.

(4) An application under subsection (3) may be made–

    (a)   where the injunction was granted by the High Court, to a judge of that court, and

    (b)   where the injunction was granted by a county court, to a judge or district judge of that or any other county court.

(5) The judge or district judge to whom an application under subsection (3) is made may only issue a warrant if–

    (a)   the application is substantiated on oath, and

    (b)   the judge or district judge has reasonable grounds for believing that the defendant has done anything which he is prohibited from doing by the injunction.

(6) Where–

    (a)   the High Court or a county court grants an injunction for the purpose mentioned in subsection (3)(a), and

(b)   without reasonable excuse the defendant does anything which he is prohibited from doing by the injunction,

he is guilty of an offence.

(7) Where a person is convicted of an offence under subsection (6) in respect of any conduct, that conduct is not punishable as a contempt of court.

(8) A person cannot be convicted of an offence under subsection (6) in respect of any conduct which has been punished as a contempt of court.

(9) A person guilty of an offence under subsection (6) is liable–

(a)   on conviction on indictment, to imprisonment for a term not exceeding five years, or a fine, or both, or

(b)   on summary conviction, to imprisonment for a term not exceeding six months, or a fine not exceeding the statutory maximum, or both.

Amendments—Serious Organised Crime and Police Act 2005, s 125(1), (4).

3A Injunctions to protect persons from harassment within section 1(1A)

(1) This section applies where there is an actual or apprehended breach of section 1(1A) by any person ('the relevant person').

(2) In such a case —

(a)   any person who is or may be a victim of the course of conduct in question, or

(b)   any person who is or may be a person falling within section 1(1A)(c),

may apply to the High Court or a county court for an injunction restraining the relevant person from pursuing any conduct which amounts to harassment in relation to any person or persons mentioned or described in the injunction.

(3) Section 3(3) to (9) apply in relation to an injunction granted under subsection (2) above as they apply in relation to an injunction granted as mentioned in section 3(3)(a).

Amendments—Serious Organised Crime and Police Act 2005, s 125(1), (5).

4 Putting people in fear of violence

(1) A person whose course of conduct causes another to fear, on at least two occasions, that violence will be used against him is guilty of an offence if he knows or ought to know that his course of conduct will cause the other so to fear on each of those occasions.

(2) For the purposes of this section, the person whose course of conduct is in question ought to know that it will cause another to fear that violence will be used against him on any occasion if a reasonable person in possession of the same information would think the course of conduct would cause the other so to fear on that occasion.

(3) It is a defence for a person charged with an offence under this section to show that–

(a) his course of conduct was pursued for the purpose of preventing or detecting crime,

(b) his course of conduct was pursued under any enactment or rule of law or to comply with any condition or requirement imposed by any person under any enactment, or

(c) the pursuit of his course of conduct was reasonable for the protection of himself or another or for the protection of his or another's property.

(4) A person guilty of an offence under this section is liable–

(a) on conviction on indictment, to imprisonment for a term not exceeding five years, or a fine, or both, or

(b) on summary conviction, to imprisonment for a term not exceeding six months, or a fine not exceeding the statutory maximum, or both.

(5) If on the trial on indictment of a person charged with an offence under this section the jury find him not guilty of the offence charged, they may find him guilty of an offence under section 2.

(6) The Crown Court has the same powers and duties in relation to a person who is by virtue of subsection (5) convicted before it of an offence under section 2 as a magistrates' court would have on convicting him of the offence.

5 Restraining orders [on conviction]

(1) A court sentencing or otherwise dealing with a person ('the defendant') convicted of an offence *under section 2 or 4* may (as well as sentencing him or dealing with him in any other way) make an order under this section.

(2) The order may, for the purpose of protecting the victim or victims of the offence, or any other person mentioned in the order, from *further* conduct which–

(a) amounts to harassment, or

(b) will cause a fear of violence,

prohibit the defendant from doing anything described in the order.

(3) The order may have effect for a specified period or until further order.

[(3A) In proceedings under this section both the prosecution and the defence may lead, as further evidence, any evidence that would be admissible in proceedings for an injunction under section 3.]

(4) The prosecutor, the defendant or any other person mentioned in the order may apply to the court which made the order for it to be varied or discharged by a further order.

[(4A) Any person mentioned in the order is entitled to be heard on the hearing of an application under subsection (4).]

(5) If without reasonable excuse the defendant does anything which he is prohibited from doing by an order under this section, he is guilty of an offence.

(6) A person guilty of an offence under this section is liable–

    (a)   on conviction on indictment, to imprisonment for a term not exceeding five years, or a fine, or both, or

    (b)   on summary conviction, to imprisonment for a term not exceeding six months, or a fine not exceeding the statutory maximum, or both.

[(7) A court dealing with a person for an offence under this section may vary or discharge the order in question by a further order.]

Amendments—:Serious Organised Crime and Police Act 2005, s 125(1), (6).

Prospective Amendments—Words in square brackets prospectively inserted and words in italics prospectively repealed by the Domestic Violence, Crime and Victims Act 2004, ss 12(1), (2), (3), (4), 58(2), 59, Sch 12, para 12, para 5(3).

5A Restraining orders on acquittal

(1) A court before which a person ("the defendant") is acquitted of an offence may, if it considers it necessary to do so to protect a person from harassment by the defendant, make an order prohibiting the defendant from doing anything described in the order.

(2) Subsections (3) to (7) of section 5 apply to an order under this section as they apply to an order under that one.

(3) Where the Court of Appeal allow an appeal against conviction they may remit the case to the Crown Court to consider whether to proceed under this section.

(4) Where –

    (a)   the Crown Court allows an appeal against conviction, or

    (b)   a case is remitted to the Crown Court under subsection (3),

the reference in subsection (1) to a court before which a person is acquitted of an offence is to be read as referring to that court.

(5) A person made subject to an order under this section has the same right of appeal against the order as if—

    (a)   he had been convicted of the offence in question before the court which made the order, and

    (b)   the order had been made under section 5.

Prospective Amendment—Subsection prospectively inserted by the Domestic Violence, Crime and Victims Act 2004, s 12(5).

6 Limitation

In section 11 of the Limitation Act 1980 (special time limit for actions in respect of personal injuries), after subsection (1) there is inserted—

'(1A) This section does not apply to any action brought for damages under section 3 of the Protection from Harassment Act 1997.'

7 Interpretation of this group of sections

(1) This section applies for the interpretation of *sections 1 to 5* [sections 1 to 5A].

(2) References to harassing a person include alarming the person or causing the person distress.

(3) A 'course of conduct' must involve —

    (a)   in the case of conduct in relation to a single person (see section 1(1)), conduct on at least two occasions in relation to that person, or

    (b)   in the case of conduct in relation to two or more persons (see section 1(1A)), conduct on at least one occasion in relation to each of those persons.

(3A) A person's conduct on any occasion shall be taken, if aided, abetted, counselled or procured by another–

    (a)   to be conduct on that occasion of the other (as well as conduct of the person whose conduct it is); and

    (b)   to be conduct in relation to which the other's knowledge and purpose, and what he ought to have known, are the same as they were in relation to what was contemplated or reasonably foreseeable at the time of the aiding, abetting, counselling or procuring.

(4) 'Conduct' includes speech.

(5) References to a person, in the context of the harassment of a person, are references to a person who is an individual.

Amendment—Subsection substituted: Serious Organized Crime and Police Act 2005, s 125(1), (7)(a), (7) (b), (SI 2005/1521, art 3(1)(m), subsection inserted by Criminal Justice and Police Act 2001, s 44(1).

Prospective Amendment—Words in italics prospectively repealed and subsequent words in square brackets prospectively substituted by Domestic Violence, Crime and Victims Act 2004, s 58(1), Sch 10, para 44; Subsection substituted: Organized Crime and Police Act 2005, s 125(1), (7)(a), (SI 2005/1521, art 3(1)(m).

CRIME AND DISORDER ACT 1998

1998 Chapter 37

PART I
PREVENTION OF CRIME AND DISORDER

Chapter I
England and Wales

Crime and disorder: general

1 Anti-social behaviour orders

(1) An application for an order under this section may be made by a relevant authority if it appears to the authority that the following conditions are fulfilled with respect to any person aged 10 or over, namely –

    (a)   that the person has acted, since the commencement date, in an anti-social manner, that is to say, in a manner that caused or was likely to cause harassment, alarm or distress to one or more persons not of the same household as himself; and

    (b)   that such an order is necessary to protect relevant persons from further anti-social acts by him.

(1A) In this section and sections 1B, 1CA, 1E and 1F 'relevant authority' means –

    (a)   the council for a local government area;

    (aa)   in relation to England, a county council;

    (b)   the chief officer of police of any police force maintained for a police area;

    (c)   the chief constable of the British Transport Police Force;

    (d)   any person registered under section 1 of the Housing Act 1996 (c 52) as a social landlord who provides or manages any houses or hostel in a local government area; or

    (e)   a housing action trust established by order in pursuance of section 62 of the Housing Act 1988.

(1B) In this section 'relevant persons' means –

    (a)   in relation to a relevant authority falling within paragraph (a) of subsection (1A), persons within the local government area of that council;

    (aa)   in relation to a relevant authority falling within paragraph (aa) of subsection (1A), persons within the county of the county council;

    (b)   in relation to a relevant authority falling within paragraph (b) of that subsection, persons within the police area;

    (c)   in relation to a relevant authority falling within paragraph (c) of that subsection –

> (i) persons who are within or likely to be within a place specified in section 31(1)(a) to (f) of the Railways and Transport Safety Act 2003 in a local government area; or
>
> (ii) persons who are within or likely to be within such a place;

(d) in relation to a relevant authority falling within paragraph (d) or (e) of that subsection –

> (i) persons who are residing in or who are otherwise on or likely to be on premises provided or managed by that authority; or
>
> (ii) persons who are in the vicinity of or likely to be in the vicinity of such premises.

(2) *(repealed)*

(3) Such an application shall be made by complaint to a magistrates' court.

(4) If, on such an application, it is proved that that the conditions mentioned in subsection (1) above are fulfilled, the magistrates' court may make an order under this section (an 'anti-social behaviour order') which prohibits the defendant from doing anything described in the order.

(5) For the purpose of determining whether the condition mentioned in subsection (1)(a) above is fulfilled, the court shall disregard any act of the defendant which he shows was reasonable in the circumstances.

(5A) Nothing in this section affects the operation of section 127 of the Magistrates' Courts Act 1980 (limitation of time in respect of informations laid or complaints made in magistrates' court).

(6) The prohibitions that may be imposed by an anti-social behaviour order are those necessary for the purpose of protecting persons (whether relevant persons or persons elsewhere in England and Wales) from further anti-social acts by the defendant.

(7) An anti-social behaviour order shall have effect for a period (not less than two years) specified in the order or until further order.

(8) Subject to subsection (9) below, the applicant or the defendant may apply by complaint to the court which made an anti-social behaviour order for it to be varied or discharged by a further order.

(9) Except with the consent of both parties, no anti-social behaviour order shall be discharged before the end of the period of two years beginning with the date of service of the order.

(10) If without reasonable excuse a person does anything which he is prohibited from doing by an anti-social behaviour order, he is guilty of an offence and liable –

(a) on summary conviction, to imprisonment for a term not exceeding six months or to a fine not exceeding the statutory maximum, or to both; or

(b) on conviction on indictment, to imprisonment for a term not exceeding five years or to a fine, or to both.

(10A) The following may bring proceedings for an offence under subsection (10) –

    (a)   a council which is a relevant authority;

    (b)   the council for the local government area in which a person in respect of whom an anti-social behaviour order has been made resides or appears to reside.

(10B) If proceedings for an offence under subsection (10) are brought in a youth court section 47(2) of the Children and Young Persons Act 1933 (c 12) has effect as if the persons entitled to be present at a sitting for the purposes of those proceedings include one person authorised to be present by a relevant authority.

(10C) In proceedings for an offence under subsection (10), a copy of the original anti-social behaviour order, certified as such by the proper officer of the court which made it, is admissible as evidence of its having been made and of its contents to the same extent that oral evidence of those things is admissible in those proceedings.

(10D) In relation to proceedings brought against a child or a young person for an offence under subsection (10) –

    (a)   section 49 of the Children and Young Persons Act 1933 (restrictions on reports of proceedings in which children and young persons are concerned) does not apply in respect of the child or young person against whom the proceedings are brought;

    (b)   section 45 of the Youth Justice and Criminal Evidence Act 1999 (power to restrict reporting of criminal proceedings involving persons under 18) does so apply.

(10E) If, in relation to any such proceedings, the court does exercise its power to give a direction under section 45 of the Youth Justice and Criminal Evidence Act 1999, it shall give its reasons for doing so.

(11) Where a person is convicted of an offence under subsection (10) above, it shall not be open to the court by or before which he is so convicted to make an order under subsection (1)(b) (conditional discharge) of section 12 of the Powers of Criminal Courts (Sentencing) Act 2000 in respect of the offence.

(12) In this section –

    'British Transport Police Force' means the force of constables appointed under section 53 of the British Transport Commission Act 1949 (c xxix);
    'child' and 'young person' shall have the same meaning as in the Children and Young Persons Act 1933;
    'the commencement date' means the date of the commencement of this section;
    'local government area' means –

        (a)   in relation to England, a district or London borough, the City of London, the Isle of Wight and the Isles of Scilly;
        (b)   in relation to Wales, a county or county borough,

Amendments—Police Reform Act 2002, ss 61(1), (2), (3), (4), (5), (7), (8), (9)(a), (b), (10), 107(2); Serious Organised Crime and Police Act 2005,ss 139(1), (2), 140 (1), (2), 141(1), (2)(a), 142(2); Anti-social Behaviour Act 2003, ss 85(1), (2)(a), (b), (c),3(a), (b), (4), 92, Sch 3; British Transport Police (Transitional and Consequential Provisions) Order 2004, SI 2004/1573, art 12(5)(b); Powers of Criminal Courts (Sentencing) Act 2000, ss 165(1), Sch 9, para 192, 168(1); SI 2005/886, art 2.

Prospective Amendments—Sub paragraph (5A) prospectively inserted by the Violent Crime Reduction Act 2006, s 59 (1).

1A Power of Secretary of State to add to relevant authorities

(1) The Secretary of State may by order provide that the chief officer of a body of constables maintained otherwise than by a police authority is, in such cases and circumstances as may be prescribed by the order, to be a relevant authority for the purposes of section 1 above.

(2) The Secretary of State may by order –

(a) provide that a person or body of any other description specified in the order is, in such cases and circumstances as may be prescribed by the order, to be a relevant authority for the purposes of such of sections 1 above and 1B, 1CA and 1E below as are specified in the order; and

(b) prescribe the description of persons who are to be 'relevant persons' in relation to that person or body.

Amendments—Inserted by the Police Reform Act 2002, s 62 (1); Serious Organised Crime and Police Act 2005, s 139(1), (3).

1AA Individual support orders

(1) Where a court makes an anti-social behaviour order in respect of a defendant who is a child or young person when that order is made, it must consider whether the individual support conditions are fulfilled.

(2) If it is satisfied that those conditions are fulfilled, the court must make an order under this section ('an individual support order') which –

(a) requires the defendant to comply, for a period not exceeding six months, with such requirements as are specified in the order; and

(b) requires the defendant to comply with any directions given by the responsible officer with a view to the implementation of the requirements under paragraph (a) above.

(3) The individual support conditions are –

(a) that an individual support order would be desirable in the interests of preventing any repetition of the kind of behaviour which led to the making of the anti-social behaviour order;

(b) that the defendant is not already subject to an individual support order; and

(c) that the court has been notified by the Secretary of State that arrangements for implementing individual support orders are available in the area in which it appears to it that the defendant resides or will reside and the notice has not been withdrawn.

(4) If the court is not satisfied that the individual support conditions are fulfilled, it shall state in open court that it is not so satisfied and why it is not.

(5) The requirements that may be specified under subsection (2)(a) above are those that the court considers desirable in the interests of preventing any repetition of the kind of behaviour which led to the making of the anti-social behaviour order.

(6) Requirements included in an individual support order, or directions given under such an order by a responsible officer, may require the defendant to do all or any of the following things—

    (a)   to participate in activities specified in the requirements or directions at a time or times so specified;

    (b)   to present himself to a person or persons so specified at a place or places and at a time or times so specified;

    (c)   to comply with any arrangements for his education so specified.

(7) But requirements included in, or directions given under, such an order may not require the defendant to attend (whether at the same place or at different places) on more than two days in any week; and 'week' here means a period of seven days beginning with a Sunday.

(8) Requirements included in, and directions given under, an individual support order shall, as far as practicable, be such as to avoid –

    (a)   any conflict with the defendant's religious beliefs; and

    (b)   any interference with the times, if any, at which he normally works or attends school or any other educational establishment.

(9) Before making an individual support order, the court shall obtain from a social worker of a local authority or a member of a youth offending team any information which it considers necessary in order –

    (a)   to determine whether the individual support conditions are fulfilled, or

    (b)   to determine what requirements should be imposed by an individual support order if made,

and shall consider that information.

(10) In this section and section 1AB below 'responsible officer', in relation to an individual support order, means one of the following who is specified in the order, namely –

    (a)   a social worker of a local authority,

    (b)   a person nominated by a person appointed as chief education officer under section 532 of the Education Act 1996 (c 56);

    (c)   a member of a youth offending team.

Amendments—Criminal Justice Act 2003, s 322; Children Act 2004, s 64, Sch 5, Pt 4.

1AB Individual support orders: explanation, breach, amendment etc

(1) Before making an individual support order, the court shall explain to the defendant in ordinary language –

(a) the effect of the order and of the requirements proposed to be included in it;

(b) the consequences which may follow (under subsection (3) below) if he fails to comply with any of those requirements; and

(c) that the court has power (under subsection (6) below) to review the order on the application either of the defendant or of the responsible officer.

(2) The power of the Secretary of State under section 174(4) of the Criminal Justice Act 2003 includes power by order to –

(a) prescribe cases in which subsection (1) above does not apply; and

(b) prescribe cases in which the explanation referred to in that subsection may be made in the absence of the defendant, or may be provided in written form.

(3) If the person in respect of whom an individual support order is made fails without reasonable excuse to comply with any requirement included in the order, he is guilty of an offence and liable on summary conviction to a fine not exceeding –

(a) if he is aged 14 or over at the date of his conviction, £1,000;

(b) if he is aged under 14 then, £250.

(4) No referral order under section 16(2) or (3) of the Powers of Criminal Courts (Sentencing) Act 2000 (referral of young offenders to youth offender panels) may be made in respect of an offence under subsection (3) above.

(5) If the anti-social behaviour order as a result of which an individual support order was made ceases to have effect, the individual support order (if it has not previously ceased to have effect) ceases to have effect when the anti-social behaviour order does.

(6) On an application made by complaint by –

(a) the person subject to an individual support order, or

(b) the responsible officer,

the court which made the individual support order may vary or discharge it by a further order.

(7) If the anti-social behaviour order as a result of which an individual support order was made is varied, the court varying the anti-social behaviour order may by a further order vary or discharge the individual support order.

Amendments—Inserted by Criminal Justice Act 2003, s 322.

1B Orders in county court proceedings

(1) This section applies to any proceedings in a county court ('the principal proceedings').

(2) If a relevant authority –

(a) is a party to the principal proceedings, and

(b)   considers that a party to those proceedings is a person in relation to whom it would be reasonable for it to make an application under section 1,

it may make an application in those proceedings for an order under subsection (4).

(3) If a relevant authority –

(a)   is not a party to the principal proceedings, and
(b)   considers that a party to those proceedings is a person in relation to whom it would be reasonable for it to make an application under section 1,

it may make an application to be joined to those proceedings to enable it to apply for an order under subsection (4) and, if it is so joined, may apply for such an order.

(3A) Subsection (3B) applies if a relevant authority is a party to the principal proceedings and considers—

(a)   that a person who is not a party to the proceedings has acted in an anti-social manner, and
(b)   that the person's anti-social acts are material in relation to the principal proceedings.

(3B) The relevant authority may –

(a)   make an application for the person mentioned in subsection (3A)(a) to be joined to the principal proceedings to enable an order under subsection (4) to be made in relation to that person;
(b)   if that person is so joined, apply for an order under subsection (4).

(3C) But a person must not be joined to proceedings in pursuance of subsection (3B) unless his anti-social acts are material in relation to the principal proceedings.

(4) If, on an application for an order under this subsection, it is proved that the conditions mentioned in section 1(1) are fulfilled as respects that other party, the court may make an order which prohibits him from doing anything described in the order.

(5) Subject to subsection (6), the person against whom an order under this section has been made and the relevant authority on whose application that order was made may apply to the county court which made an order under this section for it to be varied or discharged by a further order.

(6) Except with the consent of the relevant authority and the person subject to the order, no order under this section shall be discharged before the end of the period of two years beginning with the date of service of the order.

(7) Subsections (5) to (7) and (10) to (12) of section 1 apply for the purposes of the making and effect of orders made under this section as they apply for the purposes of the making and effect of anti-social behaviour orders.

Amendment—Inserted by the Police Reform Act 2002, s 63; subsections inserted by the Anti-social Behavious Act 2003, s 85 (1), (5), (6).

1C Orders on conviction in criminal proceedings

(1) This section applies where a person (the 'offender') is convicted of a relevant offence.

(2) If the court considers –

  (a) that the offender has acted, at any time since the commencement date, in an anti-social manner, that is to say in a manner that caused or was likely to cause harassment, alarm or distress to one or more persons not of the same household as himself, and

  (b) that an order under this section is necessary to protect persons in any place in England and Wales from further anti-social acts by him,

it may make an order which prohibits the offender from doing anything described in the order.

(3) The court may make an order under this section –

  (a) if the prosecutor asks it to do so, or
  (b) if the court thinks it is appropriate to do so.

(3A) For the purpose of deciding whether to make an order under this section the court may consider evidence led by the prosecution and the defence.

(3B) It is immaterial whether evidence led in pursuance of subsection (3A) would have been admissible in the proceedings in which the offender was convicted.

(4) An order under this section shall not be made except –

  (a) in addition to a sentence imposed in respect of the relevant offence; or
  (b) in addition to an order discharging him conditionally.

(4A) The court may adjourn any proceedings in relation to an order under this section even after sentencing the offender.

(4B) If the offender does not appear for any adjourned proceedings, the court may further adjourn the proceedings or may issue a warrant for his arrest.

(4C) But the court may not issue a warrant for the offender's arrest unless it is satisfied that he has had adequate notice of the time and place of the adjourned proceedings.

(5) An order under this section takes effect on the day on which it is made, but the court may provide in any such order that such requirements of the order as it may specify shall, during any period when the offender is detained in legal custody, be suspended until his release from that custody.

(6) (*repealed*)

(7) (*repealed*)

(8) (*repealed*)

(9) Subsections (7), (10), (10C), (10D), (10E) and (11) of section 1 apply for the purposes of the making and effect of orders made by virtue of this section as they apply for the purposes of the making and effect of anti-social behaviour orders.

(9A) The council for the local government area in which a person in respect of whom an anti-social behaviour order has been made resides or appears to reside may bring proceedings under section 1(10) (as applied by subsection (9) above) for breach of an order under subsection (2) above.

(9B) Subsection (9C) applies in relation to proceedings in which an order under subsection (2) is made against a child or young person who is convicted of an offence.

(9C) In so far as the proceedings relate to the making of the order –

    (a)   section 49 of the Children and Young Persons Act 1933 (c 12) (restrictions on reports of proceedings in which children and young persons are concerned) does not apply in respect of the child or young person against whom the order is made;

    (b)   section 39 of that Act (power to prohibit publication of certain matter) does so apply.

(10) In this section –

    'child' and 'young person' have the same meaning as in the Children and Young Persons Act 1933 (c 12);
    'the commencement date' has the same meaning as in section 1 above;
    'the court' in relation to an offender means –

        (a)   the court by or before which he is convicted of the relevant offence; or

        (b)   if he is committed to the Crown Court to be dealt with for that offence, the Crown Court; and

    'relevant offence' means an offence committed after the coming into force of section 64 of the Police Reform Act 2002 (c 30).

Amendments—Police Reform Act 2002, s 64; Anti-social Behaviour Act 2003, s 86 (1), (2), (3), (4); Serious Organised Crime and Police Act 2005, s 139 (1), (4) (a),(b), s 140 (1), (3), s 141 (1), (3).

1CA Variation and discharge of orders under section 1C

(1) An offender subject to an order under section 1C may apply to the court which made it for it to be varied or discharged.

(2) If he does so, he must also send written notice of his application to the Director of Public Prosecutions.

(3) The Director of Public Prosecutions may apply to the court which made an order under section 1C for it to be varied or discharged.

(4) A relevant authority may also apply to the court which made an order under section 1C for it to be varied or discharged if it appears to it that –

(a) in the case of variation, the protection of relevant persons from anti-social acts by the person subject to the order would be more appropriately effected by a variation of the order;

(b) in the case of discharge, that it is no longer necessary to protect relevant persons from anti-social acts by him by means of such an order.

(5) If the Director of Public Prosecutions or a relevant authority applies for the variation or discharge of an order under section 1C, he or it must also send written notice of the application to the person subject to the order.

(6) In the case of an order under section 1C made by a magistrates' court, the references in subsections (1), (3) and (4) to the court by which the order was made include a reference to any magistrates' court acting in the same local justice area as that court.

(7) No order under section 1C shall be discharged on an application under this section before the end of the period of two years beginning with the day on which the order takes effect, unless—

(a) in the case of an application under subsection (1), the Director of Public Prosecutions consents, or

(b) in the case of an application under subsection (3) or (4), the offender consents.

Amendments—Serious Organised Crime and Police Act 2005, s 140(1), (4).

1D Interim orders

(1) This section applies where –

(a) an application is made for an anti-social behaviour order;

(b) an application is made for an order under section 1B;

(c) a request is made by the prosecution for an order under section 1C; or

(d) the court is minded to make an order under section 1C of its own motion.

(2) If, before determining the application or request, or before deciding whether to make an order under section 1C of its own motion, the court considers that it is just to make an order under this section pending the determination of that application or request or before making that decision, it may make such an order.

(3) An order under this section is an order which prohibits the defendant from doing anything described in the order.

(4) An order under this section –

(a) shall be for a fixed period;

(b) may be varied, renewed or discharged;

(c) shall, if it has not previously ceased to have effect, cease to have effect on the determination of the application or request mentioned in subsection (1), or on the court's making a decision as to whether or not to make an order under section 1C of its own motion.

(5) In relation to cases to which this section applies by virtue of paragraph (a) or (b) of subsection (1), subsections (6), (8) and (10) to (12) of section 1 apply for the purposes of the making and effect of orders under this section as they apply for the purposes of the making and effect of anti-social behaviour orders.

(6) In relation to cases to which this section applies by virtue of paragraph (c) or (d) of subsection (1) –

(a) subsections (6) and (10) to (12) of section 1 apply for the purposes of the making and effect of orders under this section as they apply for the purposes of the making and effect of anti-social behaviour orders; and

(b) section 1CA applies for the purposes of the variation or discharge of an order under this section as it applies for the purposes of the variation or discharge of an order under section 1C.

Amendments—Police Reform Act 2002, s 65(1); Serious Organised Crime and Police Act 2005, s 139(1), (5), (6), (7), (8), (9).

1E Consultation requirements

(1) This section applies to –

(a) applications for an anti-social behaviour order; and

(b) applications for an order under section 1B.

(2) Before making an application to which this section applies, the council for a local government area shall consult the chief officer of police of the police force maintained for the police area within which that local government area lies.

(3) Before making an application to which this section applies, a chief officer of police shall consult the council for the local government area in which the person in relation to whom the application is to be made resides or appears to reside.

(4) Before making an application to which this section applies, a relevant authority other than a council for a local government area or a chief officer of police shall consult—

(a) the council for the local government area in which the person in relation to whom the application is to be made resides or appears to reside; and

(b) the chief officer of police of the police force maintained for the police area within which that local government area lies.

(5) Subsection (4)(a) does not apply if the relevant authority is a county council for a county in which there are no districts.

Amendments—Police Reform Act 2002, s 66; Anti-social Behaviour Act 2003, s 85(1), (7).

4 Appeals against orders

(1) An appeal shall lie to the Crown Court against the making by a magistrates' court of an anti-social behaviour order, an individual support order, an order under section 1D above,

(2) On such an appeal the Crown Court –

    (a)   may make such orders as may be necessary to give effect to its determination of the appeal; and

    (b)   may also make such incidental or consequential orders as appear to it to be just.

(3) Any order of the Crown Court made on an appeal under this section (other than one directing that an application be re-heard by a magistrates' court) shall, for the purposes of section 1(8), 1AB(6), be treated as if it were an order of the magistrates' court from which the appeal was brought and not an order of the Crown Court.

Amendment—Criminal Justice Act 2003, s 323(1), (2) (a), (b); Police Reform Act 2002, s 65(2); Sexual Offences Act 2003, ss 139, 140, Sch 6, para 38(1), (3), (a), Sch 7.

11 Child safety orders

(1) Subject to subsection (2) below, if a magistrates' court, on the application of a local authority, is satisfied that one or more of the conditions specified in subsection (3) below are fulfilled with respect to a child under the age of 10, it may make an order (a 'child safety order') which –

    (a)   places the child, for a period (not exceeding the permitted maximum) specified in the order, under the supervision of the responsible officer; and

    (b)   requires the child to comply with such requirements as are so specified.

(2) A court shall not make a child safety order unless it has been notified by the Secretary of State that arrangements for implementing such orders are available in the area in which it appears that the child resides or will reside and the notice has not been withdrawn.

(3) The conditions are –

    (a)   that the child has committed an act which, if he had been aged 10 or over, would have constituted an offence;

    (b)   that a child safety order is necessary for the purpose of preventing the commission by the child of such an act as is mentioned in paragraph (a) above;

    (c)   that the child has contravened a ban imposed by a curfew notice; and

    (d)   that the child has acted in a manner that caused or was likely to cause harassment, alarm or distress to one or more persons not of the same household as himself.

(4) The maximum period permitted for the purposes of subsection (1)(a) above is twelve months.

(5) The requirements that may be specified under subsection (1)(b) above are those which the court considers desirable in the interests of –

(a) securing that the child receives appropriate care, protection and support and is subject to proper control; or

(b) preventing any repetition of the kind of behaviour which led to the child safety order being made.

(6) Proceedings under this section or section 12 below shall be family proceedings for the purposes of the 1989 Act or section 65 of the Magistrates' Courts Act 1980 ('the 1980 Act'); and the standard of proof applicable to such proceedings shall be that applicable to civil proceedings.

(7) In this section 'local authority' has the same meaning as in the 1989 Act.

(8) In this section and section 12 below, 'responsible officer', in relation to a child safety order, means one of the following who is specified in the order, namely –

(a) a social worker of a local authority, and

(b) a member of a youth offending team.

Amendment—Children Act 2004, s 60(1), (3), s 64, Sch 5, Pt 4.

HUMAN RIGHTS ACT 1998

1998 Chapter 42

12 Freedom of expression

(1) This section applies if a court is considering whether to grant any relief which, if granted, might affect the exercise of the Convention right to freedom of expression.

(2) If the person against whom the application for relief is made ('the respondent') is neither present nor represented, no such relief is to be granted unless the court is satisfied—

(a) that the applicant has taken all practicable steps to notify the respondent; or

(b) that there are compelling reasons why the respondent should not be notified.

(3) No such relief is to be granted so as to restrain publication before trial unless the court is satisfied that the applicant is likely to establish that publication should not be allowed.

(4) The court must have particular regard to the importance of the Convention right to freedom of expression and, where the proceedings relate to material which the respondent claims, or which appears to the court, to be journalistic, literary or artistic material (or to conduct connected with such material), to—

(a) the extent to which—

(i) the material has, or is about to, become available to the public; or

    (ii)   it is, or would be, in the public interest for the material to be published;

  (b)   any relevant privacy code.

(5) In this section—

'court' includes a tribunal; and

'relief' includes any remedy or order (other than in criminal proceedings

Article 10

Freedom of expression

1 Everyone has the right to freedom of expression. This right shall include freedom to hold opinions and to receive and impart information and ideas without interference by public authority and regardless of frontiers. This Article shall not prevent States from requiring the licensing of broadcasting, television or cinema enterprises.

2 The exercise of these freedoms, since it carries with it duties and responsibilities, may be subject to such formalities, conditions, restrictions or penalties as are prescribed by law and are necessary in a democratic society, in the interests of national security, territorial integrity or public safety, for the prevention of disorder or crime, for the protection of health or morals, for the protection of the reputation or rights of others, for preventing the disclosure of information received in confidence, or for maintaining the authority and impartiality of the judiciary.

Article 11

Freedom of assembly and association

1 Everyone has the right to freedom of peaceful assembly and to freedom of association with others, including the right to form and to join trade unions for the protection of his interests.

2 No restrictions shall be placed on the exercise of these rights other than such as are prescribed by law and are necessary in a democratic society in the interests of national security or public safety, for the prevention of disorder or crime, for the protection of health or morals or for the protection of the rights and freedoms of others. This Article shall not prevent the imposition of lawful restrictions on the exercise of these rights by members of the armed forces, of the police or of the administration of the State.

POLICE AND JUSTICE ACT 2006

2006 Chapter 48

****

27 Injunctions in local authority proceedings: power of arrest and remand

(1) This section applies to proceedings in which a local authority is a party by virtue of section 222 of the Local Government Act 1972 (c 70) (power of local authority to bring, defend or appear in proceedings for the promotion or protection of the interests of inhabitants of their area).

(2) If the court grants an injunction which prohibits conduct which is capable of causing nuisance or annoyance to a person it may, if subsection (3) applies, attach a power of arrest to any provision of the injunction.

(3) This subsection applies if the local authority applies to the court to attach the power of arrest and the court thinks that either—

  (a)   the conduct mentioned in subsection (2) consists of or includes the use or threatened use of violence, or
  (b)   there is a significant risk of harm to the person mentioned in that subsection.

(4) Where a power of arrest is attached to any provision of an injunction under subsection (2), a constable may arrest without warrant a person whom he has reasonable cause for suspecting to be in breach of that provision.

(5) After making an arrest under subsection (4) the constable must as soon as is reasonably practicable inform the local authority.

(6) Where a person is arrested under subsection (4)—

  (a)   he shall be brought before the court within the period of 24 hours beginning at the time of his arrest, and
  (b)   if the matter is not then disposed of forthwith, the court may remand him.

(7) For the purposes of subsection (6), when calculating the period of 24 hours referred to in paragraph (a) of that subsection, no account shall be taken of Christmas Day, Good Friday or any Sunday.

(8) Schedule 10 applies in relation to the power to remand under subsection (6).

(9) If the court has reason to consider that a medical report will be required, the power to remand a person under subsection (6) may be exercised for the purpose of enabling a medical examination and report to be made.

(10) If such a power is so exercised the adjournment shall not be in force—

  (a)   for more than three weeks at a time in a case where the court remands the accused person in custody, or
  b)   for more than four weeks at a time in any other case.

(11) If there is reason to suspect that a person who has been arrested under subsection (4) is suffering from *mental illness or severe mental impairment* [mental disorder within the meaning of the Mental Health Act 1983] the court shall have the same power to make an order under section 35 of *the Mental Health Act 1983* (c 20) [that Act] (remand for report on accused's mental

condition) as the Crown Court has under that section in the case of an accused person within the meaning of that section.

(12) For the purposes of this section—

(a) "harm" includes serious ill-treatment or abuse (whether physical or not);

(b) "local authority" has the same meaning as in section 222 of the Local Government Act 1972 (c 70);

(c) "the court" means the High Court or a county court and includes—

(i) in relation to the High Court, a judge of that court, and

(ii) in relation to a county court, a judge or district judge of that court.

Prospective Amendments—Words in italics prospectively repealed and subsequent words in square brackets prospectively substituted by the Mental Health Act 2007, s 1(4), Sch 1, Pt 2, para 26(a), (b).

****

Schedule 10
Injunctions in Local Authority Proceedings: Powers to Remand

Introductory

1

(1) The provisions of this Schedule apply where the court has power to remand a person under section 27(6) (injunctions in local authority proceedings: power of arrest and remand).

(2) In this Schedule "the court" has the same meaning as in section 27.

2

(1) The court may—

(a) remand the person in custody, that is, commit him to custody to be brought before the court at the end of the period of remand or at such earlier time as the court may require, or

(b) remand him on bail, in accordance with the following provisions.

(2) The court may remand the person on bail—

(a) by taking from him a recognizance, with or without sureties, conditioned as provided in paragraph 3, or

(b) by fixing the amount of the recognizances with a view to their being taken subsequently, and in the meantime committing him to custody as mentioned in sub-paragraph (1)(a).

(3) Where a person is brought before the court after remand, the court may further remand him.

3

(1) Where a person is remanded on bail, the court may direct that his recognizance be conditioned for his appearance—

    (a)   before that court at the end of the period of remand, or
    (b)   at every time and place to which during the course of the proceedings the hearing may from time to time be adjourned.

(2) Where a recognizance is conditioned for a person's appearance as mentioned in sub-paragraph (1)(b), the fixing of any time for him next to appear shall be deemed to be a remand.

(3) Nothing in this paragraph affects the power of the court at any subsequent hearing to remand him afresh.

4

(1) The court shall not remand a person for a period exceeding eight clear days except that—

    (a)   if the court remands him on bail, it may remand him for a longer period if he and the other party consent, and
    (b)   if the court adjourns a case under section 27(9) (remand for medical examination and report) the court may remand him for the period of adjournment.

(2) Where the court has the power to remand a person in custody it may, if the remand is for a period not exceeding three clear days, commit him to the custody of a constable.

Further remand

5

(1) If the court is satisfied that a person who has been remanded is unable by reason of illness or accident to appear or be brought before the court at the expiration of the period for which he was remanded, the court may, in his absence, remand him for a further time.

(2) The power mentioned in sub-paragraph (1) may, in the case of a person who was remanded on bail, be exercised by enlarging his recognizance and those of any sureties for him to a later time.

(3) Where a person remanded on bail is bound to appear before the court at any time and the court has no power to remand him under sub-paragraph (1), the court may in his absence enlarge his recognizance and those of any sureties for him to a later time.

(4) The enlargement of his recognizance shall be deemed to be a further remand.

(5) Paragraph 4(1) (limit of remand) does not apply to the exercise of the powers conferred by this paragraph.

Postponement of taking recognizance

6

Where under paragraph 2(2)(b) the court fixes the amount in which the principal and his sureties, if any, are to be bound, the recognizance may afterwards be taken by such person as may be prescribed by rules of court, with the same consequences as if it had been entered into before the court.

Requirements imposed on remand on bail

7

The court may when remanding a person on bail under this Schedule require him to comply, before release on bail or later, with such requirements as appear to the court to be necessary to secure that he does not interfere with witnesses or otherwise obstruct the course of justice.

****

INDEX

References are to paragraph numbers.